MacArthur's
PACIFIC APPEASEMENT,
DECEMBER 8, 1941

Mark Douglas

Order this book online at www.trafford.com
or email orders@trafford.com

Most Trafford titles are also available at major online book retailers.

Printed in the United States of America.

ISBN: 978-1-4669-6906-3 (sc)
ISBN: 978-1-4669-6907-0 (e)

Library of Congress Control Number: 2012921708

Trafford rev. 11/17/2012

 www.trafford.com

North America & international
toll-free: 1 888 232 4444 (USA & Canada)
phone: 250 383 6864 ♦ fax: 812 355 4082

MacArthur's Pacific Appeasement, December 8, 1941
Part I
The Missing Ten Hours

Also by Mark Douglas

Pestus Fantasticus Californius
      Countryside, December 1978

Good Catch!
      Videomaker, June 1993

USS HOQUIAM PF-5 series

Of Sea Stories and Fairy Tales	TBA
Resurrected	2001
Road to Hungnam	2002
Hocky Maru	2012
Knock off Ship's Work	2012

To my hardworking editor and my helpmate: Nora-Gaye Hill Douglas, MEd, MA

A special note of appreciation and thanks go to the tireless effort of Russ Lee, to suggest additions and correct some of my gross errors of content.

Thanks also go to wonderful friends who read the early and final manuscripts.

The eminent naval historian Samuel Eliot Morison wrote that the three principles of good historical writing are vigor, accuracy, and objectivity (insofar as possible.) I believe this also applies to historical-based novels.

PREFACE

This is a work of fiction. Even so, this work is based on historical facts, gleaned from many sources. My resources are listed at the end of this book, rather than footnotes or endnotes.

After the events portrayed within, I claim with pride, my father, Commander Ivan H. Douglas, USN, LDO, Retired, 1934-1964, served in the USS SARATOGA CV-3 until November 1942; his brother, Warren E. Douglas, Machinist Mate 1/c, USNR, served in the Patrol Torpedo Squadrons in the Solomons from 1943, then the Philippines until the end of the war; Master Sergeant Richard W. Douglas, USA, served in the Battle of the Philippines in 1944 - 1945. An aunt's husband, Ray Webber, in the USAF 12th Air Force, flying in a Martin B-24 Liberator as a Tail Gunner, lost his life on an Air Raid in Germany in 1944. BGen Millington USMC, retired in 1965, after serving in the Pacific in WW2, and in the Korean War.

Much later in life, I served in the U.S. Navy 1949-1968, retiring as a Senior Chief Petty Officer. Among my duty stations was the USS Hoquiam PF-5 off the North Korean coast 1950-1951.

PROLOGUE

As planned, military action in the U. S. Commonwealth of the Philippine Isles would be in consonance with the 1935 U. S. WAR PLAN ORANGE, Revision 3 (WPO-3). When war threatened in the Pacific theater, WPO-3 was amended in 1941 as a result of the Placentia Bay, Argentia, Newfoundland meeting between United States President Franklin Roosevelt and Great Britain Prime Minister Winston Churchill, and their respective War Staffs.

This revision, renamed RAINBOW 5, included military and naval forces of Australia, Great Britain, The Netherlands (Dutch), and the United States (America) (ABDA) in a mutual defense pact. War Plan Rainbow 5 provided detailed, precise instructions the U.S. Army and U.S. Navy in the Pacific Theater would execute in the event of hostilities with Japan. If it appeared hostilities were imminent, the President of the United States, Commander-in-Chief of all U. S. military and naval forces, would order execution of Phase One, RAINBOW 5.

Phase One explicitly ordered the U.S. Army Air Force (FEAF), headquartered at Nielson Field, Manila, subordinate to the U.S. Army Far East Command (USAFFE), The Philippines, to send one Boeing B-17D Flying Fortress on a high altitude photo-reconnaissance mission over Japanese military targets in and around the island of Formosa. At the same time, the U.S. Navy Asiatic Fleet, except submarines, gunboats, PT boats, harbor vessels, and shore command, would depart for agreed upon ports in Java, Borneo, Celebes, and Singapore.

(The U.S. Army Air Force was created on June 20, 1941, but elements of the U.S. Army Air Corps remained intact until 1947 when both USAAF and USAAC were abolished and the U.S. Air Force (USAF) was born. I decided to use USAAF throughout this book.)

The President would execute Phase Two RAINBOW 5 when the Japanese attacked the U.S. or her Allies anywhere in the Pacific or Indian Ocean Theaters. Phase Two required the U.S. Army Far East Air Force to immediately launch a bombing raid on Japanese military targets with the 18 B-17Ds based at Clark Field, of the 19th Heavy Bombardment Group, targeting the Imperial Japanese Air Force (IJAF) bases and Imperial Japanese Navy (IJN) ports identified during the photoreconnaissance mission over Formosa. The U.S. Navy Asiatic Fleet would commence combined operations (ABDA) under command of Dutch General Hein ter Poorten.

Historical documents record that the United States Army Forces Far East commander in the Philippine Isles, Lieutenant General Douglas Arthur MacArthur, did not execute Phase I on December 3, 1941, as commanded by President Roosevelt, his Commander-In-Chief. He not only did not execute Phase I, he did not execute Phase II, on December 8, 1941, as commanded by President Roosevelt, MacArthur ordered Major General Lewis Hyde Brereton, CG FEAF, to unload his bombers and stand down. Why General MacArthur chose not to obey his Commander-In-Chief is a mystery to this day.

At 0755 hours, Sunday, December 7, 1941, Hawaiian Time, 1355 hours, Sunday December 7, 1941, Washington, D.C. time, and 0225 hours, Monday, December 8, 1941, Manila Time, the Imperial Japanese Naval Air Forces commenced a surprise air attack on Oahu, U. S. Territory of Hawaii. Targets included Naval Air Stations Ford Island, Barbers Point, and Kaneohe; Hickam, Wheeler, and Bellows Army Air Fields; Ewa Marine Corps Air Station, Schofield Army Barracks, casual civilian targets, and, of course, Navy ships anchored or moored at the Pearl Harbor Naval Base and around Naval Air Station Ford Island.

Most historical writers agree that for nearly ten hours, USAFFE appears to have taken no action (Rainbow 5) against the Japanese until after the Imperial Japanese Air Forces attacked civilian and military targets in the Philippine Isles. Major General Lewis H. Brereton had placed his entire command, FEAF, on full alert status when the order to execute Phase I was received.

FEAF pursuit and fighter planes, Boeing P-26A, Republic P-35A, Curtiss P-40B and P-40E, were scattered over several outlying unfinished airfields. Many of them did get into the air, acquitted themselves admirably knocking down several of the Japanese bombers and fighters, apparently without General MacArthur's knowledge.

Crude radar, extreme lack of communications training in air-to-air and air-to-ground radio command circuits and poor communications at all command levels hampered the squadrons' efforts for better results.

Inexplicably, President Roosevelt and the War Department did not relieve Lieutenant General MacArthur of his command on December 17/18, 1941, the day Lieutenant General Short, commanding the Army in Hawaii, and Admiral Kimmel, commanding the Pacific Fleet from Pearl Harbor, were relieved of their commands because of the Pearl Harbor disaster. Those two flag officers faced Boards of Inquiry, Courts-martial, and Congressional hearings several times over. There was never an investigation into Lieutenant General MacArthur's strange behavior.

Beyond belief, President Roosevelt invested Lieutenant General Douglas A. MacArthur with the Medal of Honor shortly after he arrived in Melbourne, Australia in April 1942.

The premise of this novel argues that Lieutenant General MacArthur should have been relieved of his command and sent home in disgrace to respond to an Article 70 Board of Inquiry hearing on several charges pertaining to events occurring on December 8, 1941, in The Philippines Isles, and thereafter.

I have referred to "The Soldier and the Law", Second Edition, 1943, Articles of War, and its summary of the Army Manual for Courts-Martial, MCM 1928, for Article 70 procedures and techniques.

Of course, some people named in this story are a product of my imagination. Others are extracted from my resource material.

The Battlin' Bastards of Bataan were still fighting as the Article 70 hearing begins. Events might have unfolded like this . . . . .

PART ONE

The Missing Ten Hours

Unfurl the Banners: Uncase the War Drums

Many events around the world bubbled and seethed, impacting on the War Lords of Japan, the Philippines and the Pacific War. Dates and times presented herein are in the subjects' time without reference to other time zones. The International Date Line, always confusing, is between the Philippines and Hawaii. Hawaii and east are a day earlier than the Philippines and Japan or Formosa.

**September 18, 1931
The Foreign Office
Imperial Palace
Tokyo, Japan**

(International News Service, Tokyo, Japan, 1931/09/18). The Foreign Office released a statement today, stating that saboteurs severely damaged railway beds, bridges, and the railroad signaling system belonging to the South Manchurian Railway Company. The Japanese Kwangtung Army proclaimed the Chinese had sabotaged the railway. This excuse permitted Japanese troops to invade South Manchuria on China's northeastern border.

The Japanese Army later occupied the whole of Manchuria and renamed the country Manchukuo, setting up a puppet government. This was not acceptable to the League of Nations but the Japanese pulled out of the League in 1932, ignoring the League's pronouncements.

November 1932
Democratic Headquarters
New York City, NY

(Associated Press, NYC/NY). Franklin Delano Roosevelt (FDR), on the second Tuesday of November, is elected President of the United States of America in the depth of the Great Depression. FDR will take office January 20, 1933.

January 30, 1933
The Reichstag
Berlin, Germany

(Reuters News Service, Berlin, Germany, 01/30/33). Winning 37% of the national vote, the National Socialists Workers Party (NAZI) became the largest elected party in the Reichstag (German Parliament). President Paul von Hindenburg who utterly loathed Hitler, by German law, was required to appoint Adolf Hitler Chancellor of Germany.

August 2, 1934
Berlin, Germany

(Reuters News Service, Berlin, Germany, 08/02/1934). President Paul Ludwig Hans Anton von Beneckendorff und von Hindenburg died today. A period of mourning was declared by Adolf Hitler. It remains to be seen what Chancellor Adolf Hitler and his handpicked cabinet will do.

MacArthur's Pacific Appeasement, December 8, 1941
Part I
The Missing Ten Hours

August 4, 1934
The Chancellery
Berlin, Germany

(Reuters News Service, Berlin, Germany, 08/04/1934). Chancellor Hitler and his hand-picked cabinet have passed a law declaring the presidency dormant. The role and powers of the head of state are transferred to Hitler, who has proclaimed himself "Der Fuhrer", giving him command of the German Armed Forces.

October 1935
League of Nations
Geneva, Switzerland

(Suise Wire Service, Geneva.) Haile Selassie, Emperor of Ethiopia, King of Kings, Lord of Lords, and Time Magazine Man of the Year 1935, appeared before the General Assembly of the League of Nations and begged the Members not to pass the Hoare-Laval plan to turn over most of Abyssinia to the Italian Dictator, Il Duce, Benito Mussolini, and force him to call off the invasion. The voting members ignored his plea.

General Pietro Badoglio and his Italian Army occupied Ethiopia, used Mustard Gas on the populace and Ethiopian Troops, and easily captured the Capital, Addis Ababa in May 1936. Abyssinia, or Ethiopia, was annexed by the Kingdom of Italy under Italian Military Occupation becoming the Colony of Italian East Africa.

Mid-October 1935
SS President Hoover
Manila, The Philippines

(Associated Press Manila 10/35) Major General Douglas MacArthur, family, and military staff arrived in Manila aboard the steamship, SS President Hoover. He would become President-elect Manuel Queson's Military Advisor to build the Philippines military establishment. The MacArthur's would be quartered in the Manila Hotel Penthouse on Manila Bay; special air-cooling equipment has been ordered for his quarters. His appointment as Field Marshall of the Philippines Army would coincide with the November 15th Inauguration of President Queson. MacArthur's Chief of Staff is expected to be Major Dwight D. Eisenhower.

March 7, 1936
The Rhineland
France

Der Fuhrer Adolf Hitler, directly against the Treaty of Versailles of July 1919, and the Locarno Pact of 1925, denounced the Locarno Pact, marched his troops into and occupied the demilitarized zone of the Rhineland, forcing the French troops back to France. Der Fuhrer gambled that France and Great Britain would do nothing but complain.

They complained but Nazi Germany re-militarized the Rhineland with the German Army.

July 17, 1936
Military GHQ
Madrid, Spain

(International News Wire Service, Madrid, 07/17/36) A military Junta under General Jose Sanjurjo made a declaration of opposition against the elected Second Spanish Republic. Shortly, General Francisco Franco began a protracted war against the government for control of Spain. He was assisted by Hitler's Wehrmacht and Luftwaffe, Italian Air Service, and the Portuguese Army.

The existing Spanish Royalist government was assisted by the Loyalists consisting of the governments of Soviet Union and Mexico, and private citizens of the United States volunteering as Loyalist soldiers in the Abraham Lincoln Brigade.

July 7, 1937
Yongding River Bridge
Lugouqiao, China

A Japanese soldier missed morning roll call. The Japanese Army commander accused the Chinese Army Commander across the river bridge of capturing their soldier. Desultory fighting began with potshots and sniper fire between Chinese and Japanese troops. In days, a full blown war was on. By August 1st, the Japanese Army controlled Chinese territory from Peiping to Nanking.

March 11, 1938
10 Downing Street
London, England

A State Luncheon was given in honor of Herr Joachim von Ribbentrop, German Ambassador to Great Britain, newly appointed as Germany's Foreign Minister. During the farewell luncheon, a messenger handed Prime Minister Chamberlain a note: German troops were marching into Austria for the Anschluss to fold Austria into the Third Reich. The PM abruptly rose in anger and ordered the Ribbentrops to leave immediately.

Madame von Ribbentrop warned the British to remember who their friends were.

March 13, 1938
Der Fuhrer's Private Residence
Berchtesgarden, Germany

The Austrian Chancellor, Kurt von Schuschnigg, refused Der Fuhrer's demands and resigned. Arthur Seyss-Inquart, leader of the Austrian Nazi Party, became Chancellor and invited the German Army to occupy Austria. Austria, renamed Ostmark, became another German state.

October 10, 1938
Munich, Germany

Between the UK Prime Minister Chamberlain, Nazi German Der Fuhrer Hitler, and Italian Il Duce Mussolini, an accommodation was achieved whereby the Czechoslovakian government submitted to Nazi German demands. The Czech portion was occupied by German Army troops in March 1939, and renamed Sudetenland as another state of Germany.

April 1, 1939
Madrid, Spain

On April 1, 1939, Francisco Franco became the 68th Prime Minister of Spain, Caudillo de España and Generalissimo.

1200, April 7, 1939
Rome, Italy

Italian News Service, Rome, Italy. The Italian Foreign Minister announced today that Comando Supremo, Il Duce Benito Mussolini, has found it is necessary to protect Italian interests abroad. Italian Armies, led by General Alfredo Guzzoni, are invading Albania. The minister did not answer questions.

The Albanian Kingdom was rapidly overrun. Its ruler King Zog I, with Queen Geraldine Apponyi, and infant son Leka fled for Greece, taking with them part of the gold reserves. The country was made part of Greater Italy and the Italian Empire.

"Drummers!   Beat to Quarters"

0440, September 1, 1939
Wielun, Poland

The Nazi Luftwaffe Junkers 87 Stuka dive bombers attacked and nearly destroyed this small Polish town.

Five minutes later at 0445, in Westerplatte, Danzig, on the Baltic Sea, the German battleship Schleswig-Holstein opened fire on the Polish military depot.

Also at 0445 near Mokra, Poland, Nazi troops crossed the border. Germany invaded Poland, claiming that Polish troops crossed the border and attacked a German radio station. (German criminals were dressed in Polish Army uniforms and executed on site for NAZI photographs.) In Warsaw, the Premier, on Radio Warsaw, called up the Polish Army and Air Force to resist the German Army incursion into Poland.

1200, September 3, 1939
British Broadcasting Company
London, England

Atop the House of Commons Bell Tower, the mellow tones of the bell tolled twelve.
"This is BBC London Calling. Great Britain this morning has declared war on Germany for their outrageous and illegitimate invasion of Poland."

October 14, 1939
British Broadcasting Company
London, England

"This is BBC London Calling. In a shocking disaster, a German U-boat sneaked into Scapa Flow Naval Anchorage, torpedoed and sank His Majesty's battleship HMS Royal Oak with severe loss of life. It was reported by International News Wire Service that Adolf Hitler danced with joy!"

May 9, 1940
Reuter's News Service
Paris, France

BULLETIN. The Foreign Ministry issued a terse statement confirming that German troops crossed the French border in the Ruhr Valley and are approaching the invincible Maginot Line.

1200, May 10, 1940
British Broadcasting Company
London, England

"This is BBC London Calling. Prime Minister Neville Chamberlain has resigned following the German invasion of France. King George VI has asked Winston Churchill to meet with him at 6 this evening. It is believed the King George will ask Mr. Churchill to form a new government."

May 24, 1940
British Broadcasting Company
Radio Journalist with British Troops
Portsmouth, England

"This is the BBC calling from the Naval Establishment in Portsmouth. The British Expeditionary Force in France is being recalled to England. 335,000 British, French, Belgian, Polish and some other small forces will withdraw at Dunkirk. A large French Army force is protecting the withdrawal. Most British Hurricane squadrons will return to their air bases in England in a few days; at least two squadrons will remain in the Low Countries to cover the withdrawal.

The Royal Navy is calling upon all yachtsmen and all shallow draft boats able to get close to shore to help evacuate the troops from Dunkirk beaches. It is hoped the final troops shall be taken off the beach before June 4th."

June 28, 1940
Commander, U.S. Naval Asiatic Fleet
U.S. Navy Station Cavite
Luzon, the Philippines

"Admiral, Commander Jenson from CAST is here, urgently requesting a meeting with you." reported the Admiral's Secretary, Chief Olsen.

That's odd. He's never asked for an ad hoc meeting before.

"Very well, Chief. Send him in."
Chief Yeoman Olsen, CYN, turned to the Lieutenant Commander and said, "Go right in, Commander."

Jenson opened the Admiral's door and walked in, turned and waited until the door close behind him. He turned to the admiral. "Good afternoon, Admiral. Something very important has come up you need to know about, and more important, all Navy and Air Force squadrons need to learn."
Admiral Hart's shrewd eyes looked at Lieutenant Commander Jenson carefully. "And, what have you learned from the Japanese?" he asked sharply.

"The Japs have a hot new carrier fighter plane. It is a Mitsubishi Type 0. Top level speed appears to be 340 mph, it mounts two 20mm cannons in its wings, and two 7.7mm machine guns firing through its propellers. It will be put through its paces at the IJN air field at Yokosuka, Japan." He looked at the admiral for a moment and them continued. "That is better than anything the Navy or Army Air Force has." His demeanor was very sober.

"What's your source of this information, Jenson?" the admiral asked.
"We pulled this from a JN-25 coded message, bragging to all their forces about the new Navy Carrier fighter we are going to name Zero."
"Okay, get this into the system via Officer Messenger mail to CNO as soon as possible. Meanwhile, pass it to Station 6 for their study, too."
"Aye aye, Admiral. Bye your leave, sir?" Admiral Hart nodded and turned back to his incoming basket.

MacArthur's Pacific Appeasement, December 8, 1941
Part I
The Missing Ten Hours

0945, June 29, 1940
IJN Air Base
Yokosuka, Japan

Lieutenant Tamotsu Yokoyama turned on final in his Kawasaki Type 96 open cockpit, fixed landing gear, carrier fighter, and spotted new all-metal aircraft lined up on the tarmac.

He soon found out his orders. He was to put the new aircraft, a Mitsubishi Type 0 Model 11 Carrier Fighter through its paces, "stretching the metal," so to speak.

Following all the tests and modifications thereof, he would take a section of six aircraft and supporting ground crews to IJN/IJAF Air Base at Hankow, China, and place it in combat against the Chinese Air Force, especially against the new Flying Tigers squadrons with their Curtis P-40Bs who have been shooting down our bombers and fighters.

July 10, 1940
Fighter Command
London, England

The Air Battle between the RAF and Luftwaffe begins on this date and would continue until October 31, 1940. Hermann Goring's famed Messerschmidt ME-109 and Focke-Wulf FW-190 fighters, the Messerschmidt ME-110 fighter-bombers and Dorner DO-17 bombers could not overpower the RAF with their Hawker Hurricanes and just coming on line, the new Supermarine Spitfire.

July 15, 1940
4th Composite Squadron
Clark Field
Luzon, the Philippines

Colonel Lawrence Churchill was depressed. All, that is, every type aircraft he had was so old, so out of date, the letter "Z" for Obsolete had been added to all his aircrafts' designators. Not only that, the new Second Lieutenants arriving on the transports were right out of flight school without combat training or experience and had less than 25 hours stick time.

Reading the news and listening to BBC every night about the so-called Battle of Britain and the fighters facing each other was frightening. Absolutely none of their fighters or pursuit planes were worthy of battle with modern aircraft.

The number of aircraft accidents with these new pilots was almost "okay". It was a way to write off these old aircraft. The Colonel even pleaded with the Department of the U.S. Army in Washington, D.C., to remember we also are part of the Army Air Force.

July 22, 1940
CG, Philippine Army Department
Intramurous, Fort Santiago
Manila, the Philippines

Four hundred years ago and more, Chinese pirates regularly raided the Islands of the Thieves with impunity. Exasperated, the Spanish Governor-General of the islands, now called the Philippine Isles, began building a huge fortress with high, thick walls. The walls were constructed of volcanic rock on the outside facing, and baked brick on the inner wall facing with earth packed between the two walls. This project would take nearly one hundred years to complete.

The later Spanish Governor-General named the fortress "Intramurous" meaning "Within the Walls" when it was completed in 1570. This fortress of 64 city blocks was occupied by approximately 10,000 people of all nations and races. Fort Santiago, a military fort with soldiers and cannons, brought peace to the area.

General Grunert looked up from the staff paper just presented by his Chief of Staff. "My God, Louie, get a letter out to the War Department with Churchill's complaint as an appendix. I want to make sure General Marshall understands these are the aircraft we have to fight with. They should have been—what is the navy says? They should be deep-sixed and modern fighters and bombers sent out here.

"Good Lord, Boeing P-26A Peashooters? Martin ZB-10B twin-engine bombers? Thomas-Moore ZO-19E observation biplane aircraft, and even the older Keystone ZB-3A bomber? We need to get rid of them all."

He snapped his fingers. In that letter, request permission to transfer them all the the Philippine Air Corps."

"Yes sir, General. I'll have it for your signature tomorrow morning."

"Well, okay, it's too hot to get anything done right now. Tomorrow morning will be fine." With that, the general put on his hat and headed for the Army and Navy Club in Manila.

September 3, 1940
Vichy French Foreign Ministry
Hanoi, French Indochina

(Reuters Wire Service, Hanoi, FIC 40/09/03) As reported by an unnamed French official, the Vichy government in Hanoi, Governor General Jean Decoux, has signed Accords with Japan, to allow 40,000 Japanese troops, equipment, and supplies to move into bases in northern Indochina.

1120, September 25, 1940
South China Sea
USN PBY-4 N3690
VP-104, Patrol Wing 10

"Sparks? Are you in contact with Olongapo?" Asked Lieutenant (JG) Armstrong.

"Was when I sent out our last position report about 15 minutes ago, sir." He responded.

"Standby to write." He paused allowing Grimshaw time to pick up pencil and paper.

"Go ahead, Skipper."

"Twenty ship convoy approaching French Indochina coast. Many transport ships, cargo ships, and escorting destroyers—Wait, they are throwing anti-aircraft fire at us. Chuck, get us the hell out of here now!" The Catalina banked and turned eastward, away from the convoy.

21

"The convoy is near Haiphong. Uhh, that's it, Grimshaw. Get it out."
"Okay Skipper. Give me a couple and it will be gone.

NPO3 NPO3 V N3690 N3690

V NPO3 GA
BT
JAP CONVOY MANY TRANSPORTS MANY CARGO SHIPS, ESCORTING DESTROYERS APPROACHING FRENCH INDOCHINA COAST NEAR HAIPHONG STOP THEY SHOT AT US
BT
ACK GA
V NPO3 R VA

"They got it, Skipper."
"Roger, we are continuing on surveillance."

Sunrise, September 26, 1940
Harbor Anchorage
Haiphong, French Indochina

Japanese troops, tanks, and artillery begin debarking ships off the Haiphong coast.

1000, September 27, 1940
Imperial Palace
Tokyo, Japan

Prime Minister Fumimaro Konoe convened this meeting he called *Imperial Headquarters—Government Liaison Conference.* Present were eight senior military officers and three civilian dignitaries to determine the future direction of Japan's foreign policy.

They resolved that Japan will take advantage of the European War. All land and sea territory East of India and North of Australia and New Zealand will be incorporated in what would be called the *Greater East Asia Co-Prosperity Sphere*. Most important would be the subjugation of Dutch East Indies, British and other areas rich in mineral and oil.

In the same meeting, Japan also signed the Tripartite Pact with Germany and Italy.

1200, September 28, 1940
Reuters News Bureau
Hanoi, French Indochina

BULLETIN. There is an unconfirmed report that a large contingent of Japanese Army Troops have landed near Haiphong. Further developments as they happen.

1630, October 10, 1940
The White House
Washington, D.C.

President Franklin Delano Roosevelt has signed an Executive Order setting a complete embargo on exports to Japan. This is retribution for the events in the Far East two weeks ago. This announcement was released after the Wall Street New York Stock Exchange closed for the day.

1730, December 17, 1940
Times Bureau Chief
Manila, Philippines

In an interview with Military Advisor to Philippines President Manuel Queson, Field Marshall Douglas MacArthur, in his Penthouse quarters atop the Manila Hotel, stated "he has trained 125,000 Filipino soldiers with six months basic training and more were now being trained. If he had enough time, he could make it into a fighting force. This changes the entire strategic plan in this part of the world."

Admiral Hart threw down his Manila Times newspaper in disgust.

MacArthur's Pacific Appeasement, December 8, 1941
Part I
The Missing Ten Hours

I cannot believe that blowhard said that. He knows better or should.

January 10, 1941
Sidney Huff's Cottage
Cavite, The Philippines

Huff was quite surprised when his telephone rang. It had never happened before. He placed a Commonwealth One Peso note on the page he was reading, closed his book, got up and went over to the desk where his candlestick telephone was installed.

"Hello?" He spoke.

"Am I speaking to former U.S. Navy Commander Sidney Huff?" a bland male voice asked.

"Retired Commander Sidney Huff, yes. What can I do for you, mister …?

Brusquely now, "Hold for Field Marshall Douglas MacArthur."

"What? Hello? Hello?"

Huff heard the other telephone being picked up.

"Mister Huff, this is Douglas MacArthur. How are you today?" Asked a warm, friendly voice.

"I am just fine, sir. To what do I owe this pleasure, Field Marshall?"

"Admiral Hart told me he thinks rather highly of you. You were a fine staff officer before your unfortunate heart attack and he was sorry to lose you; that he simply had no billet for a civilian. How is your health nowadays, Mister Huff?" MacArthur asked kindly.

"Well," he chuckled, "I'm not quite ready to swing a mashie yet. Other than heavy exercise, I am feeling fairly well. Why do you ask, Field Marshall?" Huff's voice was steady but very curious.

"I am not satisfied with the organization and speed over there in the Philippine Navy Section." He answered. "There is a need for someone knowledgeable in "naval" affairs to head up the effort to get that new Philippine Navy Motor Torpedo Boat Offshore Patrol Navy built, trained, and operating.

MacArthur's Pacific Appeasement, December 8, 1941
Part I
The Missing Ten Hours

"I need someone to light a fire under those Navy types and get the Filipino staff off the mark. They are falling way behind schedule." MacArthur paused here to allow Huff to respond but Huff wouldn't bite. "I'm sure you are aware that only two PT boats from Britain are in commission."

"Yes, they were building or preparing to build another forty-eight, as I recollect. The Brits certainly have their hands full and cannot build any more in Britain," answered Mr. Huff.

MacArthur cleared his throat and asked in the third person, "Would Mister Sidney Huff, Retired U.S. Navy Commander, consider an appointment to Field Marshall MacArthur's General Staff? His civilian appointment would be equivalent to a Lieutenant Colonel in the Philippine Army, same as a Navy Commander."

Surprised and amazed by the offer, Huff stammered a moment and had to clear his own throat twice. He replied in kind: "Mister Huff would be delighted to accept such an appointment, if offered."

Commander Sidney L. Huff, USN, suffered a heart attack on a Saturday afternoon in August 1940, while playing golf. That he survived was a minor miracle, accomplished by the doctors at the U.S. Navy Hospital, Canacao, at Sangley Point Naval Base.

Commander Huff had served on Admiral Hart's staff as Chief of the Port Facilities Section for U.S. Naval Bases at Olongapo, Sangley Point, Subic Bay, Cavite, and Davao. He knew his career in the U.S. Navy was over. When the local Navy Medical Board informed him he was to be medically retired and sent back to the States, he declined to leave the Philippines; he was choosing Manila as his new home of record; there was nothing for him back in the States—he had no wife or family left.

He did have a lot of civilian and military friends here and thought he could find suitable employment as a civilian in government or military service.

Mr. Sidney Huff found a very nice bachelor pad (living room, kitchenette, bedroom, bathroom, and lanai) near the naval base. He settled in his new apartment to enjoy retired life.

Five foot, eight inches tall, 142 pounds, not quite a trim figure, grey eyes, brown hair, and a pale complexion described Sidney rather well. His high tenor voice was still unsteady but not shaky. The former spring in his step had yet to return.

By mid-February 1941, the third PT boat was ready for sea trials. The fourth hull and the fifth keel were on the ways. Packard or Rolls-Royce engines had been ordered from the United States. Funding was sparse and only one set of 3 Packard engines was currently being freighted to the Philippines by sea. Sidney Huff was pleased with his efforts.

January 13, 1941
Fort Humphreys
Washington, DC

Former Air Marshall Sir Hugh Dowding, RAF, recommends the Battle of Britain air defense plan for the Philippines and Oahu, Territory of Hawaii.

It is reported that the Chief of Staff, U.S. Army will take it under advisement.

February 11, 1941
Munitions Building
War Department, Air
Washington, DC

Major Hoyt Vandenberg, USAAF, says the fabric-covered control surfaces on the Curtis P-40B with two .50 caliber machine-guns firing through the propellers, and four . 30 caliber machine-guns mounted on the wings provide inadequate fire power, and thus, are completely unsuitable for combat against a first class power like Japan.

0630, March 7, 1941
17th Pursuit Squadron

Nichols Field
Luzon, the Philippines

The squadron commander and his executive officer marched along the line of Republic P-35A Guardian pursuit planes to their own ship. This morning these two lieutenants were to fly, touching down at other emergency fields, all the way to the dusty field at Aparri on the northwest coast of Luzon. There, they would be refueled for return trip to Nichols Field, 270 air miles away.

This was the first time they had flown in their brand new Guardians, feeling rather smug they did not have to fly the Boeing P-26A open cockpit Peashooters anymore. The Peashooters were left for new, barely trained flyers arriving by ship.

0800, May 4, 1941
Headquarters
Philippines Department of the U.S. Army
Intramurous, Fort Santiago
Manila, the Philippines

General Order Number 1. The Philippine Department Air Force (PDAF) is hereby established. Brigadier General Henry B. Clagett, commanding. The Warning Service under G2 is hereby transferred to PDAF and renamed Air Warning Service (AWS).

0900, May 4, 1941
AWS O and I Center
Clark Field, Luzon

The new Commanding Officer of AWS O&I, Lieutenant Colonel Alexander Campbell, immediately moved the new central Operations and Information Center to Clark Field Operations office. His command consisted of 3 officers and 11 senior enlisted men. Campbell called his command to an initiating conference to determine just how this would work.

They taped gridded charts of the Philippines on a circular plywood table, temporarily resting on sawhorses. Three barstools were located around the table, each with a telephone operator headset and microphone. Input voice line's lamps would light up when an incoming call is detected from AWS Command, various Army and Navy command radio circuits, telegraph, teletype, and telephone lines from many phone networks, that could be switched to a headset.

Without aping the British Air Warning system, their plan was remarkably similar. All the military services would participate in the AWS through their various bases and stations. More than 400 Filipinos would call in reports to the Philippine Constabulary in their many native languages. The PC would relay the information in English to AWS, Clark Field.

A carpenter modified a six-foot ladder with a special chair for the watch officer to sit upon and overlook the plotting table. He would decide which air field and squadron would rise up and intercept the incoming enemy.

0615, May 10, 1941
27th Material Squadron
Clark Field, Luzon, the Philippines

"You got the key to this B-18?" asked the co-pilot, as they performed a walk around of this shiny, brand new medium bomber named the Bolo. This was the first delivery in the Philippines and they get to try it out.
"Yep," he answered, "do you have your copy of the Dash One (detailed instructions) for this type aircraft?"
"Yes sir."

The pilot sighed. "Okay, let's get aboard and go for a ride. We need to get up where it is cool." The B-18 Bolos are replacing the obsolete Martin ZB-10, which will become multi-engine training aircraft for the new flyers assigned to the 28th Bomb Squadron at Clark.

June 22, 1941
Reuters News Service
Berlin, Germany

BULLETIN. The German Foreign Service just announced the invasion of the Soviet Union along a 1,000 mile front across the Bug River, dividing Poland. This was necessary to protect their eastern flank from invasion by the USSR.

June 23, 1941
IJN General Staff
Tokyo, Japan

Admiral Osami Nagano, Chief of the Imperial Japanese Navy General Staff, affirmed today that the establishment of military bases in French Indochina and Thailand was necessary.

July 2, 1941
Clark Field
Luzon, the Philippines

Twenty-five Curtis P-40B Warhawks that had arrived in early May without Prestone Coolant, were now ready and being turned over to the 20th Pursuit Squadron for training. They still do not have disposable gas tanks.

July 2, 1941
Imperial Palace
Tokyo, Japan

Premier Konoe endorsed the establishment of the Greater East Asia Co-prosperity Sphere and a southward advance. Emperor Hirohito approved the policy document.

July 25, 1941
Reuters News Service
Hanoi, French Indochina

BULLETIN. Vichy French officials confirm that 40,000 Japanese troops have been landing in central and northern French Indochina without incident.

July 26, 1941
The White House
Washington, D.C.

In response to the Japanese landings yesterday in French Indochina, President Franklin Delano Roosevelt issued an Executive Order freezing all Japanese assets in the United States.

July 26, 1941
The White House
Washington, D.C.

President Roosevelt announced today he had created a new Army command in the Philippines: the U.S. Army Forces in the Far East (USAFFE). Douglas A. MacArthur has been recalled to active duty as Lieutenant General to serve as Commanding General of the newly designated command.

Sidney Huff was shocked and felt uneasy when Field Marshall MacArthur was suddenly recalled to the U.S. Army as a Lieutenant General to command all U.S. Army forces in the Far East (USAFFE). Huff continued his efforts to oversee building the Motor Torpedo Boat Division for the Philippine Navy. It was interesting, and he enjoyed a good relationship with the Filipino personnel.

MacArthur's Pacific Appeasement, December 8, 1941
Part I
The Missing Ten Hours

August 1, 1941
Air Warning Service
Fort McKinley
Manila, Luzon

      The AWS Squadron, now nearly 200 strong, consists of a secret SCR-270B Mobile Radar unit and two SCR-271 Fixed Station Radio sets. These have arrived and are being set up for testing and alignment of delicate parts. Upon completion, the squadron will be moved to and operate at Iba Field.

August 9, 1941
PM Churchill arrives on HMS Prince of Wales
President Roosevelt arrives on USS Augustus
Placentia Bay, Argentia, Newfoundland

The two leaders meet in secret with their respective war staffs, out of which comes the Atlantic Charter, among other agreements.

September 3, 1941
Headquarters, U.S. Asiatic Fleet
Naval Station, Subic Bay,
Zambales, the Philippines

      "Admiral, Commander Jenson has urgent information for you," called the Chief Yeoman outside Admiral Hart's office.
"Very well, send him in."
The chief put his phone down and turned to Commander Jenson. "You may go in now, Commander."
"Good morning, Admiral. Got some bad news for you." He said.
"Oh," raising his eyebrows. "What is it this time?"

"We have been decoding several JN-26 messages from the IJN high command. The entire Jap Navy has been placed on a war footing."

"You are just full of good news, Jenson. Pass this along to Station 6 at the Intramuro for their edification. See if they hear anything similar on their networks."

"Aye aye, Admiral. I'll be in touch." He did an about face and marched out of the admiral's office.

Hart dialed his secretary. "Chief, call a general staff meeting for 1300 this afternoon. Commander Jenson need not attend."

"Aye aye, Admiral."

September 12, 1941
Air Control Tower
Clark Field, Luzon

"Ahhh, Clark Tower this is Air Force Forty dash Three Oh Nine Two at twenty thousand, 175 knots, a flight of nine B-17D's requesting landing instructions over."

"Three Oh Nine Two, be advised Clark is closed to all traffic due to the typhoon. Return to Del Monte Field over."

"Clark Nine Two, our charts don't show a Del Monte Field. You should have our flight plan from Hickam in Honolulu. We are over Negros Island, approaching Mindoro, and close to going on thirty minute reserve fuel now. I repeat request landing instructions over."

The Control Tower Operator looked at his speaker, dumbfounded.

What the fuck? Why aren't they on the board?

He had no advance notice of this flight. Keying his microphone, he said, "Roger Nine Two. Visibility near zero, repeat, visibility near zero. Wind at surface, sixty knots, gusting to eighty knots, repeat wind at surface sixty knots, gusting to eighty knots. Altimeter setting is two nine decimal two four inches, repeat altimeter setting two nine decimal two four inches. You copy? Over."

"Roger Clark. At least the sun is shining up here. Unless you advise otherwise, when we reach Manila Bay, I will pass each ship at three minute intervals to you. Request additional lighting please. Over"

"Roger Nine Two, I will give landing instructions when you arrive here, good luck. Out.

The Sergeant grabbed his telephone and dialed Flight Operations.

"Flight Ops, Lieutenant Chesterfield, go ahead"

"Tower here, Sergeant Campbell, sir. I have a flight of nine B-17D's inbound from Hawaii . . . .

"What the hell? Tell 'em to go to Del Monte. We're socked in here."

"Two things, Lieutenant. First, they don't have charts for Mindanao or even know what Del Monte is. Second, they have enough fuel to get here. They would like extra lights on arrival, sir. Your call sir, do I tell them to crash or come on in?"

Shortly, the B-17D's began appearing at near tree top level. The first B-17D nearly took out the Tower.

The 28th Bomb Squadron was beginning to be reinforced with the latest and hottest bombers in the world.

September 29, 1941
SS American Press
Manila Harbor, the Philippines

Along with Army and Air Force personnel arriving for duty, fifty boxed Curtis P-40E Warhawk fighters were unloaded for the 17th and 3rd Pursuit Squadrons.

October 3, 1941
Headquarters, Eleventh Air Fleet
IJN Air Base Kanoya
Kyushu, Japan

Lt. Yokoyama reported to the Planners that the Mitsubishi Type 0 Carrier Fighter (Zero) can fly combat-loaded, attack, and return to base over 1,000 nautical miles, roundtrip. He explained this was based on their routine bombing missions in the Chinese theater of Operations.

Therefore, the Zeros can fly from Takao Air Base to Clark (450 NM), or Manila (480 NM), or Nichols (510 NM). Lt. Yokoyama went on to state that since this fighter was introduced in China in September 1940, his pilots have accumulated over 1,000 hours in combat, flying the Zero.

October 5, 1941
HQ, FEAF
Neilson Field
Manila, the Philippines

Brigadier General Clagett has obtained signed agreements with Britain and Australia to use air bases in Australia, Malaya, Port Moresby, New Guinea, and Singapore. Borneo is not usable in the near future. This agreement includes USAAF support personnel, munitions, and spares.

October 9, 1941
General Officers Quarters
Neilson Field
Manila, the Philippines

General Clagett's wife called from Washington, D.C., to advise him that Major General Lewis Brereton will relieve Clagett within the month. This is an unexpected blow as he expected to command FEAF and because MacArthur did not advise him of the change.

Very upset, General Clagett requested an audience with General MacArthur. General Sutherland advised him the audience was denied. He had selected General Brereton because he had more experience than Clagett. General Clagett never saw MacArthur again nor Brereton after his arrival before he flew out on the China Clipper.

2013, October 17, 1941
Hamilton Field
Marin, California

Twenty-six B-17Ds of the 32nd Bomb Squadron, on the taxiway lumbered slowly toward the apron of Runway 16, squealing and groaning as they did. The lead B-17D braked to a stop before turning on to the duty runway. It was time to run up the engines and test mags.

Lt. Colonel Eubanks checked his radio channel and picked up his microphone. "Hamilton Tower this is Air Force forty dash three zero one three at the threshhold of runway one six with a flight of twenty-six B-17s, over."

The tower operator flicked a switch that turned on Runway 16 lights. "Roger, one three, at two minute intervals, you are cleared to runway one six. Take off and climb to two thousand feet, turn left to course one five zero true and maintain level and course until over San Francisco Bay. Then turn right to course two four zero true. Commence climb to ten thousand five hundred feet. Report passing through five thousand feet, over." Eubanks copied that onto his knee notepad.

"Roger Hamilton. Climb to two thousand feet, turn left to course one five zero true until over the Bay, new course two four zero true and climb to ten thousand five hundred feet, report passing through five thousand. Over."

"Roger one three. Change to Enroute control on channel seven zero six five kilocycles after departure, over.
"Roger Hamilton, one three turning onto one six now and rolling."
"Roger one three. Safe trip."
"Hamilton one three. Off at two zero one three, over.
"Hamilton two zero one three, out."

The 26 B-17D's, bound for Clark Field in the Philippines, departed at two minute intervals, beginning the 2,000 mile journey to Hickam Field on Oahu. They are assigned to the 19th Bombardment Group, Clark Air Field, 7,500 miles away.

Sunrise, October 19, 1941

Air Warning Service
Fort McKinley
Manila, the Philippines

The first SCR-270B Mobile Radar Unit (Secret) is being deployed today to Iba Field, Zambales, on the West Coast of Luzon. This unit consists of the Operations Van, a prime mover hauling the rotating radar antenna array, a stake body truck with spare parts, and the very heavy power van with extra fuel tanks, and the commander in a General Purpose vehicle, nicknamed Jeep. Two small buses carried troops to Iba yesterday.

Second Lieutenant Arnold Wimer, detachment Commander, started the convoy immediately following breakfast. He stood up in his jeep, looked back at his convoy, and circled his arm to start engines and begin rolling.

He had hoped that General MacArthur would visit their very modern electrical machinery before they departed. At least General Sutherland should have come by. Colonel Campbell visited several times and appeared knowledgeable about this new device.

This trip is exceedingly difficult with narrow dirt mountain roads and two very shaky wooden bridges over deep gorges. For that reason, two Filipino Engineering Platoons led the way, insuring a safe trip. They might have to brace the wooden bridges.

The convoy arrived at Iba Field after dark. The Iba ground support troops had already set up tents to house the enlisted men.

1500, November 4, 1941
Pan American Terminal
Canacao Bay, the Philippines

Major General Lewis H. Brereton, USAAF, had been impressed by the flight of 42 P-40s and P35As of his new command. His new command is to be the Far East Air Force upon his official arrival at Intramuro, Fort Santiago, 1 Calle Victoria, Manila.

His command will consist of a Bomber Command, escorting pursuit and fighter groups, and a Far East Air Service Command—a battalion of 1,174 officers and men to form the AWS. A bomber group of B-24C and B-24D Liberators would be based at Aparri field. These bombers could reach the Japanese main island of Honshu and return. U.S. Army Engineers, assisted by Filipino contractors, are to begin construction and expansion of Aparri Field this month.

The B-18's would be phased out as active bombers and used to train multi-engine pilots and co-pilots, as well as becoming a passenger and freight service aircraft. Also, the P-26's and ZB-10's would be transferred to the Philippine Air Corps.

He barely had time to meet with his Chiefs of Service before being tasked to meet with the British High Command. Three days after he arrived, MacArthur sent Brereton to Darwin, Australia, to organize a place for American B-17 bombers to be stored, armed, fueled, and otherwise serviced, repeating General Clagett's efforts. When he returned, MacArthur sent him immediately to Singapore on a similar mission.

November 13, 1941
Material Inspection
Clark Field
Luzon, the Philippines

General Brereton was furious. There were no spare parts for any of his aircraft anywhere on Luzon. Not only that, there were no tools of any kind to work on the aircraft if there had been spares.

He issued orders to buy tools on the open market around Manila. Any aircraft that broke down would be used as a spare parts "bin" until such time as the pipeline from San Francisco began to bring in the required parts and tools.

1050, November 15, 1941
Reconnaisance flight over Southern Formosa
USN PBY-4 4341

VP-101, Patrol Wing 10

Lieutenant (junior grade) Dennis Folkner, USN, Pilot-in-Command, was standing behind his left seat peering down at the Imperial Japanese Air Force (IJAF) airfield.

Man o man, would you look at all those bombers. Most of them are Bettys. But what are the single-engine jobs?

"Rusty, adjust our airspeed to 90 knots. We have to get pictures of all those bombers. Looks like over a hundred of them."

"Aye aye, Skipper." Ensign Jake "Rusty" Dillon reached up to the overhead panel from where he sat in the right co-pilot's seat and fiddled with both throttles until exactly 90 knots airspeed was indicated.

Dennis returned to his seat and fastened his safety belts. Picking up his microphone, he pressed the Intercom button. "Gray, you up?" (Aerial Radioman Third Class (AL3/c).
"Yes sir, Skipper. Whatcha got?"

"Grab your camera and the telephoto lense case and hustle back to the Port Bubble. I want a lot of closeup shots of those bombers and fighters." He paused for breath and said, "Oh yes, just make sure you get really focused on those fighters. They look new. At least, I have never seen pictures of one of those, and they haven't come up to harrass us yet."
"Right, Skipper. On my way." Gray grabbed the camera and telephoto lens case and worked his way back to the Port Bubble.
"Here," he said to Seaman First Class (S1/c) Adams,"hold the telephoto case while I some some covering shots." Adams silently obeyed, watching Gray do his thing. Gray was pissed.

I don't have a GE Light Meter anymore and the Supply Officer won't issue a new one until I pay for the last one that someone stole from the case.

He held out his hand to judge the illumination. Since Lt(jg) Dennis said sharp focus, he set the f-stop to 3.5 and shutter to 1/500th of a second. He focused on the airfield and covered the base with five shots.

Changing to the telephoto lens, he picked out every kind of aircraft on the field and got several shots of each.

"Adams, ask the skipper if there is anything else he wants covered." Adams nodded, unclipped his microphone from its holder, and spoke.

"Skipper, Gray wants to know what else you want photographed."

"No. It's time for him to send our position to Olongapo. Tell him to get back up here."

"Aye aye, sir." He looked at Gray. "Go home," jerking his thumb toward the front of the aircraft. Gray nodded and worked his way forward to his radio position and strapped in.

The Navigator had already placed a slip of paper on his tiny table. It was a standard form containing the aircraft ID, time of the report, latitude and longitude at the time of the report, direction of flight in degrees, altitude, true airspeed, speed over the surface, and weather conditions. Everything was in numbers.

Gray reached in front of him and flipped the power switch on his long range radio. Watching the needles and lights for a moment, he touched his morse code key to see if the needles moved. All was in order.

NPO3 NPO3 V N4341 N4341

N4341 V NPO3 GA
V N4341 . . . . . .

Gray hunched over his key and pounded out the 25 five-character numeric words.

V NPO3 R UR MSG – RTB – GA

"Skipper, Olongapo rogers for the position report and told us to Return To Base."

"Roger that, Gray." He reached up and moved the throttles to standard patrol speed of 125 knots. "Rusty, take us up to 6,500 feet and Turn us around to course 185 degrees magnetic."

"Gotcha, Skipper."

V N4341 ACK VA

I wonder if Commander Johansen knows about the new fighter? And, I wonder why they didn't come up to hassle us, today? Well, we'll see what the Air Department Commander thinks of that fighter. Let's see, this is the 15th. Our next weekly patrol assignment begins on December 6th. Time for a little relaxation and O Club time.

1100, November 28, 1941
CINC Asiatic Fleet
Operations Center
Marsman Building, Manila

"Good morning, Admiral. We just decoded this message for you from the Navy Department, sir." The officer messenger handed Admiral Hart the classified message board. Hart signed for it and leaned forward, elbows on his desk, to read it.

/ S E C R E T / THIS DISPATCH IS TO BE CONSIDERED A WAR WARNING STOP NEGOTIATIONS WITH JAPAN LOOKING TOWARD STABILIZATION OF CONDITIONS IN THE PACIFIC HAVE CEASED STOP AN AGGRESSIVE MOVE BY JAPAN IS EXPECTED WITHIN THE NEXT FEW DAYS STOP THE NUMBER AND EQUIPMENT OF JAPANESE TROOPS AND THE ORGANIZATION OF NAVAL TASK FORCES INDICATES AN AMPHIBIOUS OPERATION AGAINST EITHER THE PHILIPPINES COMMA THAI OR KRA PENINSULA OR POSSIBLY BORNEO STOP EXECUTE APPROPRIATE DEFENSIVE DEPLOYMENT END / S E C R E T /

Admiral Hart read the message a second time very carefully and considered what it did not say.

The Chief of Naval Operations did not say to execute Rainbow 5 Phase One! Just exactly must I do? First of all, I need to get the CAST O-I-C up here to find out what is the latest poop on the Jap movements per the PURPLE code or the Navy JN-25 or the JN-26 codes. I will continue sending the Catalina PBY-4s on patrol around southern Formosa.

He picked up the war warning and walked to the outer office. "Chief, get this message to all department heads as soon as possible, and announce a meeting of all department heads in one hour. And have this message sent to the army."

"Aye aye, Admiral," responded the Chief Yeoman (CYN) (In 1949, these initials of all chiefs were reversed: CYN, for example, became YNC.) "And I want to see Commander Jenson right now, and have him read this before he comes up."

"Aye aye, Admiral."

"Commander Jameson is here, Admiral."

"Send him in."

"Good morning, Admiral. The fast answer is no war traffic in the Japanese message traffic. However, we are looking into this with Station 6 in MacArthur's headquarters and at CINCPAC to see if we missed something."

"Very well. Keep me informed of any change. Don't discuss this at the department head meeting coming up,"

"Aye aye, Admiral. Is that all, sir?"

Admiral Hart waved him out and dropped his eyes to other message traffic.

1100, November 28, 1941
LT. Gen. MacArthur's office
HQ USAFFE
1 Calle Victoria
Intramurous, Fort Santiago
Manila, the Philippines

Brigadier General Sutherland, Chief of Staff, knocked and entered MacArthur's office. "General, I think you had better read this right now. I think it's a war warning."

MacArthur looked up from his desk top. "Oh?" and held out his hand for the message.

```
FROM CHIEF OF STAFF, US ARMY
TO US ARMY PACIFIC FT SHAFTER
US ARMY FORCES FAR EAST MANILA
/ S E C R E T /      NEGOTIATIONS WITH
JAPANESE APPEAR TO BE TERMINATED TO ALL
PRACTICAL PURPOSES COMMA WITH ONLY THE
BAREST POSSIBILITY THAT THE JAPANESE
GOVERNMENT MIGHT COME BACK AND OFFER TO
CONTINUE PERIOD JAPANESE FUTURE ACTION
UNPREDICTABLE BUT HOSTILE ACTION POSSIBLE
AT ANY MOMENT PERIOD IF HOSTILITIES CANNOT
BE AVOIDED COMMA THE UNITED STATES DESIRES
THAT JAPAN COMMIT THE FIRST OVERT ACT
PERIOD END END END   / S E C R E T /
```

General MacArthur leaned back in his chair and looked at his Chief of Staff. "Dick, do I hear the sound of musketry in the distance? Better assemble the general staff right away. Uh, do you know if Hart has received this?"

"General, I don't know but crypto was working on another important message when I picked this up."
"All right. Stay on top of it and have Sid set up the staff meeting. Oh yes, fire off a message to Singapore and get Brereton back here ASAP."
"On it, General."

0800, November 29, 1941
AWS
Iba Field
Zambales, Luzon

Following the general staff meeting, the AWS Chief at Nielson Field ordered Iba SCR-270B on 24-hour alert status. Three 8-hour shifts were initiated immediately. The crews practiced monitoring FEAF flights within their approximately 150 mile radius range. Information and updating data were passed to the Air Warning Center at Nielson Field and Clark Operations for their practice.

1530, December 1, 1941
Clark Field
Luzon, the Philippines

General Brereton climbed out of his B-17 that just returned from Singapore. He was very upset. He glared at his reception committee. Waving his arms around the field, he roared at them. "Dammit, I told you to disperse all aircraft and get them painted in camouflage. At least, we do have enough paint. If I had been an attacking force, Clark would be dead. Now, get busy and clean this up. We're close to going to war with the Japanese." Fuming, he stomped off, still growling at his aide. "Damn these lazy ass peacetime staff officers."

December 1, 1941
HQ USAFFE
Fort Santiago, Intramurous
Manila, the Philippines

Huff was again surprised when Lieutenant General MacArthur, today, practically drafted him into his U.S. Army General Staff with the rank of Lieutenant Colonel. During an interim period, Huff would serve as MacArthur's Junior Aide-de-Camp, serving his personal needs, living in MacArthur's quarters, taking his meals with the family, and assisting Brigadier General Richard K. Sutherland who acted as Senior Aide-de-Camp and Chief of Staff to General MacArthur. "Something more suitable will be found later," he promised.

December 2, 1941
IJAF Formosa

Japanese authorities of the Imperial Japanese Air Force were seriously irritated at the U.S. Navy PBY-4s that had been snooping around southern Formosa since the middle of October. All Japanese forces were ordered to shoot on sight, any hostile aircraft that appeared over Formosa.

December 2, 1941
HM Naval Station,
Singapore

The people of Singapore awoke this morning and discovered huge ships in the Roads. His Majesty's Indian Ocean Fleet had arrived from the Atlantic during the night and was anchored in the Roads in front of the Singapore waterfront.

The fleet consisted of battleship HMS Prince of Wales and battle cruiser HMS Repulse, with attending escort destroyers, tankers, and cargo ships.

0905, December 7, 1941
Large Japanese convoy
Gulf of Siam, Kra Isthmus

Japanese freighters and transports began unloading troops and supplies near the Thai towns of Singora and Patani, as well as Kota Bharu at the northern tip of British Malaya.

This is the initiating act of war in the Pacific and Indian Ocean areas.

December 7, 1941
IJN and IJAF forces
Formosa

Japanese IJAF twin-engine light bombers from Kato and twin-engine medium bombers from Choshu would bomb Baguio and Tuguegarao. At the IJN air field Takao, 81 attack bombers and 54 new Zero fighters would attack Nichols and Clark Fields. At Tainan Field, 27 twin-engine bombers and 36 Zeros would also attack Clark Field.

Japanese Intelligence believed the Americans at FEAF would respond with 30 P-35s at Clark Field, 30 P-35s at Nichols Field, 25 P-40s at Del Carmen Field, and 25 P-35s at Iba Field. Most American fighters were old and not a match for the new Type 0 fighter.

Japanese Intelligence also reported they believed the P-40s were very good fighters, having faced the Flying Tigers in China in their P-40B's. They also were aware of the 35 B-17s at Clark Field and believed about 10 B-17s and ZB-10s were stationed at Iba.

The Japanese flight commanders hoped to lose less than 50 percent of their aircraft on attack. They had no knowledge of the secret radar installation at Iba being tested, nor did they have knowledge of the B-17s stored at Del Monte Field on Mindanao.

**0342, December 7, 1941
Officer of the Deck, Bridge,
USS Condor AMS-10
Pearl Harbor Entrance Patrol
Territory of Hawaii**

"Quartermaster, signal the USS Ward, I have a periscope where no 'scope should be."
"Aye aye, sir."

The quartermaster twisted his signal light toward the USS Ward and called them.

7 7 7 7

GA

V 10 WE HAVE PERISCOPE WHERE NO PERISCOPE SHOULD BE K

V 7 ACK AR

"Officer of the Deck, the Condor has a submarine periscrope out there," screamed the quartermaster.

"Very well, where away?"

"Beats the crap out of me, sir. But it is in the channel."

The OOD reached down and buzzed the Captain, Lieutenant Outerbridge.

"Captain here. What have you?"

Sir, Condor reports a periscope near the channel entrance."

"Very well. Call General Quarters."

"Aye aye, Captain," and cranked the red handle to clang GQ.

The Ward searched for an hour without success.

0030, December 8, 1941
Headquarters, Eleventh Air Fleet
Tainan IJN Air Base
Formosa

Lieutenant Commander Nomura had driven down from Takao IJAF Air Field, after discussions with Commander Yasunobu regarding radio intercepts of American pilots and air fields in the Philippines. Two flights of Japanese reconnaisance aircraft were on radio silence. Fortunately, the Americans were not talking about intercepting, or even knowledge of those flights.

As he turned into the base and parked in front of the Eleventh Air Fleet headquarters. He was dismayed by the heavy fog.

I can't even see three feet in front of the car with my headlights. Flying is completely out of the question under such conditions.

0130, December 8, 1941
IJAF Air Base
Takao, Formosa

Going back to Takao, Nomura was shocked to see the fog was even worse here.

It will not be possible to meet the departure times from the five air bases involved with the Philippines attack. This is a disaster in the making!

As the time passed for the first departure by slow medium bombers, Admirals Onishi and Tsukahara reset departure to 0400.

The fog got worse.

Now, both admirals were worried FEAF would beat them to the punch, blasting all of the air bases on Formosa with those B-17's. FEAF would know about the surprise attack on Pearl Harbor at 0230. Onishi looked at Tsukahara. "Our losses will be very high, I am afraid. We won't be able to get the Zeros up against the B-17s."

0630, December 7, 1941
Pearl Harbor Entrance Buoy
Oahu, Hawaii

WARD THIS IS ANTARES. I HAVE A CONFIRMED CONTACT OF A SUBMARINE FOLLOWING ME.

THIS IS WARD. WHERE AWAY?
THIS IS ANTARES. IT IS BEHIND MY TOW.
THIS IS WARD. CONTINUE ON COURSE. WE WILL INTERCEPT.
THIS IS ANARES. WILCO OUT.

WARD THIS IS CATALINA N4478 I HAVE SUBMARINE IN SIGHT AND AM PROCEEDING TO DROP SMOKE.
ROGER CATALINA, I HAVE HER IN SIGHT AND AM FIRING.

First depth charge missed. Second shot from the Ward hit the submarine and it sunk.

0645, December 7, 1941
Bridge, USS Ward
At Pearl Harbor Entrance

"Radio this is the Captain. Send a priority message to the Harbormaster Pearl Harbor. Quote: We depth charged and hit a submarine at the channel entrance, then depth charged that submarine again and sank it. End quote."

"Radio, aye aye, sir."

0705, December 7, 1941
USS Ward Radio Room
Pearl Harbor Channel Entrance

The radioman on the Harbor Common voice circuit, cranked up his transmitter and keyed it.

HARBORMASTER PEARL THIS IS USS WARD OVER

WARD THIS IS THE HARBORMASTER OVER

THIS IS THE WARD BREAK
WE SHOT AND HIT A SUBMARINE AT THE CHANNEL ENTRANCE THEN DEPTH CHARGED AND SANK THAT SUBMARINE
BREAK OVER

AHHH THIS IS HARBORMASTER SEND AN AMPLIFYING REPORT TO CINCPACFLT RIGHT AWAY OVER

THIS IS WARD ROGER OUT

The Harbormaster, Lieutenant Hernandez, scratched his head and wondered out loud, "What the hell do I do with this now? The two signalmen looked at each other and shrugged. Hernandez picked up his phone and dialed the Command Duty Officer at CINCPACFLT. After seven rings, he hung up.

I'll try again at oh eight hundred. I know people will be there then.

He sat back down and continued to read the Honolulu Star Sunday paper.

0753, December 7, 1941
Harbormaster's Office
U.S. Naval Station Pearl Harbor
Oahu, Territory of Hawaii

The two signalmen, Romanski, Quartermaster First Class (QM1/c) and Halstead, Signalman Third Class (SM3/c), were dressed in the Uniform of the Day, undress white trousers, white web belt with black buckle, white scivvy shirt, white hat, and shiny black shoes. They trudged up the wooden stairs from the Harbormaster office to the topside Signal Bridge. It was nearly time for Prep to Morning Colors.

Halstead trotted over the planked deck to the Signal Bag and grunted as he threw back the navy gray painted canvas cover. Grabbing the Peter signal flag ring, he fastened it to the up-haul halyard clip and bent on the flag bottom clip to the down-haul halyard ring. Then Halstead threw Peter out on the deck behind him. Grabbing the up-haul end of the halyard, he turned and watched Romanski.
"Ready," he called.

Romanski, Quartermaster of the Watch on the Signal Bridge above the Harbormaster, had his arm cocked as he watched the second hand sweep toward 12. He had previously set his wrist watch to match the official U.S. Navy chronometer in the Harbormaster's office, one deck below the roof.

As the second hand hit 12, at exactly 0755, he shouted: "Hoist Prep to the Yardarm."
(The Peter signal flag is used to signal *Prepare to render Colors*.) As Romanski yelled, he cocked his head to listen to a strange humming sound, growing louder and looked around toward the source of the noise.

Peter, pulled by Halstead, rapidly ascended to the Yardarm where two-blocked, it would wait until exactly 0800. At that time, Romanski would yell out "Execute" and Halstead would yank the down-haul side of the halyard, bringing Peter rapidly to the deck. Romanski would raise the National Ensign at the same time.

The humming changed to a strong roar as many aircraft flew low over their heads toward the ships moored in Pearl Harbor.

"Hey Ski, what the fuck is that all about? Is the Air Force scheduled for battle drills today?" asked Halstead, loudly over the multiple engines noise.

"Beats the shit outa me, Hal." Ski responded.

The small aircraft banked as they headed toward ships tied up at Ten-Ten or moored along Ford Island. Orange meatballs glistened on their wings.

Romanski sucked in his breath. "Jesus Christ," as he started running for the ladder. "Those are Japs!" He screamed.

Lieutenant Jason Hernandez, duty Harbormaster, looked out his large picture window, looking down at his harbor, wondering what the Air Force was doing this Sunday morning.

Another surprise air raid drill, I suppose.

He pulled the clipboard toward him to check for the latest hot poop when the first explosion shattered his window and shards of glass tore his face apart. Romanski and Halstead arrived just after the glass shrapnel. Lieutenant Hernandez stood holding his face and began screaming in agony.

Ski grabbed the lieutenant's head and pulled his hand away. Glancing at the numerous fragments, he yelled out, "Hal, get the First Aid kit on the double!" Halstead swerved to the locker and pulled the kit and ran the remaining few steps to Ski and the lieutenant who was moaning now. Ski gently began pulling glass shards from his face as Halstead opened the kit and began pulling 4-by-4's, ointment, and adhesive tape from the kit..

"Mr. Hernandez, I don't see any glass in your eyes. Just hang on while I remove what I can and apply some dressings." Lt. Hernandez nodded, breathing deeply and tried not to scream.

Thunderous explosions were coming, one after another along with the sound of machine guns firing. Ski glanced out the window and saw many, many planes swooping and diving over all the ships and Ford Island Naval Air Station. Black smoke started rising from many ships.

Mr. Hernandez mumbled something and Ski leaned down to hear what he was trying to say.

"Get a message out on Harbor Common that the Japs are bombing Pearl Harbor. Get it out now!"

"Aye aye, sir. Hal, you take over here. I'll get the message out."

"Got it," Hal answered. He carefully took Mr. Hernandez' head in the crook of his arm and continued pulled shards of glass from his head.

Ski rushed to the radio and grabbed the mike, flipping the transmit key.

ALL SHIPS AND STATIONS THIS NET, THIS IS HARBORMASTER PEARL HARBOR

JAP AIR RAID ON PEARL HARBOR IN PROGRESS STOP THIS IS NOT DRILL I SAY AGAIN JAP AIR RAID ON PEARL HARBOR IN PROGRESS STOP THIS IS NOT DRILL OUT

He killed the transmit key, looked at the sickening scene in the harbor and went back to the lieutenant and Halstead.

"Hal," Romanski said, handing him the keys to his car, "take Mr. Hernandez to the hospital now. He may get treatment right away. I suspect there are going to be a lot of sailors heading that way in a few minutes."

"You got it, Ski. Come on, Mr. Hernandez, we need to get down below and get over to the Navy Hospital before the crowds begin to appear." His voice was excited but quiet. Romanski looked around the office with its shattered glass.

Nothing I can do here.   Oh, hell yes there is!

He dashed up to the Signal Bridge and hoisted the American Flag. After a little thought, he also bent on and

51

hoisted AIR RAID IN PROGRESS. That accomplished, he returned to the Harbormaster office to await further orders.

0235, December 8, 1941
Message Center FEAF
Nielson Field, Manila

The cryptographer read the decrypted teletype tape. "Oh, Fuck me!" he cried. He routed the message to all FEAF headquarters

HEADQUARTERS, U.S. ARMY HAWAII
ATTENTION ALL COMMANDERS

JAPAN HAS BEGUN HOSTILITIES. CONDUCT YOURSELVES ACCORDINGLY.

0240, December 8, 1941
Admiral Hart's Quarters
Manila Hotel
Manila, the Philippines

Five foot ten inch tall Admiral Thomas Charles Hart, also known as "Terrible Tommy", was muttering in his sleep when the telephone bell startled him awake. He turned over, reaching for the candlestick telephone on the nightstand. As it rang again, he pulled the table lamp light chain on the nightstand and glanced at his alarm clock.

0240! What the hell?

He sat up in bed. Grabbing the earpiece in one hand and the candlestick in the other, he sat up in bed.
"Hart here."

MacArthur's Pacific Appeasement, December 8, 1941
Part I
The Missing Ten Hours

An excited voice responded: "Admiral, this is Lieutenant Brown, Flag Communications duty officer at Marsman. We are copying an urgent voice message from the Harbormaster at Pearl Harbor right now saying a Jap air raid is in progress, bombing ships in Pearl."

Admiral Hart sucked in his breath, shocked. "Damn! Pearl Harbor—Pearl Harbor, you say? Brown, are you sure it's Pearl Harbor? Is that confirmed?"

"Yes, Admiral Hart, but not authenticated. However, we are receiving this on Pearl's voice and morse code harbor common circuits. Pearl is repeating the air raid message now: that voice operator sounds a little excited, admiral."

"Understand." He paused to shake the cobwebs out of his head. "Let's make sure everyone's tail is up. Standby to write." There was a short pause as he thought out his messages.

"The first message goes to All Asiatic Fleet and Shore Commands, and copy CINCPacFlt, Commander Sixteenth Naval District, CINC USAFFE, CG FEAF, and CNO." He paused again to organize his thoughts and give Brown time to grab paper and pencil. "Ready? Wait, copy the Dutch General Hein ter Poorten in Java."

"Yes, Admiral, go ahead."

"Send this Operational Priority.

JAP AIR RAID ON PEARL HARBOR IN PROGRESS STOP ACT ACCORDINGLY

Is that all, Admiral?"
"That's right. Send it as soon as possible."
"Shall I encrypt it, sir?"

"No, Mr. Brown. The Japs know about the strike and we don't want to give them more opportunity to break our cipher, now do we?"

Lt. Brown chuckled with embarrassment. "Oh, yes, sorry, sir."

"Second, **EXECUTE SORTIE** to the fleet. They have their orders and know what to do, where to go.

"Third, tell the Houston I will transfer my flag back to Houston as soon as I can get out there." He paused, struggling to maintain a level mind. "Encrypt that. No need for the Jap Navy to know where I am going." He thought for a moment. "Oh yes, I will transfer my flag to the submarine Shark (SS-174) enroute to Houston."

"Aye aye, Admiral."

"Fourth, encrypt this and send to the same addressees Operational Priority.

JAP AIR RAID ON PEARL HARBOR IN PROGRESS STOP A STATE OF WAR NOW EXISTS BETWEEN THE UNITED STATES OF AMERICA AND THE JAPANESE EMPIRE STOP ALL SUBS EXECUTE UN R E S T R I C T E D S U B M A R I N E W A R F A R E A G A I N S T JAPANESE NAVY AND CIVIL MARITIME TARGETS STOP ALL SUBS ACKNOWLEDGE TIME OF RECEIPT

"Aye aye, Admiral."

"Finally, I'll grab a fast bite and be there shortly." The Marsman Building was only three hundred yards away from the Manila Hotel. Terrible Tommy's Asiatic Fleet was finely tuned and would make a good accounting in the days to come.

"Aye aye, Admiral."

The telephone went dead as the lieutenant hurried away to carry out his orders.

Admiral Hart didn't bother taking a shower and shave. He tossed his pajamas on the bed and rapidly dressed in his Whites. He made a sandwich from leftovers in the refrigerator and ate it as he hurried to his office at Marsman in the Port Area, Manila. His mind was—at the same time—numb with the horror of the attack, and moving into overdrive as he planned his moves.

0300, December 8, 1941
Flag Quarters, Neilson Field
Major General Lewis Brereton, CG FEAF
Manila, the Philippines

Major General Lewis Brereton rolled over on his cot and picked the telephone off the floor. "Brereton."

"General, CDO Major Tillotson, sir. Jap Navy aircraft are bombing Hawaii right now."

"Oh, Lord help us. Okay, sound Call to Arms and what the hell, have the bugler play Boots and Saddles. Call Colonel Eubanks to get his show on the road, get those 17's bombed up and ready to go—got that?"

"Yes sir, General."

"Have all B-17 flight crews report to the Ready Room immediately.

"Yes sir, General. Should the enlisted crews attend also?"

"Major, I believe the enlisted crews will be on the same planes with their first pilots, co-pilots, and navigators. Certainly, they attend."

The major rolled his eyes and turned pink. "Sorry, General."

"Notify AWS, all pursuit and fighter squadron commanders we are now at war with the Japs, activate war plans immediately, and take full security measures."

"Yes sir, General."

"I'll high tail it down to the Command Center as soon as I get dressed. Where are you now?"

"In the Command Center, General."

"Then, I'll see you there for a status report." Brereton hung up and began dressing.

0400, December 8, 1941
IJN Ryujo
East of Mindanao, the Philippines

In strong winds and heavy seas East of Davao, Mindanao, the light aircraft carrier Ryujo headed into the wind to begin launching its strike force of Type 96 open cockpit fighters and Type 97 attack bombers.

0430, December 8, 1941
Penthouse, Manila Hotel
Lieutenant General Douglas MacArthur
CINC USAFFE
Manila, the Philippines

MacArthur's Pacific Appeasement, December 8, 1941
Part I
The Missing Ten Hours

Brigadier General Richard Kerens Sutherland unlocked General MacArthur's front door and dashed in, waking Lieutenant Colonel Sidney L. Huff as he hurried by. Huff sat up in bed and called out: "What's the matter? What's going on?" He asked in alarm.

General Sutherland paused just long enough to switch the telephones on. He glanced at Huff icily as he turned the doorknob on MacArthur's bedroom door. "Looks like the Nips have started." He answered sharply.

Sutherland was tall, thin, dour, brusk, short-tempered, autocratic, egotistical and arrogant, a true martinet. He was the "Inner Door Guard" who tightly controlled access to MacArthur.

General MacArthur awoke as General Sutherland touched his shoulder. He swung his legs over the side of his bed and sat up, looking at his Chief of Staff.

"What is it, Dick?" He asked sleepily.

"General, I've just learned the Japs have attacked Pearl Harbor. Some of the boys heard about it on a San Francisco radio station. Apparently, there is a lot of serious damage. Really, really very bad." His response was somewhat shaky.

"I see. Does Iba Radar have any sign of air raids from Formosa?" MacArthur's response was calm and soothing.

"No sir."

"Very well. Let me know as soon as we have official word of an attack by the Japanese." He shook his index finger at his Chief of Staff. "Remember, not a shot back in anger until the first Japanese bomb drops on Philippine soil, Dick."

Sutherland nodded, "I'll bring the message over as soon as it comes in, General."

MacArthur nodded without responding and dropped back down to sleep a while longer. General Sutherland turned off the light, backed out, and closed the door.

Huff was standing in his pajamas, looking at General Sutherland. "Is that all you know, General—that the Japs have attacked Pearl?"

Sutherland stared at Huff for a moment, pulled out his cigarettes and lit up. Finding an ashtray, he sat down in an overstuffed chair and stared at MacArthur's door. "That's all we know."

Huff picked up the phone and started to dial.

Sutherland looked up sharply. "Who the hell are you calling at this hour?"

"We need to open the message center and radio room for hot traffic, general." Huff commented mildly.

"No! Don't do that. MacArthur will order them open in his own time."

"General, we're at war now. Isn't it our responsibility to help General MacArthur prepare for war?"

Sutherland looked at Huff in exasperation. The General just reminded me—making finger quotation marks—'not until the first Japanese bomb drops on Philippine soil'."

Kee-rist, that's all I need, The General nailing me to the wall for opening the Comm Center.

0500, December 8, 1941
Penthouse, Manila Hotel
Lieutenant General Douglas MacArthur
CINC USAFFE
Manila, the Philippines

The telephone began to ring. Huff started for it but Sutherland raised his hand and pointed to himself. He got up and moved to the desk with the telephone, and picked up the ear piece.

"Sutherland here." He spoke crossly. The phone hissed with radio static.

"This is General Gerow, G3 of the Chief of Staff. I thought General MacArthur would be in his command center by this time. What is he doing in his quarters?"

"This is General Sutherland, Chief of Staff. What can I do for you?"

"General, I want to speak to General MacArthur, please."

"General, the General is indisposed at the moment. I repeat, I am his Chief of Staff, what can I do for you?"

"Nothing. Unless his indisposition is in the latrine, get him on the phone now, General Sutherland. General Marshall asked me to call him."

"Very well, General. Just a moment." He laid down the phone, hurried into MacArthur's bedroom, and touched his shoulder.

Angry at being disturbed again, MacArthur asked coldly, "What is it, this time?"

"General, General Gerow, G3 of Marshall's staff is on the phone and insists on speaking to you."

"Dick, you turned the phone on, against my orders?"

"Yes sir, General. What with the Jap attack on Hawaii, it seemed the proper thing to do."

Grimly, MacArthur got out of bed, put on his old West Point maroon bathrobe and strode out to the telephone. He sat down at the desk and snatched the phone ear piece up to his ear.

"MacArthur here. What is it you want that you could not obtain from my Chief of Staff, Gerow?" He snarled.

"You did not respond to the order to execute Phase One and apparently your transmitters are down. You did not respond to an urgent message send over an hour ago to execute Phase Two of Rainbow Five. General Marshall is giving you a direct order to execute Phase Two immediately! I require you to answer the order now." General Gerow's voice was nasty.

MacArthur was building into one of his angry responses, but decided a cold answer was best. "My army is ready to meet the enemy, general. There's your immediate answer. Good day." and hung up. He turned and glowered at Sutherland and Huff. "The gall of Marshall, ordering me to do anything." He moved toward his bedroom, calling over his shoulder. "I am going back to bed for a while."

Sutherland and Huff exchanged glances. "General, isn't it time to go to your command post. The war appears to have started." Sutherland suggested.

General MacArthur stiffened, then said, "Very well. I shall shower and shave, then we will go to headquarters." he responded petulantly.

0515, December 8, 1941
Penthouse, Manila Hotel
Lieutenant General Douglas MacArthur

CINC USAFFE
Manila, the Philippines

Someone began pounding on the penthouse outer door. Lt. Colonel Huff almost ran to the door, followed by General Sutherland. Huff was alarmed and Sutherland was irked by anyone calling at this hour. Huff opened the door. General Brereton was standing there.

"I went to headquarters to get General MacArthur's signature on the order to execute Phase Two. Not there, I came here. I need to see him, right now."

"No, you do not see him right now. Return to Nielson and you can talk with him later."

Brereton decided to take the bull by the horns and began moving by Sutherland and Huff. Sutherland stood in his way. "You are not seeing him now, Brereton. Leave at once! the Chief of Staff ordered.

Brereton was not having any of that. He pushed, then shoved. But now, Huff and Brereton blocked his way. The three of them argued and got nowhere. Major General Brereton gave up angrily and left.

0521, December 8, 1941
Choshu IJAF Air Base
Southwestern Formosa

The fog began lifting about 0500—lifted enough the squadron of 18 Mitsubishi Type 97 twin-engine medium bombers (Betty) could safely take off. They lifted off heading southeastward toward Northern Luzon and their assigned targets.

0530, December 8, 1941
Kato IJAF Air Base
Southwestern Formosa

MacArthur's Pacific Appeasement, December 8, 1941
Part I
The Missing Ten Hours

After being delayed from the reset 0400 departure, 25 Kawasaki Type 99 twin-engine light bombers departed from Kato for Tuguegarao in Northeastern Luzon. As this attack force passed the northern tip of Luzon, they saw an ancient warning practice put to use by Filipinos: a succession of mountain top signal fires marched ahead of them down the Luzon coast!

0600, December 8, 1941
Headquarters, USAFFE
Intramurous, Fort Santiago
1 Calle Victoria
Manila, the Philippines

General Brereton arrived to discuss immediate FEAF plans with General MacArthur. General Sutherland told him MacArthur was in conference and not to be disturbed. He angrily discussed his plan to send all his available B-17's to bomb Japanese Navy and Air Force installations on Formosa. Sutherland agreed this was a good idea but could not give the go ahead without MacArthur's approval. Brereton returned to his headquarters.

0600, December 8, 1941
Status of all aircraft
All FEAF Fields

Clark Field .

20th Pursuit Squadron.

First Section of 18 P-40Es were manned, ready, and lined up to take off as soon as they were given the order.

Second section of 18 P-40Bs were on deck, ready to go.

Eighteen B-17s were being fueled and armed for flight to Southern Formosa as soon as MacArthur signed the order.

The 10 B-18s were in stand down status. They would not fly to Formosa.

MacArthur's Pacific Appeasement, December 8, 1941
Part I
The Missing Ten Hours

Iba Field.

3rd Pursuit Squadron's 18 P-40Es were manned, ready, and lined up to take off as soon as they were given the order.

AWS SCR-270B was tracking an unknown number of aircraft flying toward Central Luzon, apparently for Manila.

Nichols Field.

17th Pursuit Squadron's 18 P-40Es and

21st Pursuit Squadron's 18 P-40Es were manned and set at each end of the runway, waiting for orders to take off.
All P-35As were positioned on the side at the middle of the runway, manned and ready, waiting for orders.

Rosales Field.

34th Pursuit Squadron's 24 P35As waited for the order to take off, as were 12 P-40Bs.

Aparri Field.

A flight of 3 P-40Es sat at the end of the dust covered runway, waiting for fuel trucks and orders to take off.

Del Carmen Field.

34th Pursuit Squadron's 18 P-40Es were fueled, armed, and ready to fire their engines and take off.

0600, December 8, 1941
Davao Field,
Mindanao, the Philippines

Taking off from IJN aircraft carrier Ryujo in a driving storm, the open cockpit IJN Type 97 attack bombers flew towards Davao to strike at the joint Navy/Air Force field and any targets of opportunity.

The attack bombers dropped their 132-pound bombs on Davao air field, hangar, fuel farm, and radio station. These were followed by IJN Type 96 fighters which strafed the area. Departing here, both flights headed into the Gulf of Davao looking for targets.

Spotting two PBY-4s moored near shore, these were destroyed. The seaplane tender, USS Preston, shot down two Type 97 attack bombers and damaged one Type 96 fighter.

MacArthur's Pacific Appeasement, December 8, 1941
Part I
The Missing Ten Hours

0615, December 8, 1941
Above an unnamed Filipino fishing village
In a small bay
at the very northern end of Luzon

To conserve their surprise attack, the rear gunners in the twin-engined bombers were ordered to strafe all villages along their line of flight.

The small Filipino pushed his smack into the quiet water and looked up at the noisy chatter in the sky. Many airplanes were flying overhead to the south. He heard and saw funny little water columns that seemed to be walking towards him. When they reached him, he was slammed down on the beach, numb with shock and pain.

Jose Cortino began screaming in pain from two bullets that sped through his body into the sand behind him. His woman, Angelina, bringing his water and balut, froze in shock. She dropped Jose's food and ran screaming toward him, only to fall dead from a couple bullets.

The village jefe hearing the aircraft and machine gun noise, then screams, came out of his hut. Instantly, he jumped behind a palm tree and waited until all the aircraft were gone. Determining there was nothing he could do for Jose and Angelina, the jefe ran to the telephone hutch nailed on a palm tree less than a month ago and called the Police Constabulary (PC) about 30 miles south of his barrio.

0627, December 8, 1941
FEAF dirt strip
Aparri, Luzon

Three U.S. Army Air Force Lieutenants, flight gloves and leather helmets stuffed in their horsehide jacket pockets, huddled together near their P-40E Warhawk fighters, smoking cigarettes nervously, watching the dirt road leading in to this damned dirt air strip. No doubt about it: this is a dangerous place. As a fighter lands—or takes off—the dust blown up makes it dangerous for following fighters until the dust settles. That lasts five to ten minutes depending upon wind conditions.

MacArthur's Pacific Appeasement, December 8, 1941
Part I
The Missing Ten Hours

The strip is too narrow for two fighters to land or take off together.

These air strips are so new, bulldozer tracks still show. There are absolutely no facilities of any kind nor buildings, not even phone lines back to the Air Group. The Flight Leader looked around this strip in disgust.

Meanwhile, they are watching and listening for the fuel truck and armorers with .50 caliber ammo for their machine guns. That may take a while for a couple of reasons. First, the roads are extremely primitive—carabao trails. Second, because every emergency dirt strip, freshly carved out of the jungle has at least three fighters that need to be serviced and airborne to defend against a possible Japanese air attack.

And this is going to be a B24 base? HA!

Their fighter radios are ineffective while sitting on the ground. They can only pray the Japs don't discover their presence here.

First Lieutenant Roger Bailey, USAAF, Flight Leader, looked at his two Second Lieutenant wingmen. "This may take a while. Since we are on the edge of the beach, why don"t we enjoy the surf. There are no natives around to steal our ships. (There were two chuckles.) Not only that, we can hear the trucks when they show up."

The surf, rolling in from the South China Sea, was about a hundred feet from where they stood in the dirt. Bailey strolled over to the high tide line and looked up and down the beach for natives or boats.

Absolutely nothing in sight except a very long beautiful beach. Oh my God, this is one of the places the Japs could land if they invade. The Colonel needs to know about this. And, if they do land here, they have an air strip ready made for use. Mother Goose!

"Gentlemen, gentlemen. Have you looked at this beautiful beach? Isn't it lovely? Think of having your beautiful girl friend here with no one around, except Jap soldiers landing from their ships!" His voice was romantically emotional as he began, and turned snarlingly rough as he realized the landing was not only possible, but probable.

MacArthur's Pacific Appeasement, December 8, 1941
Part I
The Missing Ten Hours

"Think of strafing Jap troops landing on this beach, and then, Jap fighters occupying this strip. I bet their engineers would oil down this strip in no time flat." His wingmen looked over the strip and beach and agreed by nodding their heads. "Okay, when we finally get gassed up and machine-guns loaded, we are going to make a practice high speed pass over this beach. I lead, and you two follow at 500 yard intervals." They looked around again and nodded. "That way, if we survive that long, we can wreak havoc on the Japs—at least for a few minutes."

The two Second Lieutenants looked at him strangely and nodded again. They all turned their heads back to the strip as they heard engine noises.

0640, December 8, 1941
U.S. Naval Hospital Canacao
U.S. Naval Base, Cavite
Manila Bay, the Philippines

Navy Nurse Harrington was on the Graveyard shift. It was a quiet night. All of a sudden, she heard a commotion in one of the hospital offices.

What is going on? There is supposed to be quiet about the decks in this hospital.

Suddenly, she saw lights coming on in the Officer's Quarters across the way. People were running around shouting.

What on earth is going on?

A moment later, a seaman in teeshirt and scivvy shorts burst into her ward shouting the Japs were bombing Honolulu!

Why would the Japs bomb Honolulu? What the hell is he talking about?

MacArthur's Pacific Appeasement, December 8, 1941
Part I
The Missing Ten Hours

Across Manila Bay at Sternberg Army Hospital in Manila, Nurse Redmond was called to the phone. A friend told her Pearl Harbor was being bombed. She did not believe it. But her friend insisted it was true.

At Fort Mills Army Hospital on Corregidor, a Nurse decided to write up a shopping list of things she would need from the PX: face cream, tooth powder, comb, bath towel, kotex, shampoo. Kleenex, and chocolate candy.

At Fort McKinley Army Hospital just outside Manila, doctors and nurses were issued helmets and gas masks. Two women coming off the nightshift, stuffed their helmets and gas masks in their golf bags and headed to the links.

0715, December 8, 1941
Headquarters, USAFFE
Intramurous, Fort Santiago
1 Calle Victoria
Manila, the Philippines

General Brereton arrived a second time to obtain approval for his B-17 bombing run on Formosan targets. Sutherland had no news for him and would not let him into MacArthur's office. After some frustrating conversation, Sutherland said he would ask, and slipped sideways into MacArthur's office, carefully not permitting Brereton to see inside MacArthur's office, closing the door behind him. After a moment, he returned. "MacArthur said no. We are not to make the first overt act of war." he said, solemnly.

Brereton protested. "You've got to be kidding. The Japs have already made the first action at Pearl Harbor, and we hear of strafing of native villages up North. Baguio has been strafed and bombed. Davao was bombed and strafed an hour ago. What more does he need?" He yelled.

0719, December 8, 1941
PC Regimental Headquarters
Northern Luzon Sector
The Philippine Isles

MacArthur's Pacific Appeasement, December 8, 1941
Part I
The Missing Ten Hours

The PC Capitan looked at his sector map of Northern Luzon. He had marked six villages that had been struck with machine-gun fire and bombs by unknown aircraft. From the last strike, he knew they were Japanese bombers of an unknown type.

He picked up his EE-5 phone and cranked. It was time to call Philippine Army headquarters and report these incidences. There were no good roads going up into that jungle area. He ordered a Mounted Philippine Army Scout patrol on horses with pack mules to head north and assist each of the villages. Several deaths were reported along with many injured men, women, and children.

0740, December 8, 1941
HQ FEAF
Neilson Field
Manila, the Philippines

Back at FEAF headquarters at Nielson Field, Brereton reiterated his conversation with Sutherland. Discussing the situation with his staff, they decided to mount the three B-17 reconnaisance mission as soon as possible.

0744, December 8, 1941
HQ FEAF
Neilson Field
Manila, the Philippines

"Operations Center, Miller speaking, sir.
"This is AWS O-and-I Iba. We show a large flight of aircraft over Lingayen Gulf heading towards Clark Field."
Miller sucked in his breath.

Oh shit!

"General, O-and-I is tracking a large flight of aircraft over Lingayen Gulf heading towards Clark, sir."
Brereton acknowledged the information with a nod and called Clark to get the fighters up and the bombers away.

While he was on the phone to Clark, General Arnold, Air Force Chief of Staff, was on another phone line waiting for Brereton to bring him up to date on what had transpired on Oahu. He did not want a repeat of that disaster. Brereton reassured him they were taking action and precautions.

0815, December 8, 1941
IJN Bombing Squadron
Over Baguio, Luzon

Seventeen Kawasaki Type 97 heavy bombers at 13,000 feet, lined up on Camp John Hay and proceeded to drop their 220 pound bombs on barracks and other buildings. Their latest intelligence indicated that MacArthur would be in residence at his Summer HQ. Completing their bomb run, the squadron turned gracefully to the right to the north, and headed home. No damage to any aircraft.

0818, December 8, 1941
Tainan IJN Naval Air Base
Southwestern Formosa

The fog finally dissipated and after final briefings, the aircrews manned their twenty-seven Type 96 old land-based twin-engined bombers, each loaded with twelve 132 pound bombs, roared down the runway, one-by-one, and headed due south.

0819, December 8, 1941
U.S. Army Hospital Camp John Hay
Baguio, Luzon, the Philippines

Nurse Bradley was abruptly summoned to Headquarters. She learned the Japanese had struck Pearl Harbor and expected here shortly.

MacArthur's Pacific Appeasement, December 8, 1941
Part I
The Missing Ten Hours

This is impossible! A well-marked hospital with bold Red Crosses on the roof. They won't attack us.

The air raid siren wailed. A few moments later, Japanese bombers attacked with bombs and machine-gun fire on Camp John Hay Hospital. Minutes later, civilian dependents and Filipino civilians began entering the hospital for treatment. Nurse Bradley was one of the wounded needing treatment.

0825, December 8, 1941
Tuguergarao Field
Luzon

Twenty-five Kawasaki Type 48 bombers, lined up and dropped their bombs on this air field. They were relieved that no American interceptors came up to greet them with machine gun fire. Following their drop, the bombers wheeled and headed back to Kato Air Base, Formosa.

0830, December 8, 1941
20th Pursuit Squadron Operations Tent
Clark Field
Luzon, the Philippines

"Lieutenant! Get your Second section outta here now. Go to Tarlac at 15,000 feet. Intercept the Japs and knock the crap out of them."
"Yes, sir, Captain. We're gone." He raced out of the tent, circling his right index finger high over his head. Engines began coughing into life.

His crew chief held his parachute out and helped strap him into it. The Lieutenant grabbed his gloves, helmet, goggles and oxygen mask, climbed into his P-40B and stood on his seat. Pulling his canvas helmet on, he looked both ways at his eighteen P-40Bs where his pilots were straining to watch what he did.

He pointed North and looked back and forth as pilots nodded their heads. He put his thumb on his chest and pointed sky high. His pilots were still nodding their understanding. He dropped in his seat and strapped in.

He returned his crew chief's salute, released the brakes and began taxiing out to the runway. As he reached the runway, he glanced over at the tower and saw a green light flashing at him.

Advancing his throttle to take off power, he reached over and pulled his canopy shut and locked. At 60 knots, he raised the tail and soon was airborne.

He flipped a switch to raise the wheels and responded to the sudden veer because the wheels did not retract equally. He checked his rear view mirror for his squadron. Some were still on the ground but moving right along toward take off.

They will all form on me and the two flight leaders in a few moments. We'll see how nervous they are once we have formed up.

0830, December 8, 1941

34th Pursuit Squadron
Del Carmen Field
Luzon, the Philippines

Just South of Clark, AWS ordered the squadron of 18 P-40E's into the air at 17,000 to cover Clark Field.

0845, December 8, 1941

19th Bombardment Group
Clark Field
Luzon, the Philippines

Per Colonel Eubanks after consultation with General Brereton, all B-17s and B-18As were ordered to take off, clear the area, and patrol within radio range of the Control Tower. This was very dangerous because pursuit planes of three squadrons and all the bombers, were attempting to take off in all directions. In many cases, narrowly averting collisions.

MacArthur's Pacific Appeasement, December 8, 1941
Part I
The Missing Ten Hours

0850, December 8, 1941
HQ, FEAF
Neilson Field
Manila, the Philippines

General Brereton called HQ USAFFE to find out if MacArthur had changed his mind. Sutherland ordered Brereton to hold off bombing Formosa targets for the moment.

0900, December 8, 1941
Upstairs, various altitudes
P-35As, P-40Bs, P-40Es, B-18As, B-17C/Ds

These young pilots, mostly Second Lieutenants with little or no combat training prior to arriving in the Philippines, were looking for Japanese planes to shoot down.

Most of the airplanes machine guns had never been fired because .50 caliber ammunition was in short supply. Six machine guns shooting at the same time was noisy and slowed the aircraft from the recoil.

To a man, they were nervous, some scared, and a few sick. But they stuck it out, circling, looking for the enemy, and watching their wingman who was watching their First Lieutenant Squadron Leader, also without combat experience.

They were finding their aircraft were not such hot ships. Getting above 15,000 feet meant using oxygen, which was a pain. The P-40Es were sluggish and got worse—the higher they got—very slowly.

Squadrons had been ordered over Manila, Iba, Clark, and off to the northland. They lost communications with their air field and sometimes with their mates in the air.

0900, December 8, 1941
On the Ground
FEAF pilots and crews
the Philippines

MacArthur's Pacific Appeasement, December 8, 1941
Part I
The Missing Ten Hours

Some squadrons of pursuit planes, fully loaded and ready to go, were anxiously waiting their orders to take off, which never came.

The P-40Bs in the 3rd Pursuit Squadron at Iba could hear of bombing action by the Japanese coming over their radios.

At Nichols Field, the P-40E pilots of 21st, 3rd, and 17th Pursuit Squadrons never heard a word of bombing or combat with the enemy nor order given to take to the air.

Finally, in disgust, the squadron commanders called all the pilots to the Group Operations tent and fed them Coca Colas and sandwiches.

0930, December 8, 1941
IJN Naval Air Base
Takao, Formosa

Twenty-seven Type 1 bombers lifted off, heading for Clark Field.

A few minutes later, the second flight of 27 Type 1 bombers took off for Iba Field.

A few minutes after that, the third flight of 27 Type 1 bombers took off, also for Iba Field.

Later, 53 Mitsubishi Type 0 Carrier Fighters, swarmed the runways and headed south to protect their bombers from American fighters, which would be waiting for them.

0945, December 8, 1941
IJN Naval Air Base
Tainan, Formosa

Twenty-seven Mitsubishi Type 0 Carrier Fighters , feet pressed against their brakes, waited for the signal to take off. All the bombers had left an hour before. Now, fully loaded with fuel, drop tanks, and ammunition, these fighter pilots were anxious to get on with it. The signal appeared. Pairs at a time, the fighters lifted into the air, heading south.

MacArthur's Pacific Appeasement, December 8, 1941
Part I
The Missing Ten Hours

1000, December 8, 1941
HQ, FEAF
Neilson Field
Manila, the Philippines

General Brereton put in another call to General MacArthur. He got General Sutherland.

"I need to talk with General MacArthur, Sutherland. Put me through to him," he ordered.

"I told you before, the General is busy in conferences. Your orders remain the same. The entire USAFFE command is still in a defensive stance," Sutherland said, quietly.

"That's not possible. We are NOW being bombed here in the Philippines. Aparri, Camp Hays, and Davao have all been struck. There is death, injury, and damage. Dammit, put me through."

"Comply with your orders, General!" Came the terse response.

Brereton slammed down the phone and turned to his Chief of Staff, "Colonel Brady, I want a note on record of that conversation with Sutherland. And Eubanks, get your bombers ready to go."

Eubanks rushed out to his 'private' B-18A and headed back to Clark Field to recall and load all the B-17s for strikes on Formosa.

1014, December 8, 1941
HQ, FEAF
Nielson Field
Manila, the Philippines

Brereton looked at his phone as it buzzed again, and picked it up.

Brereton here," he said, brusquely.

"This is General MacArthur, Lewis. How are you doing over there?" he asked in a kind voice.

Good heavens! It's Mac himself.

"Good morning General. Clark has not been bombed yet. All of my B-17s are standing tall, ready to go as soon as they are bombed up." He paused. MacArthur was listening. "Colonel Eubanks is preparing a reconnaissance flight to Formosa right now. I have him also preparing the bomb flight information. I want to attack Formosa this afternoon." he held his breath, waiting for MacArthur's response.

There was silence on the line for a moment. "Well General, that is your decision to make."

Screw you, Sutherland!

"Thank you, sir. I hope to have the attack force in the air before Noon."

Brereton called a general staff meeting. He related his conversation with General MacArthur. "We need a detailed plan of attack against the IJN and IJAF air bases and IJN harbors." The staff completed his order by 1045, and he signed the order.

Two squadrons of B-17s would be loaded with 100 and 300 pound bombs and depart, arriving on target at dusk. Two squadrons of B-17s would move from Del Monte Field, Mindanao, to San Marcelino on Luzon's west coast, thence to Clark Field in the dark hours to refuel and prepare for bombing Formosa at daybreak tomorrow.

1100, December 8, 1941
Clark Field
Luzon, the Philippines

Lt. Col. Eubanks and his Operations Chief, hurried in to get the reconnaissance flight on the way. The B-17s circling away from Clark have been ordered to return. Meanwhile, the fighters are running out of fuel and need to return to the field and refuel.

As the B-17s landed and returned to their dispersal sites, their crews went off to lunch. The gas trucks came out and began fueling the bombers.

P-40Es and P-40Bs came in for refueling about the same time. The 17th Pursuit Squadron from Iba Field moved up to the hangers and parked their ships wingtip-to-wingtip while they waited to be refueled.

All the fighter jocks were shocked to learn of the bombings at Baguio and Tuguegarao. They had seen nothing nor heard anything on their radios.

1120, December 8, 1941
AWS Radar Operations
Iba Field
Zambales, Luzon

The duty radar 'scope operator could not distinguish the number of aircraft or their altitude of the flights coming in from Formosa. He could, however, see the several flights coming in from different directions. This data was passed to the Air Warning Service at Nielson FEAF Headquarters and Clark Operations by teletype machine.

The Japanese military commands had no information about this secret device. Under ideal conditions, the SCR-270B could pick up targets as far away as 150 miles.

1130, December 8, 1941
Air Warning Service Operations
HQ FEAF
Nielson Field
Manila, the Philippines

The Air Staff, including the Commanding General, Lew Brereton, were watching the big map board being updated, minute by minute. Reports were coming in from Filipinos all over Northern Luzon. Brereton smiled when he learned that one tile on the board indicated the mountain top signal fires marching south following one of the Japanese flights.

As the board was brought up to date, the three operators wearing telephone operator headsets with microphones, passed information to one of the other operators, or reached out and pushed a tile. Their information was coming in on voice radio, telephones, teletype, and notes passed from the AWS duty officer.

MacArthur's Pacific Appeasement, December 8, 1941
Part I
The Missing Ten Hours

1130, December 8, 1941
HQ, 19th Bombardment Group
Clark Field
Luzon, the Philippines

Forty First Pilots and Co-Pilots of the 14th, 28th, and 93rd Bomb Squadrons were assembled in the auditorium, chattering amongst themselves as they nervously awaited the Group Commanding Officer.
The door swung open. "Attention on deck!" came a loud voice.

The assembled officers straggled to their feet as Lt. Col. Eubanks strode in. "As you were, gentlemen. Be seated," announced Eubanks.
"We now have our written orders for the recon mission. Three ships and crews of the 30th Bomb Squadron will fly this mission," He pointed to three First Pilots.

"You, you, and you may leave now for lunch. Be back here at Noon with your crews for mission briefing."

As these First Pilots and their Co-Pilots got up to leave, Eubanks turned to the remaining officers and told them to arrange for fueling their thirteen B-17s and loading fourteen 300-pound bombs on each B-17. You will take off at 1400 hours which will bring you over your Formosan targets about dusk.

No special cameras were stored at Clark. The Reconnaissance flights were delayed until 3 cameras were flown in from Nichols Field.

1145, December 8, 1941
3rd Pursuit Squadron
Iba Field
Zambales, Luzon

"Roger Clark. 3rd Pursuit to Point Iba at 15,000 feet. Is that correct?"
"Correct Iba. Get them up."

"Roger Clark. Wilco out."

The radio operator wheeled in his chair and handed the message to his commanding officer. It read: "Point Iba, 15,000 feet." The First Lieutenant looked at it for a second.

Translated, I think that means get my ass in gear with the squadron, climb to 15,000, and go over to Point Iba a few miles away and wait for the Japs.

He ran out of the Operations tent and gathered his flight leaders to give them instructions. All of the P-40Es would protect Iba Field by circling at Point Iba a few minutes away in a line to intercept the incoming Japanese flight. Flight A would be followed by Flight B, and finish up with Flight C.

Flight A took off from the south end of the field. Flight B at the north end, did not want to taxi through all the dust, so they took off *to* the south. Flight C, P-35As, dispersed in the middle of the field, had dust all over. The C Flight leader took off, not followed immediately by his flight. When they did take off, they joined B Flight, instead.

Somehow, some of the pilots in the 3 flights heard a radio call from Clark ordering them to head to Manila. The remainder stayed at Point Iba.

1145, December 8, 1941

21st Pursuit Squadron
Nichols Field
Manila, the Philippines

The order came from 24th Group Operations. Take off and protect Clark Field. Flights A and B of twelve P-40Es took off and raced toward Clark, about 50 miles away. The squadron commander was heading for 24,000 feet.

No sooner had they gotten slightly north of Manila, still climbing, when a change of orders reached them. Reverse course and take a position above Manila Bay midway between Corregidor and Cavite to intercept incoming Japanese airplanes.

Flight C of six P-40Es was having trouble with their engines. These were among the latest arrivals from the

States. When they got airborne a few minutes later they could not find the other twelve ships nor did they hear the change of orders.

Two of these new ships began throwing oil on the windshields, so they returned to Nichols Field. The remaining four followed the only orders they knew about: protect Clark Field.

1155, December 8, 1941
AWS, Iba Field
Zambales, Luzon

The SCR-270B Radar Operator, tensely explained to his relief there were two large groups coming south. One group was plotted directly in line for Clark Field 43 miles away, and the other large group was aimed at Iba Field, 35 miles away.

"We are about to get bombed here. Before you take over, get this information to Operations at FEAF headquarters, right now. Also," he looked around for the oncoming runner, "sound the air raid alarm on the siren, right now." He looked around at his relief. "Me and my runner are going to stay here until the last possible moment." He was silent a bit.

The air raid siren sounded hollowly outside.

"Whatever you do, don't let anyone hide under the power truck. It is loaded with gasoline for the generator."

1155, December 8, 1941
AWS Operations Room
Nielson Field
Manila, the Philippines

General Brereton was keeping track of the incoming enemy flights. He was called to the telephone.

"This is Sutherland. General MacArthur wants to be brought up-to-date since you and he last talked an hour and a half ago."

"General, we are tracking two main flights on the SCR-270B at Iba AWS Station, heading for Clark and Iba but there is no actual contact with the enemy." Brereton thought about it for a moment and added: "watchers up the length of Luzon had been giving reports of sightings of large groups of high flying airplanes. That's all we have at this time."

"Thank you, General. I will pass that along to The General." Brereton grunted, hung up and turned back to the plot table.

1205, December 8, 1941
24th Pursuit Group Operations
Clark Field
Luzon, the Philippines

As the teletype message from Iba AWS appeared, that operator called to his C.O. "Captain, AWS says a large enemy force is less than 43 miles out, aimed at Clark Field, sir." His voice was calm as he announced disaster in the making.

The Captain called out, "Okay, Private." He turned to a pilot fidgeting behind him. "Get your 17th Pursuit up and patrol over Manila. The enemy is coming in from the west."

The pilot ran out circling his army above his head to mean 'Start 'em up and take off'. The 15 pilots raced to their P-40Es , which had been fueled, serviced, and armed with a full load of .50 caliber machine gun shells for their six guns. As they taxied out, they received their orders in their earphones. "Head over to Manila to intercept the Japs."

1210, December 8, 1941
20th Pursuit Squadron Operations
Clark Field
Luzon, the Philippines

The First Lieutenant, C.O. of the 20th was hanging around the Operations Room, waiting for orders to take his squadron of P-40Bs to the air. Group had said there were conflicting reports of where the enemy was located.

1215, December 8, 1941
IJN Tainan Air Base Squadron
9,000 feet, 65 miles north of Clark Field

The group leader, signaled his force of 34 Mitsubishi Zero carrier fighters to don their oxygen masks and began climbing to 22,000 feet over the Kawasaki Type 96 twin-engined slow, light bombers just ahead of them. The fighter pilots were uneasily peering in every direction looking for the American fighters. There were none in sight.

1235, December 8, 1941
20th Pursuit Squadron Operations
Clark Field
Luzon, the Philippines

A crew chief, hearing the hum of aircraft engines, looked up and spotted the high flying V of Vs formation and screamed out, "Oh shit, Japs!"

The C.O. told him to run up the red flag and ran for his P-40B. In short order, engines were started and the fighters began moving to the runway. Another pilot looking up noticed the Japs were lined up with the runway. Bombs were beginning to fall.

Someone started cranking the manual air raid siren. Soldiers ran for the slit trenches that Colonel Eubanks insisted be dug, vacating hangers and other buildings as bombs began exploding around them.

The dying began at Clark Field.

People received punishing shrapnel wounds. The bombs did not differentiate between officers, enlisted men, or Filipino and Filipina workers. Some people were blown apart; others lost arms or legs.

Fighters still on the ground and most of the bombers and buildings were exploding and burning. A few P-40Bs tried to taxi out to take off and were blown to bits or began burning as leaking gasoline spilled over the aircraft pushed by the wind from the propeller.

The 200th Coast Artillery Company had a major problem with their 3-inch rounds. Each round had to be cleaned of green corrosion before they would fit into the breech block.

To make matters worse, the fuses were frozen and had to be broken loose with a wrench to set the time. It really did not matter: most rounds were duds to begin with; most of the fuses were dead. Those rounds that did explode at the highest altitude were still way below the Jap bombers.

The 192nd M3 Stuart Tank Battalion and the 193rd Half-Track Battalion were trying to get their act together without much success. A pilot whose plane was shattered ran up to the Sergeant-in-Charge and told him to line up the tanks looking down the runway. Perfect shots, no deflection angles. The sergeant passed that word along. Stuarts began moving into the correct position to fire their guns at the Japs.

1237, December 8, 1941
28th Bomb Squadron Operations
Clark Field
Luzon, the Philippines

A B-18A was taxiing to the fueling station as bombs began exploding.

"Holy shit! Let's get out of here," exploded the Co-pilot."
The Navigator, frantically cranking down the flaps, asked "Where the hell can we go?"
"Rosales, yeah, Rosales" as he jammed the throttles to take off power. Staying low just above tree level, they flew toward Rosales Field, a small auxiliary air field.

Two B-17s, one from Del Monte Field, Mindanao, and the other, returning from patrol, did not know of the attack until they individually broke out of the overcast and saw the utter destruction in front of them.

Wheeling about, they got out of the area while trying to find out where to go. The Clark Tower operator, hiding on the floor, advised them to go to Del Monte. One had enough fuel and headed south. The other B-17 did not have enough fuel and decided to hide behind the tall volcano, Mount Pinatuba.

1238, December 8, 1941
IJN Kawasaki Type 96 Light Twin-engined bombers
Over Clark Field
Luzon, the Philippines

Their mission completed, the bombers wheeled southwest heading to Tainan, Formosa. No anti-aircraft fire had reached them. No fighters came up to fight with them. The bombers were safe and the flight crews began breathing again.

1238, December 8, 1941
IJN Mitsubishi Zero Carrier Fighters
Over Clark Field
Luzon, the Philippines

It was the fighters turn. The Zeros came down from 22,000 feet at a shallow angle to strafe the field. In short order, all aircraft, damaged or not, were strafed first with 20-mm canon fire and then with 7.7-mm machine guns. They even made splinters of three fake B-17s in front of Bomber Group Operations.

P-40Es were responding in pairs to the call for help. The first pair shot down two of the Jap fighters. The first Zero had its tail shot off and the second one simply fell on its side to the ground.

The P-40Es were no match for the faster, more agile tight turning Zeros but could dive away from them to the ground. Indeed, one pilot noticed he exceeded 500 mph on his dive to the treetops.

Of one P-40E's six .50 caliber machine guns, only one was firing. Even so, he saw his Zero smoking and heading into the jungle below. Another P-40E's guns would not fire.

One of the flying B-17s got into it, surviving pass after pass from several Jap Zeros. As soon as the pilot could, he dropped to 500 feet so the Japs couldn't get under him.

The other surviving B-17 was hiding behind Mount Pinatuba.

A P-40B managed to get off the ground as the strafing continued. A zero got him and watched him spiral into the ground. Two P-40Bs attempted to fly but were strafed and burned before even getting to take off air speed.

Two B-17Ds on the ground by the 19th Bombardment Group Operations office were still viable. However, as the First Pilot of one and the Navigator of the other started to taxi, three IJN Zero fighters spotted them and it was all over.

One of another B-17D's gunner manned a twin .50 caliber machine gun and managed to keep the Zeros away from his and another B-17D nearby.

The Coast Artillery was firing, or attempting to fire, their 37-mm canons. Most of those rounds were duds, too. Several canons jammed.

A second flyer whose plane was burning, ran up to a Half-Track and pointed out the Jap's circular pattern. The half-Track moved into position along the length of the main runway and began firing his twin .50s with success. He saw one Zero dive into the ground and another smoking after it passed him.

The IJN group leader above Clark recalled his aircraft to the rallying point. In a few minutes, the reformed squadrons, less those lost in combat, wheeled northwest, heading back to Formosa.

1240, December 8, 1941
AWS Iba Field
Zambales, Luzon

The 'Scope operator reported the Japs were almost over Iba Field. "Ir's time to bail out and head for the slit trenches. But, Jeez, don't crawl under the Power Truck." So saying, he scrambled out of the SCR-270B Operations Van and looked for a slit trench. None had been dug at Iba. He dived behind a palm tree and hoped to survive.

1240, December 8, 1941
Takao IJAF Bomb Group
Over Iba Field
Zambales, Luzon

At 20,000 feet, the lieutenant leading a force of 51 Mitsubishi Zero Carrier Fighters, watched the flight of Kawasaki Type 1 twin-engined light bombers begin their bomb run on Iba. He was puzzled because there were many American fighters on the ground, and none in the air he could see.

Moments later at 1244 hours, the bomb group at 23,000 feet began dropping 132-pound bombs from each of the 27 bombers. As the group completed their bomb run, they dropped to 16,000 feet and wheeled right to head out to sea on their way home to Takao Air Base on Formosa.

Immediately behind the Takao bomb group, the Kanoya Air Base Group of 26 bombers began dropped one 1,100-pound bomb and six 132-pound bombs on Iba Field. They also gracefully wheeled right and headed out to sea for Kanoya Air Base on Kyushu.

None of the bombers were shot at or damaged in any way.

1244, December 8, 1941
Iba Field
Zambales, Luzon

Low on fuel, several P-40Es were coming back from Manila Bay to refuel. They had not seen or heard of any action to this point. As the first fighter landed, bombs began exploding at the far end of the runway, coming toward him. A bomb blew the tail assembly off his plane.

Three other P-40Es were descending to land and did not see the runway explosions. Two were blown apart and one escaped. Some pilots apparently thought it was another war drill. They simply kept coming. Another two veered off, heading over the sea near the field.

1247, December 8, 1941

3rd Pursuit Squadron
Iba Field
Luzon, the Philippines

A straggler P-40E returning to refuel, suddenly found himself in the Jap Mitsubishi Zero strafing run. He fired on the Zero in front of him and saw it beginning to smoke.

Suddenly tracers were zipping ahead of him. He pulled out of the formation and headed for the sky. No one followed him. Low on fuel, he aimed at Rosales Auxiliary Field in hopes of finding fuel thereafter.

Another P-40E returning to Iba, saw the Zeros strafing the field and took them on. He got hits on 3 Japs. On his 3rd pass, only a few of his guns operated. On his 4th pass, none worked and he headed to sea.

1250, December 8, 1941

17th Pursuit Squadron
Over Manila Bay, Luzon

The Minesweeper USS Lark, fired at the P-40Es and reported that seventeen Jap fighters were circling above them.

Another group of P-40Es over Cavite were also being fired upon by Navy gunners on their ships. Fortunately for all, they missed.

1300, December 8, 1941
Zeros of Tainan Air Group
Over Del Carmen Field
Luzon, the Philippines

Eighteen P-35As of the 34th Pursuit Squadron were coming up to attack the Japs! The Guardians managed to shoot down 3 Zeros without any of the P-35As being shot down. All sustained damage; some would no longer fly.

The Tainan Air Group returned to Clark Field and found a mixed group of P-40s and P-35s at 14,000 feet circling the field. Only two or three of the American fighters escaped this attack. The Air Group also fired two B-17s and four B-18s, before departing seaward, heading for home.

At 1315 hours, on the way to the rally point, a P-40B came up and blew another Zero out of the sky.

1330, December 8, 1941
Clark Field
Luzon, the Philippines

Two P-40Bs, independently, circled the field looking for a spot on the runway that was not cratered from the Jap bombs. Each finally landed safely, only to find out that the Coast Artillery had been trying to shoot them down as they circled the field.

Aircraft recognition was not high on anyone's list of things to memorize, this day.

1330, December 8, 1941
Nichols Field
Zambales, Luzon

One-by-one P-40Bs and P-40Es, low on gas, landed at Nichols, glad to be on the ground. They exchanged stories. Uppermost in their minds: the P-40s were outclassed by the Zero. They could dive away steeper and faster, but in level flight and tight circling the Zero had them cold. They were amazed the P-35As actually shot some of the Zeros out of the sky.

1330, December 8, 1941
Clark Field
Luzon, the Philippines

It appeared the Japanese had withdrawn, clearly the winner. Every available vehicle, including horse- and carabao-drawn carts were picking up wounded soldiers and civilian workers, and carrying them to Fort Stotsenburg Hospital, about 1,000 yards away from Clark Field. Later, bodies and body parts would be collected and carried to the hospital for identification where possible, and burial.

It also appeared every building was damaged or destroyed by bombs and machine gun fire. One B-18A, hidden under trees away from the runways had survived without a scratch. The 30th Bomb Squadron Operations tent was not damaged, either.

1500, December 8, 1941
Nichols Field
Zambales, Luzon

Eighteen P-40Es circled the field, stunned by the damage. They had been flying over Manila Bay since they took off about 1230 hours. They had not fired a shot, heard anything on their radios nor saw smoke from all the damaged air fields.

1500, December 8, 1941
20th Pursuit Squadron
Clark Field
Luzon, the Philippines

Of the 23 P-40Bs assigned to the 20th, only three survived the bombing and strafing attacks. Four pilots had been killed attempting to take off; 3 were badly burned by exploding gasoline in their aircraft tanks. Five enlisted crewmen were killed; six were badly wounded.

1500, December 8, 1941
Rosales Field

MacArthur's Pacific Appeasement, December 8, 1941
Part I
The Missing Ten Hours

Luzon, the Philippines

There was an ample supply of gasoline to fill the four P-40Es, plus the two that had landed in a riverbed at Lingayen Bay. The question of how to fill their tanks from 55-gallon drums was answered by getting a ride into the town of Rosales and locating funnels, buckets, hoses, chamois cloths, and cans to transfer from the drums into the cans and then into the aircraft tanks.

1500, December 8, 1941
19th Bomber Group Operations
Clark Field
Luzon, the Philippines

Lt. Col. Eubanks wanted an accounting of all his B-17Cs and B-17Ds. As he and his executive officer rode around the field in a damaged car, they found his B-17D with slight damage, one other hidden B-17C and a B-17D without damage, and as they watched, another B-17D came in to land.

In all, of the nineteen B-17s an even dozen were completely destroyed, three could be repaired, and two were repaired before the end of the day. Ten aircrewmen had been killed. Twenty-one other non-flying personnel had been killed.

1550, December 8, 1941
Headquarters, USAFFE
1 Calle Victoria
Intramurous, Fort Santiago
Manila, the Philippines

General Brereton arrived and finally after two failed attempts to meet face-to-face with General MacArthur, Sutherland ushered him into MacArthur's private office. MacArthur had already heard about the Clark destruction from Brereton's phone call to Sutherland a little after 1300 hours. Before that call, he had expounded on an attack on Formosa in the early hours tomorrow morning. Since then, Brereton had complete knowledge of his bombers destruction and cancelled his plans to bomb Formosa tomorrow.

He no longer had fuel, bombs, or machine-gun ammunition at Clark for the Del Monte B-17s. None of the P-40s had drop tanks to make a round trip flight to Formosa protecting the B-17s anyway. Realistically, the P-40s cannot reach the B-17 bombing altitude.

Late afternoon and evening
December 8, 1941
Central and Northern Luzon
The Philippines

First Sergeants pulled out their little pocket notebooks and began to count noses. Who survived unwounded and were present? Who were killed in action? Who were wounded in action? Who are missing in action, presumed blown apart? Who took off for the hills?

Doctors and their assistants went around ascertaining bodies that were alive or dead. If alive, render first aid on the spot and move them to a hospital. If dead, identify the bodies and record the information. If only scattered body parts were present, gather the parts for burial.

All command leaders, Navy, Marines, Army, and Army Air Force were trying to get their people and respective Filipino civilian workers fed and bedded down for the night. Everyone was afraid the Japs were going to attack again tonight. Tents were set up deep inside the jungle where they could not be seen from the air.

Screams and moans still filled the air as the sky darkened. Fires flickered around the various military sites. Wood, fuel, cordite, and burning body smoke filled the air.

0640, December 9, 1941
Approaching Keelung, Formosa
USN PBY-4 4671
VP-104, Patron 10
Naval Air Station Olongapo

MacArthur's Pacific Appeasement, December 8, 1941
Part I
The Missing Ten Hours

Subic Bay, the Philippines

Allen Clark AL2/c, got up from his Radio Desk, put on his gloves, helmet and goggles, and quickly got into position on the Starboard Bubble. Sliding the glass bubble open, he unlocked the .50 caliber machine-gun, loaded the belt into the breech, safed the gun, and swung it out ready to fire.

The Port Gunner picked up his microphone, "Skipper, we are manned back here and ready for action," was his nervous but cheerful announcement.

At least, we are going to hit these bastards in their own backyard!

The PBY banked and dropped to a low altitude, not acceptable back in the States. At 50 feet, they were hard to see.

"Okay crew," the Lieutenant (jg) yelled, "we're going to bomb any ship we can get next to and skedaddle back to Olongapo. Gunners: Guns Free!"

Clark unsafed his machine gun, closed the bolt and began looking for targets. As he spotted a small harbor vessel and began to fire, the PBY rose to cross a cargo ship. "Bombs are away," called the Co-Pilot.

Clark and the other gunner had a new target now and began shooting as two bombs exploded on the cargo ship.

Back at 50 feet, anti-aircraft fire hit their tail assembly. Losing control, the PBY hit the water, flipped tail over nose, and began sinking upsidedown.

As they went under water, Clark and the other gunner knew they would drown if they didn't evacuate *NOW*. Water was rushing in from several directions, including the bubbles. Clark got out and swam to the surface, jerking at his Mae West CO_2 bottles to fill the watertight envelopes, looking for the rest of the crew.

He waited a moment, realizing he was the only one to get out alive. Clark swam to shore in his bright yellow life vest. He took it off and hid it in the brush by the beach. His gray flight suit was okay but he tucked his white hat into a knee pocket. Crouching, he headed inland.

A Jap soldier jumped up in front of him, rifle aimed at his gut, shouting at him. Clark raised his hands and waited. The Jap soldier pushed and shoved him around, forcing him to his knees. As Clark watched, the soldier drew his sword and raised it over his head.

You're not slicing my head off, asshole.

Clark tackled the soldier, grabbed the sword, and stabbed the Jap through his chest. Breathing heavily, he watched the Jap die. Clark began running away from there as quietly as he could.

In about fifteen minutes, a Jap patrol found him and ordered Clark to surrender. He raised his hands over his head and stood still.

Captured on the second day of the war, he was shipped to northern Korea to work in the coal mines until the end of the war in September 1945.

[I served under Chief Warrant Officer (CWO3) Allen Clark at Naval Communications Station, San Francisco between 1956 and 1958. He was famous in the Communications Center for always repeating "Get that message through." Again in the '90s before he died, we worked together at the De Anza College Television Studios where he produced TV shows for cablecast. I was his Floor Director. This is when I heard of his action at Keelung, Formosa.]

December 9, 1941
GHQ, USAFFE
1 Calle Victoria,
Intramurous, Fort Santiago
Manila, the Philippines

Yesterday's savage, numbing air strikes across the island of Luzon and other islands in the archipelago are beginning to sink in. The Japanese IJAF and IJN Air Armada based on Formosa had struck Clark at the lunch hour.

Lieutenant General MacArthur's staff is continuing to receive new and revised spot reports from every Army unit able to communicate, even as the enemy attacks again. Many units have not reported their situation. Efforts to contact those units continue. Aparri, Luzon, in the far north reported single-engine planes bombing and strafing the unfinished dirt fighter strip as early as 0830, yesterday.

The Commandant, Sixteenth Naval District, headquartered at U.S. Naval Base Cavite Navy Yard, messaged the Chief of Naval Operations (copy to USAFFE) summarizing reports received from Naval elements as far south as Davao, Mindanao.

IJN Jap planes from an unknown aircraft carrier had bombed two moored Consolidated PBY-4 Catalinas and the Davao airfield at 0615. The destroyer seaplane tender USS William B. Preston DD-344/AVP-20, reported it had shot down 3 dive-bombers and damaged a two-engine bomber.

ComSixteen also reported major damage to their port facilities and warehouses this morning; 243 torpedoes were destroyed; many fires still raging out of control due to lack of water pressure for fire hoses. Navy handybillies—shipboard damage control suction pumps—are pumping salt water from the bay providing low pressure water to the fire hoses. Secondary explosions continue unabated at Cavite Navy Yard. However, all seven Manila piers are damaged but still usable.

Only 3 B-17D survived intact at Clark Field after the 1235 hours air raid. Air Force fuel and ammo dump stores and equipment, including the new secret SCR-270B radar at Iba Air Field, were destroyed. The count of killed and wounded soldiers and civilians continue.

General MacArthur's war room was next to his private office. An enlarged National Geographic map of the Isles, protected with a sheet of clear acetate, covered one wall. Colored pins and miniature flags mark where U.S. military and naval forces are located. Enlarged military maps of the main islands of the Philippines covered another other wall. A major oil company road map of the Philippines is taped to the last wall.

Red crayon X's mark known destroyed buildings, bridges, rails, and facilities based on spot reports. The largest red X's mark Clark Field, struck at 1235 hours, and Iba Field, struck a few minutes later. Twelve of the Boeing B-17C and B-17D Flying Fortress heavy bombers are now forlorn, smashed hulks lying burning in their revetments or under trees where they were camouflaged.

MacArthur's Pacific Appeasement, December 8, 1941
Part I
The Missing Ten Hours

Three fake plywood B-17s in front of 19th Bomb Group HQ where they had been lined up had been blasted into smithereens. Eighteen B-17D's are safe at Del Monte Air Field in Mindanao, out of IJAF range.

The high-octane gasoline fuel farm is a smoking ruin; all aircraft fuel lost. Aircraft fuel at Nielsen Field was not bombed. Ammo bunkers storing machine gun shells still crackle, firing in all directions. Bomb storage bunkers are completely destroyed. Hangers, shops, and barracks are destroyed or heavily damaged. It is apparent that Japanese intelligence had pinpointed all their targets with highflying reconnaissance aircraft.

An unknown number of the Curtis P-40 Warhawk pursuit planes managed to get up and shoot down or damage high-speed Japanese pursuit planes of an unknown new type and a few Mitsubishi Betty twin engine high altitude bombers.

The many dead and wounded, including the Filipino work force, have been removed to Fort Stotsenberg military hospital for treatment or burial. Reports coming in are confused and difficult to sort.

The U.S. Army Hospital, Camp John Hay, at Baguio with large red crosses on building rooftops, was bombed and machine-gunned by the Imperial Japanese Air Force at 0819 hours. Another report stated the hospital was also bombed at 0838.

The U.S. Army Far East Air Force (FEAF) 19th Heavy Bomber Group is no longer an effective fighting force. The Pursuit and Fighter Groups are marginally so.

Filipino Constabulary Police continue to call the Philippine Imperial Palace with names of villages in northern Luzon that have been strafed with machine-guns by Japanese bombers, reporting on killed and wounded civilians. Several detachments of Philippine Scouts (Mounted), with pack-horses, have been dispatched to contact the remote villages and assist villagers along the Japanese air routes.

Admiral Hart, Commander-in-Chief, U. S. Asiatic Fleet (CINCUSNAF), sortied most of his fleet to Borneo on December 3, 1941, when the Commander-in-Chief, President Roosevelt, executed War Plan Rainbow 5 Phase I. Admiral Hart and the rest of his staff departed for Java early yesterday morning soon after the Imperial Japanese Navy Air Force began its attack at Pearl Harbor, in accordance with War Plan Rainbow 5, Phase II. Other ships, submarines, PT Boats, and auxiliary craft meant to stay behind were moored or anchored in the harbor at Cavite.

For several weeks, Admiral Hart's Scouting Force of amphibious Consolidated PBY-5A's and water-borne PBY-4's had been skirting Formosa, looking at ports and air fields. This information was gathered and forwarded to Chief of Naval Operations, and copied to FEAF.

December 9, 1941
GHQ, U.S. Army Forces, Far East
One Calle Victoria,
Intramurous, Fort Santiago
Manila, the Philippines

Lieutenant General Douglas Arthur MacArthur moved impatiently between his war room rocking on his shoes and sitting at his desk in his private office. He studied the marked up military charts, smoking cigarette after cigarette, his eyes following enlisted men and junior officers with dread as they hurried in to bring the military maps up to date.

General MacArthur had made an unusual decision, allowing his general staff to bring the latest information directly to his maps and charts as soon as spot reports were received, without waiting for permission from Sutherland or Huff to enter. He would have been irritated if the constant noise and chatter in the headquarters area bombarded his ears through an open doorway.

He hated Admiral Hart for deserting him and had called him a coward in the face of the enemy. It did not matter that Admiral Hart, CinC Asiatic Fleet, had obeyed his orders. Hart's departure with his tin boats angered MacArthur.

He saw no good news: only news of more destruction and death. A few U.S. Army and Philippine Scout platoons were still out of touch with their company commanders.

MacArthur reached out with his foot and pressed a hidden buzzer. The door opened and Lieutenant Colonel Sidney L. Huff appeared still dressed in yesterday's uniform, haggard from being up since General Sutherland woke him at General MacArthur's quarters to announce the Jap raid on

MacArthur's Pacific Appeasement, December 8, 1941
Part I
The Missing Ten Hours

Pearl Harbor. As Junior Aide-de-Camp, Huff lived in MacArthur's quarters and his and his wife's beck and call.
 "Yes, General?"

Lieutenant General MacArthur looked up from the dispatches on his desk and looked at Lieutenant Colonel Huff. "Get hold of Skinny, Sidney. I want to talk to him."
"Right away, General," he said, backing out and shutting the door.

Wish he would make up his mind whether to call me Sid or Sidney!

Brigadier General Jonathan Mayhew Wainwright IV, Cavalry, USA, was tall and thin, hence the nickname "Skinny". He had a leathery complexion from years in the saddle as a cavalryman. Like most American military personnel, he had been ordered to send his wife Adele back to the States as war clouds loomed in the Far East. Skinny moved into Flag Officers Quarters (FOQ) to be closer to his troops and because his family quarters echoed with emptiness.

He commanded the Philippine Division—way undermanned and not well trained—that would spearhead the defense of Southern Luzon. MacArthur recently added two Philippine Army divisions who also were not trained and had almost no equipment. Indeed, the Army medical staff was busy treating Filipino feet that were not used to shoes. Nevertheless, Skinny was proud of the men he commanded and they loved him.

It was his task to prevent an enemy landing on the Lingayen Gulf beaches. If that failed, he was to fall back, in proper order, into the Bataan Peninsula, there to hold and protect Manila Bay until the Navy returned with troops and war supplies.

Huff picked up his phone, wiped the sweat from his face—his handkerchief was sopping wet—looked across the open area at the switchboard, and waited for the operator to answer.

"Connect me with General Wainwright, Corporal Wynn," Huff ordered, again wiping sweat dripping from his forehead with his free hand and rubbing it on his trousers. The GHQ air conditioning plant had been wiped out in the first bombing raid on this fortress.

MacArthur's Pacific Appeasement, December 8, 1941
Part I
The Missing Ten Hours

"Right away, Colonel," answered the Corporal. There followed a series of clicks and buzzes in the telephone system. The line suddenly jumped louder as a phone was answered.

"General Wainwright's Headquarters, Major Ellison, Aide-de-Camp speaking sir," was the clipped response on a noisy signal wire line.

"This is Lieutenant Colonel Sidney Huff, General MacArthur's Junior Aide-de-Camp, Ellison. My general wants to talk with your general, Major." He shouted into the noisy line.

"The General is about ten minutes away, Colonel. Do you want to hold or wait for my call back?" he asked.

Huff thought about it, briefly. "Please call back as soon as General Wainwright returns, Major," he responded while looking at his wristwatch. He jotted the time and information in his pocket journal.

"Will do, Colonel Huff." The noise dropped as the major hung up. Sid hung up and automatically knocked on MacArthur's door. Hearing a muffled response, he opened, peered through the doorway and said, "General Wainwright is away from his desk. He should be back in about ten minutes, General." Huff hesitated. "Is there anything I can do, sir?"

General MacArthur looked at Huff and shook his head without speaking. Huff nodded, backed out the door, and shut it, returning to his own desk.

1430. December 9, 1941
GHQ, U.S. Army Forces, Far East
One Calle Victoria,
Intramurous, Fort Santiago
Manila, the Philippines

As he started to sit down, the switchboard operator called to him.

"Hey, Colonel, I got a General Gerow from the Chief of Staff War Plans for General MacArthur on the RCA radiophone. Do you want to take it, sir?"

Huff frowned and shook his head.

A Navy Petty Officer would have never said 'Hey'.

He pointed to the door to send it in to The General, as he turned and reached for the door.

"General, General Gerow, War Plans, is on the Radio telephone. We're patching it to you now."

Lt. Col. Huff reached into his shirt pocket and withdrew his green pocket journal and pencil again to note the time and name of the caller. He didn't know the subject, however. He reached for the Army Register and looked up the general. Brigadier General, Leonard Townsend Gerow (VMI '11), currently serving as Chief of War Planning, Army Chief of Staff.

MacArthur drew in a deep breath and sighed, opening the drawer and taking out the radio telephone. When it rang, he stood—and picked up the handset; his thoughts were more nimble when he was standing or walking. He jammed his left hand into his back pocket, gazed at the far wall, frowned intensely and spoke.

"MacArthur here. What can I do for you, Gerow?"

"General, we have not received any sitrep yet on the Japanese attack in your command."

"Ahhh, yes. We shall get that TWX'd this afternoon, Gerow. Still assessing damage here, you know." MacArthur said, as he twiddled with his yellow pencils.

"Was there severe damage anywhere?" Gerow asked.

MacArthur considered that question carefully.

Had they seen a message from the Navy?

"Without all the information, Gerow, I hesitate to give a definitive answer. Let us say there was moderate damage overall."

The line was quiet for a moment. "General, were any facilities completely destroyed?"

MacArthur glanced down at his clean desk. "I do not have any information in front of me that indicates complete destruction of any facility, Gerow. We understand the Navy got hit pretty hard at Cavite and the Air Station at Olongapo. Is there anything else?" MacArthur allowed irritation in the sound of his voice.

"Just get the damage assessment TWX'd in as soon as possible, General. General Marshall and the Commander-in-Chief are waiting for them."

MacArthur's Pacific Appeasement, December 8, 1941
Part I
The Missing Ten Hours

"Very well, Gerow, as soon as I can." MacArthur hung up the phone. He considered Gerow's call for a moment and returned to the damage reports on his desk.

MacArthur worked steadily on reports coming in from all points. He looked up in irritation at a loud and heated argument outside his door and listened to the struggle.

The door burst open, banging hard against the wall. Major General Lewis H. Brereton, his face red with sweat and anger, glasses fogged over from the heat, bulled his way into MacArthur's private office dragging Huff and Sutherland with him. He began screaming as he struggled with Sutherland and Huff. He glared at them. "Get your hands off me," he grated. Faces of soldiers and officers looked through the open door.

"Damn you, MacArthur. All but three of my B-17s at Clark were destroyed by the Japs and most of the P-40's. . ." MacArthur jumped to his fee and slammed down his pencil on the desk. "You come to attention, Brereton. How dare you address me that way?"

". . . and almost every other aircraft, too. You're going to . . ."

"Be silent," roared MacArthur, his voice rising higher, "and come to attention, I say."

". . . pay for this, you miserable whelp! I've sent a message to General Arnold charging you with treason."

"Get him out of here." MacArthur looked at Brereton with mingled anger, disgust, and alarm. "I didn't authorize any transmission to Washington from you, Brereton."

"Didn't have to, MacArthur. I sent it over Air Force radio channels in the clear." Brereton yelled triumphantly, as he was being dragged out of the office. The door shut in his face.

"Damn you, Sutherland, I said take your shitty hands off me," Brereton snarled as he struggled in their grip.

"Not until I have you out of GHQ, flyboy," said Sutherland through gritted teeth. "Go back where you belong."

Brereton struggled in their grip, continuing to berate Sutherland and Huff while he was forcefully ejected from Headquarters, Sutherland smiling wickedly. Officers and soldiers stood frozen in shock by this display.

Damn flyboys think their shit don't stink. That ought to teach him to mind his betters.

MacArthur hunched his shoulders and paced back and forth for a few minutes as he considered the consequences of Brereton's intemperate actions. Finally, he sat back down and began working his way through damage reports again.

A soft knock landed on his door as it opened a crack. "General, General Gerow in Washington is on the radio phone for you again."

"Very well, patch it in here," said MacArthur with a calm and unruffled voice.

His phone rang and he picked up the handset. "General Gerow, how are you?"

"Just fine, General MacArthur. I'm calling to remind you we have not received your situation reports yet. We need to get a quick estimate of damage from the air attacks."

"Oh, yes. Well, we suffered light to medium damage, General. Our troops are prepared and ready for battle with the Japanese forces."

"You suffered no major damage, then?"

"No, barely any damage in Manila," repeated MacArthur.

General Gerow paused. "No damage at Iba or Clark, General?"

"We're getting battle damage assessment a little later. Sun has just come up here, you see." MacArthur allowed irritation to creep into his voice.

"Very well. Send us a follow up report by TWX as soon as you can. That's all I have for now."

"Thank you for the call, General," and hung up the radiophone.

Huff opened the door and announced, "General Wainwright is on the phone for you, General."

MacArthur snatched up the phone and got right to the point. "Jonathan, I want you to take command of the Northern Luzon Ground forces immediately. Who do you recommend to take command of the Southern Force?"

The phone line was silent for a long moment as Wainwright considered the order. "Very well, General. I'll take a brief break to turn over command of Southern Luzon Ground forces to Brigadier General Parker."

"He's an excellent leader, Jonathan. Good choice. Set up your forces according to my Beach Defense War Plan and deny the Japanese landing forces a foothold."

"We'll do our best, General. I'll give you an update before sundown."

MacArthur's Pacific Appeasement, December 8, 1941
Part I
The Missing Ten Hours

Major General Jonathan Wainwright thoughtfully pushed the EE-5 handset back in its leather holder. "Ellison, we have work to do," he called through the door. Major Ellison came through the door with his eyebrows raised in question. "What's up, General?"

"I've just been given command of the Northern Luzon Ground forces. Gather the staff for a meeting and call General Parker. I need to talk to him."

"Yes sir, right away, General."

1400, December 9, 1941
Tainan IJAF Medium Bomber Group and Zero Escorts
Downtown Manila, the Philippines

The hum grew louder. People looked up from where they stood, walked, or rode, and scanned the sky. "Oh God, there they are, almost right on top of us!" screamed one man.

Some people shrieked but everyone looked for shelter because the bombs will soon be falling on them. Relieved, they watched the huge number of bombers continue on their way, heading directly for the big U.S. Naval Base at Cavite.

1405, December 9, 1941
Tainan IJAF Medium Bomber Group and Zero Escorts
Approaching Cavite Naval Base at 23,000 feet

The bomber commander did the military pilot search —up, down, left, right, behind—to see if any enemies were diving on them. His Zero escorts were far above him, weaving back and forth.

No enemy fighters coming up. What s wrong with these Americans? Don't they know we are at war now?

He nudged his bombardier. "Find our targets."

A few minutes later, twenty-four Betty bombers unloaded their one 1,100-pound bomb and 23 132-pound bombs on the Naval Base, causing greater destruction. On completion of the bomb run, the flight wheeled toward the China Sea and headed North to their base at Kato, Formosa. On the second attack, they had destroyed the Naval Base and most of its assets.

Eleven Consolidated PBY-4 patrol bombers survived the raid. They returned from offshore, refueled, and departed for Netherlands East Asia in the Celebes to fight another day. Sadly, some of their friends were shot down or survived in Japanese prison camps.

1430, December 9, 1941
Headquarters, Asiatic Fleet
US Naval Station Cavite
The Philippines

Following a grim, frosty, eyeball-to-eyeball meeting with MacArthur earlier yesterday, Hart learned of the incredible disaster at Clark and Iba. Hart decided to save his Asiatic Fleet to fight another day. MacArthur called him a coward, abandoning his army to the enemy. Hart didn't bother to answer the blowhard; he just walked out.

Hart immediately caused the Heavy Cruiser Houston, the two Light Cruisers Marblehead and Boise, two of the three Submarine Tenders, and thirteen World War One (as it was now called) destroyers, to get underway for the Celebes Netherlands East India ports as the Asiatic Fleet's new base, and for protection against japanese air raids.

He also ordered Captain Wilkes, his Chief of Staff and Commander, Submarines Forces Asiatic Fleet to distribute the twenty-three new Fleet class submarines, based at Cavite, along the probable Japanese convoy routes from Formosa and French Indochina to the Philippines, and attack.

Besides tugs and harbor tankers, this left six gunboats, formerly of the China rivers, six S-class submarines also from the China Station, and a squadron of Patrol Torpedo Boats (PTs).

The Naval Station Cavite consisted of the 16th naval District Headquarters, the naval Hospital, twenty-eight PBY-4s at NAS Olongapo. (PBY-4 Catalinas were floatation only.)
Cavite also contained gasoline, diesel, and ship oil fuel farms, warehouses filled with submarine and aircraft supplies,

including a very large number of new, super-secret torpedoes, and the usual assortment of barracks, mess halls, and clubs.

Navy, Marine (augmented by the China 4th Marines), and civilian personnel were also present.

Unfortunately, the Department of the Navy did not believe it necessary to also provide anti-aircraft batteries of any kind. That was Army business. Only light machine guns on the harbor craft were available.

Admiral Hart ordered the remains of the Naval Station destroyed. He understood the Japanese would take over in a very few weeks.

0800, December 10, 1941
Japanese Amphibious Force One
Aparri Beach
Northern Luzon, the Philippines

The barges loaded with Japanese Army troops and supplies began heading to shore as the cruisers and destroyers continued to shell the landing zones. American and Filipino troops backed off the beach until the shelling stopped, then moved forward into their battle positions to beat back the Japanese Army.

By Noon, the Aparri Field was secure. Japanese Navy and Air Force aircraft now had a base on Luzon.

0830, December 10, 1941
Japanese Amphibious Force Two
Vigan Beaches
Central Luzon, the Philippines

The second invasion force met with stronger opposition from the American and Filipino troops but the beachhead was secured within two hours. The assault troops pushed the American Army troops out of the way and continued their march.

MacArthur's Pacific Appeasement, December 8, 1941
Part I
The Missing Ten Hours

1230, December 10, 1941
The Waters off French Indochina
North of Singapore, Malaya

The few survivors of the ruthless air attack by the Japanese Navy torpedo and dive bombers clung to wreckage, floats, or were in the few lifeboats that had not been destroyed. They wondered who knew that His Majesty's HMS Prince of Wales and HMS Repulse had just been sunk, drowning more than 800 seamen. Where was the American air coverage they were supposed to have?

0600, December 11, 1941
Main Japanese Invasion Force
Legaspi Beaches
Southern Luzon, the Philippines

Before the Japanese troops began to embark in their barges, an S-class submarine torpedoed and sunk one of the smaller Japanese troop ships. Although Japanese destroyers depth charged the area, the American submarine got away with minor damage.

This thrust northward toward Manila was intended to crush the American forces between the earlier landings in the north in a pincer movement.

0445, December 12, 1941
USS Seawolf, Fleet Submarine
Off Aparri Landing Beaches
Northern Luzon, the Philippines

Lieutenant Commander James Byrne, the Captain, had been stalking this Japanese Seaplane Tender for two hours. In the pre-dawn light, he was about to attack and sink it. Several destroyers were cruising back and forth but had not sensed the Seawolf.

"Down 'Scope," he ordered, and turned to his Executive Officer. "What do you have on the Is-Was,

102

Ed?" (The Is-Was is a complicated circular slide-rule designed to set up submarine targets, such as this.)

"We have a solution. Angle on the bow, Port 3 degrees. 1,500 yards distant; at anchor. I see the runtime to be 56 seconds, Captain."

"Okay. This will be a final look before shooting. Open Outer doors one, two, and three. Ready tubes one, two, and three in a five degree spread." The Torpedo Officer whispered instructions to the Forward Torpedo Room Chief on his headset.

A quiet clunk sounded three times as the Outer doors of the three torpedo tubes pulled inward exposing the business end of the tubes with their torpedoes.

"Tubes one, two, and three are ready, Captain" replied the Torpedo Officer.

"Up 'Scope." The Captain squatted and followed the periscope tube up. "Hold it there, Chief." The Chief of the Boat (COB) pressed the red stop button.

The Captain looked in the eyepieces, refocussed, check his target, and spun completely around looking for destroyers that might be charging. Then, "Ready—Fire one, two, and three." The Seawolf bucked as each torpedo was expulsed from its tube with high pressure air.

"Close outer doors. Down 'scope. Down planes ten degrees. Make our depth 250 feet, right turn 15 degrees to new course 265. Rig for silent running." The usual sliding clunk as the doors pushed out to hide the tubes, sounded throughout the Boat.

He peered over the Exec's shoulder to see the Stop Watch second hand sweeping toward 56 seconds. Passing 60 seconds, he frowned and called down through the open hatch: "Sonar, anything?"

"No, Captain. I heard the screws stop but that's all."

"Very well. Listen for those destroyers. They ought to be heading our way."

"Aye aye, sir. Not a sound, so far."

The Captain waited ten long minutes. "Up planes five degrees. Make our depth 60 feet, turn left to base course 185 degrees, reduce speed to 3 knots.

The two men on forward and after planes (similar to elevators on aircraft), called out "aye aye, sir—60 feet." The helmsman called out "returning to course 185." Another man turned the annunciators to 3 on both electric engines. "Engine Room responds three knots, Captain."

"Very well."

The Chief of the Boat who had been monitoring all this action very carefully, finally announced "The Boat is at sixty feet, Captain."

"Up 'Scope, but I don't want more than six inches up there, Chief."

He squatted and came up with the periscope. First, he swept in a circle for danger from the destroyers, then checked his target. Nothing was happening there. No one was running around peering over the side.

"Ed, I know damn well those torpeodes should have struck that tender. Ready tubes four, five, and six. Open Outer Doors on tubes four, five, and six." The Captain and Exec did their little dance as they set up for the next shots at the seaplane tender. Once again, there was a good shooting solution. They fired all three tubes and dropped to 250 feet to wait for the explosions.

There were no explosions.

The Captain was embarrassed and pissed.

There was no way I missed the ship six times. Once or twice, maybe, but not six shots

"Ed, reverse course and ready after tubes seven and eight. By God, we are going to kill that ship."

There were no explosions. The Seawolf retired out into the Indian Ocean and sent a seething message to the Commander Submarine Force, Asiatic Fleet, reporting the failure of eight torpedoes with the new (secret) magnetic exploders.

The S-class Boat at Legaspi with Contact exploders was the only successful attack from the Asiatic Fleet submarines.

December 13, 1942
GHQ, U.S. Army Forces, Far East
One Calle Victoria,
Intramurous, Fort Santiago
Manila, the Philippines

MacArthur's Pacific Appeasement, December 8, 1941
Part I
The Missing Ten Hours

General MacArthur studied the overlays of Northern Luzon one more time, took his hands out of his back pockets and walked to his door, opening it. "Dick—Sid, would you come in here please," he said.

They looked at each other apprehensively; something in his voice bothered them. Together, they rose from their desks and followed MacArthur back into his office.

"Shut the door, Sidney. Sit down, both of you." MacArthur began pacing the floor from one wall to the other and stuck his hands in his back pockets, all the while staring at the ceiling as he thought.

MacArthur continued to pace from wall to wall.

Sutherland and Huff, watching General MacArthur, glanced at each other now and then, worry lines showing. The General sighed and took a deep breath, then paced some more before beginning to speak. He was glancing at them from the side of his face.

He is embarrassed! thought Sutherland.

"Gentlemen, as hard as it is, I've got to pull our forces back to the Bataan Peninsula. Skinny and Brigadier General King? Well, I expected more, they are not doing as well as they should." He paused for a moment to study their faces. "The enemy is pushing hard to encircle Major General Wainwright's troops. Brigadier General Parker is doing his best to prevent that."

He paused and wheeled to Huff. "Sid," he ordered, "you get hold of Brigadier General Drake immediately—right now—and tell him we are going to execute War Plan Orange Three within the day." He turned to Sutherland. "Dick, you get hold of Colonel Casey and order him to begin blowing bridges, roads and rails ahead of the enemy. He is to make sure our troops are safely across the bridges before he sets the charges."

Brigadier General Sutherland flinched as though struck by a blast of wind.

My God, Casey has been blowing everything to slow the Jap advance since the eleventh. Has he forgotten this?

Huff swallowed and nodded.

"Sid, you emphasize to General Drake he has to move the supplies back into the original Bataan depots just as fast as he can. What he cannot move, he is to advise Colonel Casey to blow up or burn."

"Yes sir," Huff agreed as he turned and hurried out the door to his phone.

General MacArthur looked at the closed door for a moment, shook his head, turned to Dick Sutherland and placing his hand on Chief of Staff's shoulder, guided him to the door. "Dick, you call Casey as fast as possible. Then, let's quickly determine the movement order of troops back into the Bataan positions."

MacArthur looked at him grimly. "We have to hold out long enough for the Navy relief force to get here from the States." He paused again. "I don't think they will make it in time."

"Would you repeat that, Colonel Huff?" General Drake said in a shocked voice.

"I said General MacArthur said he is going to execute War Plan Orange Three within the day. You need to move all those Beach Defense supplies back to Bataan where you got them, General." Huff said.

"My God, I'll never get those supplies out of the Beach Defense zone. Much of it has already been blown up or burned to prevent capture as we retreat. You tell General MacArthur I got the message and am on it now, but damned if I know how much I will be able to move."

General Drake slammed his EE-5 phone back in its case, and yelled out, "Sergeant Major!" Then, with the weight of the war upon him, he leaned over his charts to see what had not been burned or blown up.

Colonel Huff hung up and turned to General Sutherland. "General, General Drake says most of the supplies have already been torched or blown up to keep the Japs from getting them. He will move what he can but it won't be much." General Sutherland looked shocked and swallowed several times before he knocked on MacArthur's door. He knew the end was near.

**1600, December 13, 1941
GHQ, USAFFE**

MacArthur's Pacific Appeasement, December 8, 1941
Part I
The Missing Ten Hours

1 Calle Victoria
Intramurous, Fort Santiago
Manila, the Philippines

"Generai Sutherland, Drake here, President Queson refuses to allow us to use the railroad to move supplies back into Bataan. Further, he will not permit our food supplies to move, either. Will you or The General intercede? Otherwise, we are going to lose a tremendous amount of material."

"Drake, use trucks. Carry out your orders. Is that all?"

Stunned, General Drake swallowed and hung up.

0930, December 14, 1941
GHQ, USAFFE
1 Calle Victoria
Intramurous, Fort Santiago
Manila, the Philippines

Major General Lewis Brereton, CG FEAF, stood at attention in front of Lieutenant General Douglas MacArthur's desk. His face was glacial with contempt as he stared at his Commander-in-Chief.

MacArthur handed Brereton a signed general order. "Brereton, I have disbanded the Far East Air Force. You and the fourteen B-17s at Del Monte are to fly to Australia to save them. You will receive new orders from the Department of the Army G1.

"As all the remaining aircraft have been destroyed, your remaining forces are transferred to the Army in the Infantry unless they have some other specialty of use to the Army. Any questions?" MacArthur asked, casually.

Trembling with rage, Brereton about faced and marched toward the door.
"Brereton, I require you to respond and salute. I have not dismissed you."
Major General Lewis Brereton paused, did not look back and left MacArthur's office, leaving the door open.

MacArthur's Pacific Appeasement, December 8, 1941
Part I
The Missing Ten Hours

0700, December 18, 1941
GHQ, USAFFE
1 Calle Victoria
Intramurous, Fort Santiago
Manila, the Philippines

The putrid stench of death that began ten days ago swirled in the wind and rain. Most of the bodies had been removed to cemeteries, but swelling donkey, horse, and carabao carcasses with legs sticking out at hideous angles were scattered over the shattered roads, buildings, and fields. Nearby columns of oily smoke and fire were visible in the tropical downpour.

Secondary explosions still could be heard from the now destroyed Cavite Navy Yard as well as several other points around Manila Bay and the city. There would be no air raid on Manila today because of the stormy weather. The relative humidity would climb into the middle 90's.

A drab brown 1939 Plymouth Army sedan moved swiftly along the highway, weaving and dodging bomb craters and debris. Lightning flashed on the three white stars on ragged red flags attached to both front fenders called attention to an Army Lieutenant General in the automobile. They rippled and snapped in the breeze as the automobile weaved and raced along the bomb-shattered streets from Manila Hotel, General MacArthur's penthouse residence.

Lieutenant General MacArthur snapped his fingers.

That's it! General Homma plans to live in my quarters, if he can take over Manila. That's why my hotel has not been bombed. The gall of that bastard.

He fumed as he continued to think about it. MacArthur looked up as the driver slowed and turned.
The pennants fell limp as the sedan began climbing the short hill through the Intramuro narrow entrance to Fort Santiago where miserable sentries posted in the rain with rifle muzzles pointed down, water pouring off their flat helmets, gave dispirited rifle salutes.

The Army sedan pulled under the bomb-damaged portico at the U.S. Army Forces Far East, General Headquarters, stopping next to the sandbagged entrance.

MacArthur's Pacific Appeasement, December 8, 1941
Part I
The Missing Ten Hours

Sentries posted at GHQ sprang to attention as the sedan came to them.

A sergeant, equipped with leggings, helmet and sidearm, leaped from the driver's seat, ran around the sedan and opened the rear door. He stood at attention and saluted as Lieutenant General Douglas A. MacArthur stepped out of the sedan, starched and pressed khaki uniform wilting in the downpour.

Setting his favorite gold-encrusted headgear firmly on his head, Lieutenant General Douglas A. MacArthur turned and looked grimly at his bomb-blasted 1941 black Cadillac, taken out in the first attack on Manila on December 8. His eyes swept around to the oily smoke and flames still rising from military targets around Manila bay. The Japanese Air Force had struck hard ten days ago and again and again since then to soften the American Army before the Japanese Army invaded the shores of Luzon.

General MacArthur returned his driver's salute with his gold marshal's baton. It was a gift from Philippine President Manuel L. Queson, presented the day he was appointed Philippine Field Marshal. President Queson was unhappy with MacArthur now and probably would like to take back the gold baton.

Lieutenant General Douglas MacArthur marched inside. Never smiling, he acknowledged greetings dourly from officers and soldiers alike raising and shaking his gold baton in their direction, nodding here and there as he made his way into his office, shut the door, and immediately walked into his war room.

"That will be all, Roberts—ah, sorry, Corporal. Levinson, is it? We'll get that overlay updated in a little while." (Day before yesterday, bomb shrapnel had killed Corporal Roberts, his previous orderly.)

"Yes sir, General." Corporal Levinson stuck the crayons in his mouth and a wiping rag in his pocket. Clutching reports in one hand, he hastily backed down off the rickety ladder and dropped his pieces of paper and crayons in a basket below the Luzon map.

He tiptoed quietly across to the door, glanced at the general and left, closing the door softly behind him. Closing his door didn't do much good; noise, smoke and stench still crept into MacArthur's private office and war room.

MacArthur picked up his ivory cigarette holder and pushed a Chesterfield into the end. He struck a sulpher match with his thumbnail and waited until all the sulpher burned off before lighting his cigarette. He disliked the taste or smell of sulpher and claimed his tobacco smoke was much healthier without that taste. All of his cigars had been destroyed on December 9th. He blew out the match and laid it carefully in the clean ashtray positioned on the right rear edge of his desk. Then drew smoke directly into his lungs and let the smoke trickle from his nostrils.

MacArthur strolled into the Map Room and leaned back against his small desk. He surveyed the situation maps, cigarette holder clenched in his teeth while he gripped the near edge of the desk with stretched out arms. The new clerk had changed his war map this morning. Slowly turned around, MacArthur shook his head, walked back into his office and sat down.

His very large wooden desk fairly glowed with wax. There was nothing on it except a polished brass shell casing—with cigar cup holders—ashtray and six yellow pencils with sharp points. He idly pushed the pencils around into different patterns, doodling as it were, while he studied an overlay of Northwest Luzon to see what progress the Imperial Japanese Army made overnight advancing from Aparri and Vigan. They came ashore just a few days ago and were pushing his troops back into Bataan, most of them properly retreating, a few fading into the jungle.

Richard K. Sutherland, MacArthur's Chief of Staff, had been promoted to Brigadier General when MacArthur made the assignment. Sutherland's uniform was immaculate, kept that way by a Filipino servant. He believed he was superior to all other beings except The General.

Right now, Sutherland sat at his scarred desk immediately outside MacArthur's office to the left of his door, nervously puffing on a cigarette. He glanced at Huff sitting in the outer office area.

I wonder what task Huff should undertake now?

Sutherland's senses had been outraged when MacArthur had drafted a medically retired Navy Commander into the Army as a Lieutenant Colonel. Sidney Huff, MacArthur's new Junior Aide-de-camp could not really be called an Army officer. Sutherland growled under his breath.

Huff wasn't even a real Aide-de-Camp yet. He ought to be

returned to Cavite and work on his Filipino PT Boat Navy, except Cavite was destroyed.

Huff sat at his small desk outside General Sutherland's office: the outer door guard as it were, as a glorified messenger boy and Sutherland treated him that way. Huff's uniform was wrinkled and not up to any military standard because he could not afford a Filipino servant to look after his clothes. Huff looked haggard, still not in good health. MacArthur had ordered Sutherland to teach Huff the finer points of his new duties.

General Sutherland still eyed Huff with distaste. "Huff, why don't you see if there is any pastry left to go with that coffee you're bringing back to us."

"Right away, General Sutherland."

Lieutenant Colonel Huff heaved himself out of his chair wearily and headed toward the coffee room without another word. General Sutherland smiled thinly as he watched Huff walk slowly to the coffee room. There was only one stale bear claw left and Huff ate it with relish before heading back with two mugs of coffee.

A general may order me to bring coffee to him, but I'll be damned if he can eat the last bear claw.

For that reason, Lt. Col. Huff could not answer the phone when it rang; he was carrying coffee back to General Sutherland.

Sutherland looked at the phone nastily and picked it up. "Sutherland speaking," he said, in a bored voice.

Huff was supposed to answer the telephone. Who the hell was bothering him this time of morning?

"Sutherland! This is Marshall. Is MacArthur there?" General Sutherland, stunned, snapped to attention in his chair, swallowed and said "Let me check, General. I believe he is. . ."

"You tell MacArthur to get his ass on the phone right now, Sutherland, and you tell him I said that." General Marshall's voice roared in harsh anger. That anger came through loud and clear on the tinny voice radio circuit.

"Yes sir, General Marshall."

MacArthur's Pacific Appeasement, December 8, 1941
Part I
The Missing Ten Hours

He jumped up, knocking over his chair, and gave a hard double knock on The General's door, then burst in.

Sutherland cleared his throat and squeaked. He cleared his throat again and tried again with a shaky voice. "Sir, General Marshal is on the radio telephone and ordered me to tell you to get your ass on the phone." He stood at attention, eyes aimed six inches above MacArthur's head to avoid the rage he knew from experience would follow.

General MacArthur's head jerked up in shock. He leaped to his feet almost knocking over his chair. "Did George really say that?" he asked, his voice rising sharply.

Sutherland swallowed and nodded. MacArthur stared at the map of Luzon for a moment. He grimaced, shook his head, walked back to his enormous desk and sat down. Opening his top left drawer, he removed the telephone and said, "Patch the radio phone circuit in here, Dick. No one else is to listen or know about this call." He paused and looked at Sutherland. "Except General Homma's Intelligence boys, of course," he said wryly.

General Sutherland walked with long strides to the switchboard and spoke to the Corporal.

"Corporal Wynn, patch that call from General Marshall to General MacArthur's office phone. When he answers, you make sure you disconnect your earphones and then forget you heard about the call. That's an order, Corporal. Clear?"

"Yes sir, General." The Corporal did not think well of Brigadier General Sutherland.

Everything you say is an order, Genrul!

The Corporal's hands moved surely and smoothly, plugged three patch cord metal ends into the proper holes and toggled the ringing lever. He toggled his own phone circuit lever off, pulled his patch cord out, took his earphones off and sat back to watch the little white light above General MacArthur's phone line.

General Sutherland was sweating as he pulled his Camel cigarettes from his shirt pocket and offered one to the corporal. Taking one himself with shaking hands, he aped The General, striking a sulfur match with his thumbnail, listening to the shushing sound of sulpher burning, and waiting until all the sulpher burned off before lighting his own cigarette. Then he leaned over the top of the switchboard to light the corporal's cigarette. Sutherland smoked rapidly in short puffs and watched the signal light.

Lieutenant General Douglas A. MacArthur glared through bloodshot and scratchy eyes at the phone on his desk, broke a cigarette trying to insert it into his cigarette holder, then jammed another Chesterfield into his cigarette holder, waiting for the call to be transferred. He struck the sulpher match with a trembling hand and lit the cigarette.

Is Marshall going to tell me how to run my war with Japan again? Last time we talked, I told Marshall what I thought of that miserable whelp Hart, running away at the first sound of battle.

The phone buzzed. He mashed the cigarette in his brass ashtray, turned and snatched up his handset with a sweaty hand. He forced a hearty greeting: "It's a beautiful morning here in Manila, George. What can we do for you today?"

"Is this Lieutenant General Douglas Arthur MacArthur?" a very cold, saw-toothed voice asked through the hissing and fading radio telephone signal.

Frowning, MacArthur responded curtly, as he studied the ceiling. "Yes, who is this?"

"This is General George Catlin Marshall, Chief of Staff of the United States Army, General. Can you hear and understand me?" The very cold raspy voice continued.

"Yes, I can, George," said a slightly subdued MacArthur.

"MacArthur, you have lied and avoided following orders for the last time," he snarled.

MacArthur bolted upright in his chair as his face turned dark red in anger. "Now wait just a god damned minute. Who the hell do you think you're talking to, Marshall?" He surged forward in his chair and clamped the telephone receiver to his ear.

"You are hereby recalled immediately to Fort Belvoir, Alexandria, Virginia, to face an Article 70 Board of Inquiry into the disaster of your command. Bring your general staff out with you, especially General Brereton. Do you understand what I just said?" demanded the calm, icy voice.

"What the hell are you talking about, George? Is this necessary?" snapped MacArthur. Sweating because of the humidity, he tried to light a cigarette as he absorbed what General Marshall was saying.

"MacArthur, you will address me as General Marshall. You will arrange to fly out tonight in a B-17—if there are any left, otherwise by the next submarine. You will keep this headquarters informed of departures and arrivals all the way to Washington. You and your staff will be met at Bolling Field in Washington and transported to quarters at Fort Belvoir under house arrest. This movement is secret. You are to talk with no one. Is that clear?"

"I'll advise Skinny he has command while I am gone," rejoined MacArthur, angrily.

"MacArthur, you are not listening. You are not returning to the Philippines. You are relieved of your command on my recommendation to the Commander-in-Chief. He heartily agrees."

"Now just a god damned minute, George . . ."

"Address me as General!" Marshall snapped. "You are fired, MacArthur. Do you understand that? You're fired! I doubt if you will ever hold command again. Major General Wainwright is hereby promoted to Lieutenant General and assumes command as Commander in Chief, USAFFE. We can only hope he can pull this debacle of yours into something positive."

General MacArthur was building up to a spectacular rage. He screamed heatedly, "You horse's ass! You weren't a good regimental commander, and you certainly haven't got the balls to be a good Chief of Staff, much less be a pimple under a good McClellan saddle. Obviously you do not have all the facts before you. Go back to your staff and get a better reading on the real situation out here. How the hell can you relieve me at a time like this?"

General Marshall took an audible breath and gritted his teeth. "MacArthur," he said evenly in flat, measured tones, "if you do not follow your orders and leave the Philippines tonight, I will have you stripped of your rank and pulled out in irons tomorrow as a private. Is that clear enough for you?"

"Yes sir, General," came MacArthur's crisp reply.

You son of a bitch! Goddamn you all to hell, Marshall!

"Good. Now get Skinny over there and hand over the reins to him. Alert all your staff and move in secret. I require you to respond."

MacArthur's Pacific Appeasement, December 8, 1941
Part I
The Missing Ten Hours

"Yes sir, General Marshal, sir. My staff and I will be on a B-17 tonight for Del Monte, Australia, Hawaii, San Francisco, and Washington, D.C."

"Very well. One more thing: as you leave Manila, you are reduced in rank to Colonel."

The radiophone went dead in MacArthur's ear. He sat motionless, his face nearly purple in fury. A scream of rage rose from deep within him. MacArthur threw the telephone across the room, bouncing it off the wall so that it fell to the floor in several pieces.

The light went out much sooner than Brigadier General Sutherland expected, even before he finished his cigarette. The Corporal looked at the general with raised eyebrows. General Sutherland shrugged. The corporal reached up and pulled the patch cords out. A muffled scream and a crash sounded from Lieutenant General Douglas MacArthur's office. Sutherland and the Corporal looked at the door and each other, shrugging.

I wonder what happened?

Sutherland was curious at the brief call and whether he should go back to the office. His wait stretched into long minutes.

General MacArthur's door finally opened very slowly, just enough so that MacArthur standing in the doorway could motion for Sutherland to join him. Stubbing his cigarette in the corporal's ashtray, Sutherland returned to join MacArthur who motioned him to shut the door.

General MacArthur's face was white and he appeared to be shaking with rage. He looked at Sutherland and with a harsh voice barely under control said, "You personally go get Skinny and bring him here immediately. I have been relieved of my command . . . "

"My God, General!" Sutherland gasped, and turned pale.

MacArthur ignored him and continued. "Lieutenant General Wainwright is the new Commander-in-Chief. My staff and I are to report to Fort Belvoir, Virginia, to face a Board of Inquiry as soon as transportation can be arranged." He looked directly at Sutherland. "You and I will sit down and determine which of my staff, if any, will go with me—that is, besides you,

Brereton, Willoughby, and Huff. "

"Me, sir? Why me?" asked a stunned Brigadier General Sutherland.

"Because you are my Chief of Staff, Sutherland," MacArthur snarled. MacArthur paused, then spoke as if in a dream world. "Tell everyone to pack one small bag for each person. No papers, logs, or journals of any sort. We will fly to Del Monte on Mindanao tonight, then on to Brisbane. Is that clear?" He cleared his throat and spoke just above a whisper. "Oh, yes, as soon as my aircraft takes off for Del Monte, I am reduced in rank to Colonel."

General Sutherland gulped, took a deep breath, and spoke rather raggedly. "Yes sir, get Skinny—I mean Major General Wainwright—back here right away. Should I tell him . . . ?"

"Lieutenant General? No," shaking his head. "Just get him back here. Then go over to Nielson Field and arrange with Brereton for the best two of the three B-17's remaining to fly all of us to Del Monte tonight. Remember, one bag each of personal effects, no papers of any kind. From there we either fly on or wait for a submarine to take us out."

"General, aren't you going to take logs and messages with you for defense?" He stuttered, grasping at an unreal situation. "Sorry sir, but at the Board of Inquiry you must have a defense."

MacArthur tilted his head back and looked down his nose at him with a thin smile. "Can't afford the extra weight, Dick, can we? We only have the two B-17Ds left that can fly our party out of here. Now, send Sid in to see me." MacArthur herded him out of his office and shut the door.

Sutherland blinked his eyes several times, looked at the closed door for a moment and rushed away.
"Dear God, they'll crucify us for sure."

"FIFE AND DRUM CORPS: PLAY THE ROGUE'S MARCH!"

1930, December 18, 1941

MacArthur's Pacific Appeasement, December 8, 1941
Part I
The Missing Ten Hours

Manila Hotel
Manila, the Philippines

Lieutenant Douglas A. General MacArthur, his wife Jean, son Arthur, and servant Ah Chew, Brigadier General Sutherland, Colonel Willoughby, and Lieutenant Colonel Huff stood in the twilight under the canopy outside the Manila Hotel, protected from the drumming torrential rain, lightning, crackling thunder, and whipping wind.

Jean had cheated and gathered all his medals and other personal papers. Ah Chew whimpered and held young Arthur close to her. This annoyed Sutherland because Jean did not return to the States when everyone else was ordered to leave, including his own wife, and he bitterly thought Ah Chew should stay here.

Let Jean take care of her son.

Colonel Willoughby, numb with worry, thought his Army career was going down the tubes when the hearing was over.

Huff shivered in the driving monsoon rain. He hoped he would not drop into a malarial fever again, as he had long before. He just wanted to take care of Jean and Arthur, as well as his general.

They were waiting for a covered Army truck to carry them to Clark Field. Major General Brereton, their pilot, would help them settle down in the B-17 that would take them to Australia. Philippine President Queson and his family would meet them at Clark Field and fly out in the other B-17. There was a strong fear the Japanese would execute Queson if he remained in the Philippines.

Colonel Willoughby heard the truck first and blinked his flashlight to direct the truck to them. The brakes squealed as the truck swerved and stopped in front of them, splashing water on their shoes and bottoms of their uniform trousers.

MacArthur looked back at the hotel and up toward the penthouse, blinking at the raindrops in his eyes, where they had lived since 1935.

I hope General Homma enjoys the fruits of my labor, up there.

MacArthur's Pacific Appeasement, December 8, 1941
Part I
The Missing Ten Hours

MacArthur pulled himself up into the truck bed, turned and helped his wife Jean, son Arthur, and servant Ah Chew, climb in. He sent them to the front of the truck bed and followed them, sitting where he could look after them. The others climbed in and Sutherland stomped twice on the truck bed with the heel of his shoe.

The truck started off with a jerk. Jean began crying, and Ah Chew began wailing in concert; Arthur joined, crying in sympathy and fright. Those were the only sounds besides the engine as the covered truck jolted and bounced its way along the rubble-strewn highway, twisting and turning in and out of potholes and bomb damage. It was a long, jarring 50 mile ride to Clark Field.

Two gasoline tanker trucks were parked forward of the wings of the two B-17s. Gasoline hoses were pulled up on top of the wings as the ground crew topped off the fuel tanks. The sky was in full darkness now, with heavy rain and strong wind. The ground crews purposely strode under the B-17s, checking everything. They knew their boss, Major General Brereton, and the other pilot would make the final walk around after they were finished.

The Army trucks containing Lieutenant General Douglas MacArthur and party, and Philippine President Queson and party, finally arrived, pulled up behind the two B-17D bombers, and stopped. Lieutenant Colonel Huff was the first to jump down from the truck bed. He turned and helped the others get off the truck. Queson's party was already out of their truck. The tropical rain still poured steadily with gusty wind, lightning and thunder.

Major General Lewis Brereton grimly saluted Lieutenant General MacArthur, and President Queson. "Mr. President, General, this is a long flight from here to Australia, mostly over water. All machine guns have been removed in exchange for fuel." He glanced at the ladies and, looking at General MacArthur and President Queson, said, "some mattresses, pillows, and blankets have been put on board for your group. There are no seats since this is a combat aircraft."

He paused, looking straight into MacArthur's eyes. "The radar technicians got the radar at Iba back up. It's only fifty percent effective, but they can't see any Jap aircraft over the Philippines. Any questions, General?"

"Ah yes, Brereton. Is there any food or refreshments available? That sort of thing?" asked MacArthur, quietly.

MacArthur's Pacific Appeasement, December 8, 1941
Part I
The Missing Ten Hours

Brereton looked at the three women and children, and nodded. "There is water and Kool-Aid to drink and I had the cook make up some sandwiches—as much as we could scrape up." He thought for a moment. "Oh yes, there is a piss tube for the men. I brought an open five-gallon milk can for the women. Is that all, General? We need to get airborne very soon."

MacArthur looked at the huge bomber. He had never been close to a B-17 to inspect this new war machine. "How do we get on this thing?" He asked, leaning over and peering at the bottom.

Brereton cracked a smile, pointing to the side of the bomber at an open hatch. "You enter through that door in the side, General," he indicated, grimly enjoying himself. "I climb in under the nose, to be on the flight deck at the controls. You and your group will stay back here in both aircraft. Once we are airborne, General MacArthur, I am in command."

MacArthur looked down his nose at Brereton and slowly nodded. He looked at everyone and growled irritably, "Well, get on board this thing. Help the women, Huff, Sutherland," he ordered, waving his hands toward the door. President Queson, staff and family moved off to their own B-17. He was going into exile in Australia, or maybe the U.S.

All four engines were ticking over at idle. The aircraft engineer, Technical Sergeant Roger Elliot, came up behind General Brereton and Co-pilot Captain James Englemann in their aircraft seats. "General, they are all seated on the deck or laying down and strapped in, as best as we could, sir. All four engines look in great condition. Your crew is all aboard at their stations or helping our guests, sir."
Brereton looked back at him and smiled. "Thanks, Elliot. Take your station."

T/Sgt Elliot moved to the Engineer's Console, sat down and strapped in. Brereton looked out his side window, pointed a flashlight at the other B-17 and flicked it on just once. That co-pilot responded with one. Brereton twisted the other way toward the Control Tower mounted on a six by six truck and flicked it on and off twice. The control tower operator had been waiting for that. He promptly flashed a green light at the two bombers.

"Sergeant Elliot, taxi power on Two and Three, please," ordered Major General Brereton.
"Yes, sir. Two and Three coming up, General."

MacArthur's Pacific Appeasement, December 8, 1941
Part I
The Missing Ten Hours

Elliot started the two engines that moved up smoothly to taxi power. Major General Brereton's feet reached forward and released the brakes. The ship moved slowly along the taxiway and rolled to the threshold at the end of the runway, brakes and landing gear squealing and howling as they do, then turned to line up on a darkened runway.

General Brereton picked up his microphone and checked to make sure he was on Intercom. "Sergeant Thompson, you on?" He asked.

"Yes sir, General," Thompson replied.

"Sergeant, make sure all your transmitters are disabled. Inform me when completed. We will not be transmitting on this trip to Australia, until we approach Del Monte to top off fuel."

"General, we are silent. The morse code key and microphone are disconnected as well; the transmitter power is turned off. Our receivers are on, sir."

"Very well, thank you."

He looked out his window checking on the second B-17. The other B-17 stopped on the runway threshold waiting for General Brereton's aircraft to get airborne. The few trucks along the runway began turning on their lights marking the runway sides; a small bonfire flared up, lighting the end of the runway. There were no runway lights because the severed power cables had not been repaired.

"Let's test those mags one more time, Sergeant Elliot," Brereton ordered, as he set the brakes on.

"Yes sir."

"Brakes set."

T/Sgt Elliot throttled up each engine in turn for left and right magneto check. After testing each, he set the four engines magneto switches to "Both".

"Everything checks out, General," reported Elliot.

Brereton looked to his right at the co-pilot. "Captain, give me twenty degrees flaps."

"Flaps extending to twenty degrees, General."

"Okay, time to go. Give me the Landing lights, Captain. As soon as we are airborne, I'll call to extinguish the lights."

"Yes sir." The Captain reached up to the panel and lit the Landing lights.

Brereton looked over his shoulder at Elliot. "Give me take off power now on all four engines, Technical Sergeant Roger Elliot. We're leaving this country for home. Next stop is

MacArthur's Pacific Appeasement, December 8, 1941
Part I
The Missing Ten Hours

Del Monte Field on Mindanao. We'll top off the tanks there and continue to Darwin, and then Brisbane, Australia."
"Roger that, General."

Sergeant Elliot moved the four throttles smoothly up to full take off power, watching all four sets of dials, gauges, and meters. With the plane shaking and straining to go, engines roared at full power, eager to go; then exhausts began flaring bright blue with raw gas in the darkness. Brereton kicked the brakes off. With a louder roar, the B-17 rumbled and bumped its way down the repaired runway. At 80 knots, Brereton pushed the control column forward to lift the tail. As the B-17's speed rapidly increased, the bomber finally rose in the dark sky.

The passengers, uncomfortable even before the plane moved, were frightened by the strange sounds and roar of the engines. Little Arthur wailed with terror, held tightly by his mother Jean, no less frightened.
"Lights out now, Captain."
Englemann grunted as he reached to a panel above their head and flicked a switch. It was suddenly dark out there.
"Wheels up, Captain."
"Yes sir." He reached to the central console and found the wheel lever. Moving them forward, pistons forced hydraulic fluid to move through chambers, which caused a strange moaning as the wheels moved out of the slipstream.
"Wheels are up. Flaps to zero, General?" the Captain asked.
"Do that." As the flaps retracted to zero the outside sound changed until only the engines on climbing power were left. As the B-17 reached 5,000 feet, General Brereton leveled off.

"Elliot, throttle back and set for cruising at 5,000. I don't want to go into the real cold air, so we'll stay here."
"Roger that, General."
The second B-17 rolled off the tarmac onto the runway and repeated the performance.
The sound of the B-17s faded away.
The truck lights flicked off one-by-one as the trucks moved off the airfield to new assignments.

The Control Tower operator pulled the main power switch off, dropped to the ground, and walked away. He didn't bother to lock the door. There would be no more flights from Clark Air Field.

MacArthur reached up to his collar tips and removed the 3 stars from each wingtip. Thoughtfully, and with bitter taste in his mouth, he began trying to attach Colonel eagles to his collar tips. Sutherland reached out in the gloom. "Here, General, allow me."

Colonel MacArthur smiled up at Sutherland. "Why thank you, Dick. This is the first time I've worn eagles since the War to End All Wars." He paused. "Why don't you keep the stars for luck?" Sutherland, now senior to MacArthur, shook his head. "Oh, no, General. You keep them and expect to put them back on."

MacArthur leaned back against the vibrating aluminum hull and peered out into the darkness.

Is this the end of my Army career? If the results of the Article 70 hearing go against me, I shall never be able to run for the Presidency of the United States. Wonder what Mother would have advised?

MacArthur continued to look into the blackness as the airplane began to jink around in roughening weather.

It was a gamble. We could have beaten back the enemy and make him pay dearly for all the real estate. Drake let me down when all those supplies were needed back on the peninsula and he let them rot behind the beaches. And the treachery of the Philippine Department of Transportation not letting me use the trains to move supplies. Trucks couldn't get back because Casey was blowing bridges too fast—pretty cowardly to move backwards that fast.

The B-17 continued to buck, rise and fall, buffeted by the storm as they flew southeastward toward Mindanao. Jean, young Arthur, and Aw Chew wailed and were violently sick. The navigator, a young Second Lieutenant, crawled back to MacArthur to explain the situation: "It's the tropical storm, General. We cannot fly above, below, or around it.—Sorry, sir." MacArthur grimly hung on and nodded to the navigator.

"Button Two on the radio console, Captain," ordered Brereton.
"Yes sir," leaning forward to the middle console and pushing Button Two in until it illuminated. "You got it, General."
Brereton pulled the mike from its clip, hesitated, and pushed its intercom button. "Sergeant Thompson, you on?"
"Yes sir, General."

MacArthur's Pacific Appeasement, December 8, 1941
Part I
The Missing Ten Hours

"I need power on AN/ARC-37 now." Thompson leaned forward, reconnected the antenna, and flipped the power switch. As soon as the lamps came on full, he touched the key momentarily to make sure it was ready to transmit. "General, you got '37 now, sir."
"Thank you, Thompson." Now Brereton pushed the transmitter button on the mike.

"Del Monte Tower, this is Air Force four zero dash three zero one four, a flight of two B-17s from Clark, 25 miles northwest of your station at five thousand. Request landing instructions over."
"Del Monte Tower?"
"Del Monte Tower?"
"Thompson, are we on the right enroute freq for Del Monte Tower?"
"Yes sir, General. They may not be manned at this time of night."
"Okay, we'll drop gradually to five hundred with all lights on, buzz them, and see if that wakes them up!"

"Okay Captain, turn on all the lights, wheels down, fifteen degrees flaps."
Englemann grinned at General Brereton as he went through the motions. "This'll make their hearts go pitty pat."
Brereton nodded. "Eliot, give me take off power now, please."
"Five hundred feet, General."
"Here we go"—four engines thundering, all lights burning, Air Force forty three zero one four buzzed Del Monte Field.
"WAKE UP DOWN THERE!" roared Brereton as he laughed. "Okay, clean it up and go dark."
Three minutes later, a breathless, angry voice called "Who the hell is up there?"
Brereton grinned at Englemann and picked up his mike again.
"Lousy voice procedure, Charlie. This is Brereton with a secret flight of two B-17s, three zero one four and three zero two one for landing instructions over."
"Standby until I make sure all guns are safed, General."
Runway lights appeared moments later.
"At one minute intervals, two B-17s are cleared to land. A Follow-me truck will guide you to the fuel depot."

MacArthur's Pacific Appeasement, December 8, 1941
Part I
The Missing Ten Hours

"Roger Colonel. See you on the ground." Flicking the Intercom button, he said: "Eliot. Once we are at the fuel depot, get the guests off the plane to stretch and walk around."
"Roger that, General."

"General Brereton," said the colonel, saluting. "Is this a surprise inspection? We did not receive a flight plan for you."
"We decided to come in blind; less chance of the Japs finding out our passenger list. Otherwise, this is your ordinary gas station visit for gas, oil, and windshield polishing."
"Well, we can certainly—my god. Isn't that General MacArthur?" He exploded when he saw the Chickens on his collars. "COLONEL!" he shouted. "What the hell is going on, General?"
"Secretly, he is enroute secretly, to Washington secretly, to face an Article 70 Board of Inquiry, secretly. Am I getting that fact across to you?"
"Yeah, I got it—I mean yes sir, General. I understand this is all hush hush but what did he do?"
"You know too much, already. Make sure your people who do see our guests keep their mouths shut and carefully censor all outgoing mail. Bye the way, Lieutenant General Wainwright is now CinC USAFFE."
"WOW!" The colonel slowly shook his head. "I'd better get this program modified and get you out of here. Do you want a flight plan to Darwin? Several of our ships have been flying down there."
General Brereton thought it over. "Yes, but no names or titles on the Special Information line in the flight plan."
"You got it. Just two more Seventeens to Australia."
"Thank you, Colonel. New subject. FEAF is being disbanded. The remaining B-17s—that is, yours—and the only one left at Clark, will fly to Australia for new assignments." He paused while he dug out the general order disbanding FEAF.
"Unless you know of any PBY-5As that can land here, I'd be very careful about any further flyovers. All my ships except the one remaining B-17 at Clark, are gone. My troops are being turned into Infantrymen or other specialties. So, when you fly out, try to take as many of your ground forces as possible."
"That bad? Holy Toledo!"

"Worse than that. I see Captain Englemann is heading towards us. Must be ready to go. Good luck to you and your command, Colonel." He turned, heading back to his ship. The Colonel called after him: "You, too, General."

0715, January 13, 1942
Special Flight 0001
Bolling Field
Anacostia, Virginia

"Bolling Tower, this is Air Force Special flight zero zero zero one, a C-46 at 5,000 feet, 20 miles from your station requesting landing instructions. Notify the Provost of our arrival. please. Over". General Brereton grimaced as he prepared to finish his duty.

"Special zero zero zero one. Inflight notice. Provost will meet you in front of Operations. A flagged truck will guide you there. Over."

"Zero One. Acknowledged. Over"

"Bolling. Descend to 1,500 feet and call for further instructions. Over"

"One. descend to 1,500 and hold; advise for further instructions. Over"

"Bolling roger out."

"Bolling Special One at 1,500 feet. Over"

"One. Turn left to 165 degrees and descend to 500 feet. Advise when field is in sight. Over"

"Roger Bolling. I have you in sight at 500 feet. Over"

"One. You are cleared straight in on runway 18. Hold at end of rollout. An MP truck will guide you to Operations. Over."

"Bolling Special One. Roger. On the ground at 0715."

A very tired Major General Brereton held, waiting for the MP truck to turn around and lead them to Operations. When he began driving to Operations, Brereton followed in the C-46. As soon as he shut down the engines, Special 0001 was done. He'd have to wait for the Provost to do his business with his passengers before he departed for BOQ.

A Corporal Flight Attendant, cracked and opened the passenger section of the cargo hatch. A Colonel wearing crossed pistols on his lapels, entered with a brief case. He glanced around until he recognized Colonel MacArthur, and approached.

"Colonel MacArthur? He asked politely.

MacArthur swiveled in his seat. "Yes, Colonel?"

"I am Colonel Adams, Provost Marshal of the Washington District. I remind you that you are under arrest and will be escorted to Fort Belvoir, Virginia, to stand before an Article 70 Board of Inquiry hearing. Is that your understanding?"

"Yes, Colonel."

"Then, I must advise you that anything you say may be taken down and held against you in the hearing or in any court-martial that may follow. You will be provided counsel, or choose one of your own choice, at your expense."

"Very well, Colonel. I understand. What of my family? May I put them into the Williard Hotel in the District?" MacArthur gently asked.

Colonel Adams nodded. "We will provide transportation for your family and baggage in a few minutes. However, I must advise you that your wife may not attend the Article 70 hearing. Is that clear?"

MacArthur sighed and nodded his understanding.

Colonel Adams stood and addressed the remaining passengers who had been absorbed in that conversation. "As you are all party to the Article 70 Board of Inquiry, you heard me advising Colonel MacArthur of his rights. Is there any need of me repeating that for any of you?"

One-by-one, each silently shook their head negatively.

"Very well, with the exception of Mrs. MacArthur and son and servant, you will board the Military Police bus at the foot of the steps." He turned to General Brereton: "you may follow at your leisure, General."

MacArthur hugged Jean MacArthur and Arthur and said good-bye and left the aircraft. The rest of his staff followed.

o-0-o

08/24/12, 9/17/12,

PART II

The Article 70 Hearing

CHAPTER ONE

Judge Advocate General Corps

Founded July 29, 1775, by General George Washington, the Judge Advocate General Corps (JAG) has been a vital component of the United States Army for more than one hundred sixty five years, as of December 1941. JAG is the oldest law firm in the United States.

As the judicial arm of the U.S. Army, the JAG Corps is charged with prosecuting and defending military law as defined by the U.S. Army Articles of War. Comprised of more than 500 highly trained and experienced attorneys on December 7, 1941, the JAG Corps provided legal services to commanders, civilian staff, active-duty soldiers, and retired Army service personnel. Officers of the Corps are the chief officers of court-martials and courts of inquiry. Major General Myron C. Cramer, JAG, USA served as Judge Advocate General, December 1, 1941 – November 30, 1945.

0815, January 23, 1942
Munitions Building
U.S. Army Judge Advocate General Corps.
Washington, D.C.

Colonel Leroy Quentin MacIntyre, JAG, USA, dashed out of the rain storm into the Munitions Building and slammed the door in the face of strong wind. Water dripped from his raincoat onto the hall floor as he walked to his office. Colonel MacIntyre entered his office, shaking his rain-drenched brimmed felt cover and placed it on the shelf. He followed that with his soaked raincoat, carefully placing it onto a coat hanger in the coat rack. Then one finger at a time, Colonel MacIntyre removed his wet leather gloves. He rubbed his cold wet hands briskly together, wiped them on his butt automatically, and adjusted his tunic and Sam Browne belt. Pulling a comb from his back pocket, he combed what was left of his thinning brown hair. Ready to face the world, he looked around for his usual morning cup of steaming black coffee.

No coffee?

"Good morning, Colonel."

"Memory loss this morning, Sergeant Waters?" smiling at Waters. with green eyes and black hair with streaks of gray beginning to show. Staff Sergeant Waters who had been with Colonel MacIntyre for several years, stood in the open doorway without his coffee. He stood five feet nine inches tall in his stocking feet, weighed in at 168 pounds, He had entered the U.S. Army in 1917 from Midland, Texas, and served in the trenches in the Great War to end all wars.

Following Armistice Day, Waters was reduced in rank to Corporal from Master Sergeant. He completed high school education, finally. A skill with writing and typing gave him an opportunity to apply for transfer to the Judge Advocate General legal field. There he stayed, very slowly advancing in rank to Staff Sergeant. Even then, it was his great skill with legal papers that helped him advance.

"Good morning, Sergeant, what's on your mind?" Colonel MacIntyre asked, miming holding his coffee cup and looking pointedly for his coffee.

"Sorry, sir. General Cramer wants to see you in his office right now, sir. Colonels Obrey and Van der Wendt, and Captain Millington and Lieutenant Worthington are already informed."
MacIntyre groaned quietly.

I thought I'd have a few days off before being assigned to another court-martial.

"Any idea of who is on the hot seat this time, Sergeant Waters?" he asked, eyeing him curiously.

Waters shook his head slowly. "Oh no, sir, the General is playing his cards very close to his vest this morning," he answered soberly. "I noticed he hadn't opened his briefcase yet," he commented helpfully.

MacIntyre sighed, tugged at his tunic bottom, pulled his zippered notebook from his desk drawer and walked down the hall to the general's office. He grimaced as he opened the general's door. Everyone else arrived ahead of him and were standing, waiting his arrival. He hated that. General Cramer had only been in command less than two months and already knew that nugget of information. He liked to needle MacIntyre once in a while. "Glad you could join us, Roy," he said, pleasantly.

MacIntyre nodded. "Good morning, General. Sorry to be late, sir."

Major General Myron Cady Cramer, Army Judge Advocate General, ruddy-faced with a shock of brown hair with slivers of gray, and brown eyes, looked at the officers standing before him, his rimless bifocals glinting in the gray sky through the window. His expression was grave.

"Be seated, gentlemen, this will take a few minutes. I selected you because you have finished your last assignment." He looked at each of them as he lowered himself into his massive chair. "That is correct, isn't it? Your desks are clear?" A chorus of affirmatives came in response.

He cleared his throat and frowned. General Cramer removed a key ring from his pocket, selected a tiny key, and unlocked his briefcase. He lifted some folders from the briefcase and laid them on his desk, glancing at them as he closed, locked, and set his briefcase on the floor.

General Cramer opened the top folder. With all eyes on those folders because of this unusual behavior, he spoke. "Good," he said, tapping the folders with his finger. "What we have here is secret and you must guard the information carefully."

He looked all five officers in turn to make sure they caught his meaning. "A secret Article 70 Board of Inquiry has been ordered and will be conducted upon a former general officer." He paused for a moment, looking at each officer. He had their undivided attention.

"The officer in question allegedly failed to obey at least three lawful orders. In addition to accepting a very large sum of money from a foreign power, he lied about the status of his forces, and may have committed treason by not following orders."

His subordinates' eyes snapped back and forth at each other as they sucked in their breath in shock. He waited for the hubbub to die, and continued. "This officer and his staff are under house arrest here in Fort Belvoir—incommunicado—without telephones."

General Cramer rocked back in his chair studying his staff, then continued. "They looked pretty haggard from travel when I served them last night, and read them their rights. They have been here almost two weeks, taking Physicals, getting their service records up-to-date, and being fitted into new uniforms. Amazingly—so far—their presence has not leaked out to the press. We want to keep it that way, which is why they do not have private access to telephones at this time."

He looked at their bewildered faces. General Cramer handed out folders as he made assignments. "Colonel MacIntyre, you will prosecute; Captain Millington, you will assist and Captain-designee Worthington, you will be investigator. Colonel Van der Wendt, you will defend. Pick someone from the pool to assist in your defense. Colonel Obrey, you will be the Trial Judge Advocate conducting this hearing. Gentlemen, this case is of such magnitude, it is going to take all your wits to successfully judge, prosecute, or defend."

"General, who ordered the Article 70 board?" asked Colonel Van der Wendt.

"President Roosevelt! He wanted to go directly to a General Court-martial. He is really pissed. He wanted to throw the key away but this gentleman is very powerful. Admiral Leahy, FDR's special assistant, wrote up the charges and specifications for the Commander-in-Chief." There were rapid exchanges of glances.

This is really serious.

"The officer in question is Colonel Douglas Arthur MacArthur." As one, the officers leaned back in shock. "Roosevelt fired him at the same time as Lieutenant General Short and Admiral Kimmel but kept it secret. MacArthur was personally informed by General Marshal over an open RCA radiotelephone circuit." The General chuckled. "I'll just bet Marshall enjoyed that." (The two generals, George C. Marshall and Douglas A. MacArthur, had despised each other for years.)

He looked at each of his officers in turn. "Ordinarily, this would not be an easy task. It is made more difficult by the fact MacArthur has too many hero worshippers up on the Hill and around the Country." He paused to let them collect themselves. He, too, had had a hard time grasping the accusations.

"And, as you heard, he has been reduced to the rank of Colonel, by order of the Chief of Staff, General Marshall." The general leaned back, put his hands behind his head and rocked gently in his chair as he watched his senior staff for a moment. For once, there were no wise cracks.

Leaning forward after they settled down, he tapped the folders on his desk with his finger to emphasize what he was going to say. "Gentlemen, repeating, this is classified secret and will remain so until the convening authority signs off the results of this Article 70 hearing. Now, any questions?"

Colonel Van der Wendt got his hand up first, nervously blinking. "General, I'd like to be recused. I happen to detest MacArthur and some of his past actions."

"Eric, it isn't going to matter too much because MacArthur has a very expensive lawyer retained by powerful friends who" he paused and raised his fingers in quote signs "somehow learned MacArthur was here and under serious charges: his name is Mr. John Engelson, Esquire, of the Engelson, Engelson and Engelson Law Firm. You will be assisting and doing yeoman duty for Mr. Engelson, which is why you didn't get Worthington."

The general's voice was matter of fact as he explained that. "Obviously, some people know that Mac is here. Hopefully, they took the Secrecy Act oath to heart. Trials are stacking up and General Marshal has advised me this hearing," making quote signs with his fingers again "will start in one month or less."
"Not much time, General," complained Colonel Obrey.
"That I know, Jim. You will have your hands full making sure the hearing runs smoothly," said the general.

The general turned to MacIntyre, pushing a very bulky file box across the floor with his feet. "Roy, this contains copies of logs, messages, records of phone calls, and the like from the War Department and Navy Department that should get you started on the Article 70 investigation. Make sure Van der Wendt gets a copy."

Colonel MacIntyre looked down at a box with several thick file folders and soberly nodded.

"That will be all, gentlemen."

The officers stood, came to attention, saluted, and filed out of the general's office, heading toward their offices. Lieutenant Worthington stooped and groaned as he picked up the file box. "Hey, this is heavy."

Van der Wendt grimaced. "You gentlemen know anything about John Engelson, Esquire?" Everyone shook his head.

"I think I am going to have my hands full with John Engelson." He waved and turned off to his office.

Colonel Obrey nodded and waved back.

"You'll find me in the Law Library if you have questions. I have some research ahead of me." He headed down the hall to his own office, brow wrinkled in thought.

When the others walked into MacIntyre's office, he motioned Millington to shut the door. As the door clicked shut, the Colonel looked at his junior officers. "For the course of this hearing, none of what we do strays from your mouth into someone's lovely ear.

First thing: Staff Sergeant Waters. We need a very trustworthy NCO clerk to help us out. He's been with me for several years and I trust his discretion." He paused. "Unless one of you gentleman has another NCO in mind." Millington and Worthington looked at each other and shook their heads.

Colonel Mac opened his door, "Sergeant?" and motioned his clerk into the office when he looked up from his desk.

"Yes sir, Colonel. What can I do for you?"

The colonel sat back down in his chair and motioned the other two to sit. "Drag your chair in, Sergeant Waters, we have a rather large order on our hands. An Article 70 hearing of a senior officer."

Waters nodded. With wide-eyed innocence on his face, with raised eyebrows he asked, "Yes sir. That would be former Lieutenant General Douglas A. MacArthur, Colonel?"

"Holy shit, Waters. How did you know that?" Tom asked.

"The Colonel is aware us lowly NCOs have Top Secret Clearances?" he asked, with a toothy smile.

"The Colonel is aware," he responded with amusement.

I should have known Waters would know.

Millington nodded, chuckling.

"Well, the order for his Article 70 has been making the rounds of the office." Waters smiled as he looked at the Colonel and Captain Millington. "You won the toss and I won the $100 pool," replied Waters.

"What pool, Waters?" asked Worthington.

Still smiling broadly, Waters said, "We clerks put up a pool on which team would get the job as Prosecution Judge Advocate. I knew my team would win. When do we go to work, sirs?"

Roy, Clint, and Tom started laughing and Waters joined in.

"Well, Waters, we would be ever so grateful if you could come up with additional copies, so we all know what page we're on." Roy turned to Tom. "Tom, I'm glad the General assigned you as Assistant. Your Infantry background will be an important asset.

Millington smiled, nodding agreement.

"As investigator, Clint, you can use Waters to help you find all these people." Worthington acknowledged, raising his hand.

"And, Waters, you'll be the mule that carries us. I believe whatever we find within this box of files will provide all sorts of follow up material." He thought for a second. "Oh, Waters, get an extra copy for Colonel Van der Wendt, please."

"Colonel, I'll go rustle up some copies right now, if that's okay with you," said Sergeant Waters, picking up the big box of records.

"Do it, and collect your bounty while you're at it."

"Yes sir," he laughed, closing the door behind him.

The Colonel pointed at Worthington. "Clint, your Army Air Corps experience and knowledge of those Boeing B-17C/D Flying Fortresses and pursuit planes are going to provide important background information. You'll need to tell us what all those zoomies have to say about things in the Philippines and convert it into English."

Lt. Worthington nodded and added, "Yes sir. I think there were 48 antiquated Republic P-35A Guardians and some biplanes, also. I'm not sure what the Navy had at Subic Bay but you can count on some Consolidated PBY-5A Catalinas amphibious patrol planes, plus some PBY-4 water-only Catalinas and probably those old F3A-3 Brewster Buffalos."

CHAPTER TWO

Colonel Eric Van der Wendt, veteran of more than sixty courts-martial, as trial judge advocate or defense counsel, had prevailed in forty-three of those cases. Eric was upset and feeling a little bit depressed after reading the proposed charges and specifications and other available information about MacArthur's misbehavior—make that alleged misbehavior. Eric let out a great sigh and stared out his window, rather glum about the probable outcome of MacArthur's Article 70 hearing.

Folders and charts lay in sorted piles on his worktable. Eric picked up his Bode China teacup with piping hot Earl Grey Tea and took a sip while he stared at his worktable.

I'm glad I am going to be second chair. Let the great John Engelson, whoever he is, take his lumps on this one. MacIntyre was going to rip out MacArthur's guts and stuff 'em down his throat.

His door swung open without a knock; Eric looked up, eyes flashing fire.

Who the hell is coming in without knocking first?

A smiling civilian stood there looking around his cramped office with curiosity—a sympathetic smile growing on his ample face—and finally, at him. He was dressed in a three-piece wool suit, dark blue with pinstripes, white shirt and red tie, a homburg—of all things—and held a cherry wood cane in hands holding what looked like doeskin gloves, to complete his ensemble.

"Colonel Van der Wendt, I believe? I am John Engelson. We have some serious work to do." He held out his business card to the colonel.

Eric stood, smiling as he accepted the card and studied it while he shook hands and tried to size up Engelson. "Pleasure is mine, Mr. Engelson. Won't you come in and sit down?" Eric asked.
"No," said Engelson, softly. "I had in mind taking you to lunch at one of my favorite restaurants, a hofbrau of some note in Arlington, to get acquainted and begin planning strategy." He pointed around

Eric's worktable with his cherry wood cane. "Looks like you have been doing your home work, too."

Eric glanced back at his worktable and shrugged. "It doesn't look very good for our side."

Engelson looked at him steadily for a moment as if trying to make up his mind, licking his lips. "Is he a fallen hero, Colonel?"

Eric's laugh was nasty. "No, not at all. He's a backstabbing grandstander, in my book. It's just the idea of a general officer like MacArthur even being charged with treason that eats at my belly," shaking his head.

"From what I have picked up, Colonel, MacArthur is a theatrical ham and quite the snob, very class conscious. However, he is not guilty of any charge yet, Colonel. We have to operate on that premise, even if neither of us has a large respect for him."

Engelson paused as if searching for the right way to say something.

"On a different note, Colonel, whenever we go to lunch or dinner for strategy conferences or even travel to interview prospective witnesses, I take the bill. I am being very well compensated for my services. You are not."

Eric thought about that for a minute and nodded his head.

It certainly did not fall into the illegal category.

He smiled and nodded to Engelson. "My name is Eric, sir."

Maybe he's not such a bad fellow, after all.

Engelson smiled, "John to you. Ready to leave, Eric?"

"Certainly, John, after you," as Eric waved him out the door, stuffing his brief case with some of the papers and grabbing his felt visored cap.

CHAPTER THREE

"Put that box on the table, Clint. We need to sort it out," MacIntyre said. Sergeant Waters rushed to help Clint lift the big box onto the long table.

Lt. Worthington grunted as they lifted the heavy cardboard box onto the table. Col. MacIntyre leaned over the box, and then straightened up. He was silent for a moment as he studied the box. He leaned back over and began rummaging through the files, checking file names.

"Okay," the colonel said, looking up. "Clint, you take all of these Army Air Corps—or the new name, Army Air Force—files and see what you can build—photos, organization, who or did anybody get into action; Tom, you take the Infantry files and try to build the Order of Battle; and I'll handle the Headquarters files. Let's see if we can make sense of things. Establish a timeline, if possible. Okay? Eventually, we'll interlace the three timelines to get a better overall picture—perhaps different color inks for better source identification."

He turned to Sergeant Waters. "Waters, among other things, you will be responsible for producing the finished time line. I believe that will be critical."

"Got it, Colonel."

They all nodded and began pulling files. Roy claimed the middle of the worktable, with Tom at one end and Clint at the other end.

Clint stiffened and sat up straight. He stared at the wall for a moment, then whispering almost to himself: "my God, they were using Boeing P27A Peashooters, Seversky P-35A Guardians and Curtiss P-36 Hawks. I thought all their pursuit jobs were Curtiss P-40Bs and P-40Es Warhawks."

Louder, he said, "Intelligence had rumors of a new high speed Jap fighter. These guys faced them and lost." He shook his head. "The hottest Army Air Force fighters—the Warhawks, were lumbering jackasses going against a racehorse of a Jap fighter. The best we've got is second or third class."

He laughed as he thought of something. "Hey, fellas, that P27A Peashooter. Do you know how it got its name?"

Everyone shook their head and looked at him.

"You'd probably have to see a picture of it, but to aim at an enemy plane, the pilot looked down a long narrow tube—the sight. Looked like a kid's peashooter." Clint looked around for laughter and grins. Shaking their heads and pointing down at their paperwork, Tom spoke up. "Only a zoomie would think of that. Back to work." Clint was crestfallen.

They used yellow lined pads to write questions for further research, jot down notes, and begin to construct timelines. Colored crayons or pencils marked certain parts of various papers. Every so often, one would suck in his breath or curse as something else came to light. Uncomplimentary mutterings lit up the air above them.

Into the second week of research, Tom stuffed the last pages back into its file folder and that back into his box. He stood and stretched, rubbed his numb butt, looked around at the Colonel and Clint, and left the room.

Thomas Enright Millington, was the fourth generation Infantryman with this name and first of the Millingtons to graduate from West Point ('29). His genes carried the distinctive Millington longish face, thin, straight nose, blue-green eyes, and thin brown hair.

Roy had laid his copy aside. He was tapping his pencil like a drummer as he studied his legal pad, already into the third page of notes.

I wonder if the whole Army is as fucked up as MacArthur's command? Or is it the fault of Congress? Toss in the War Department and stir!

Tom returned with a short stack of paper. He soon hung it on a hook on the wall. A big red 30 was on the front page.
"I had the print shop run off a count down for us." He ripped pages off until number 16 was exposed. "That's how much time we have until we better be ready for the hearing, Colonel."

"Hey, Sergeant Waters," the Colonel called. "Drag your chair back in here and join us. Bring your pad, too," he added.
"Right away, sir." He picked up his chair and carried it in, bumping the door shut with his hip.

"Sergeant, we need you to track what we are doing because of the very short fuse. And don't be afraid to offer any comments or suggestions, either. This is going to be a real hassle to get it done right." He held up their hen-scratched timeline for him to see. "And see if you can make this look professional."

"Yes sir, Colonel." Staff Sergeant Waters said, dropping his gaze to look at the floor. "I most certainly will. I've got a personal interest in this. My cousin Alfred, Aunt Lorraine's only son, is, or was, a Corporal in a .30 caliber air-cooled machine gun squad in the Fourth Marines somewhere on Luzon. I was the one who talked him into joining up. We don't know if he is alive or dead." His voice was husky as he finished.

The colonel looked at him for a moment. He asked softly, "I gather you have your own copy of the Preliminary charges?"
Waters nodded without comment.
"Tell me, Sergeant Waters, what is your take on the hearing?" asked Lt. Worthington.

MacIntyre held up his hand, palm out. "Clint, first things first," said the Colonel. "Have we all finished our first reading? I want that out of the way so the four of us are on the same page. Juniors first," he said nodding at Staff Sergeant Waters.
"Yes sir, Colonel, three times now."
"Only once, Colonel," Said Lt. Worthington.
"Yes, I have," replied Capt. Millington.
"Me too. Let's get a full round of initial impressions, starting with you, Waters."

Staff Sergeant Waters looked at his hands for a moment. "Did you notice the Fourth Marines are not included in MacArthur's USAFFE Table of Organization? And, he never mentioned them in the Order of Battle. Besides, shouldn't they have been under the Sixteenth Naval District?" He looked at the three officers staring at him and shifted in his seat.

"Sorry, Colonel, that personal note just slipped out. Anyway, I believe MacArthur has a lot to answer for or try to explain away. Part of the Philippines Treasury gold that was shipped to Australia on the submarine disappeared in Sydney.

The Colonel snapped to attention and leaned forward. "What did you say, Waters? Disappeared?"

"Just that, Colonel. All the strapped, bound wooden boxes carrying the gold were counted carefully as they came on and off the submarine and went into armed army trucks. Somehow, one of the trucks did not arrive at the Australian bank, sir." Sitting down, he jabbed a finger in the air and announced, "CID and their Australian counterparts are working on the missing box or boxes of gold bars—who got 'em and where'd they go?"

"Did you know those gold bars are darned heavy, sirs? I had an opportunity to lift one at Fort Knox once. A guard, an old buddy from the trenches snuck me in, had me wear special white cotton gloves, and let me lift one of the bars." He slowly shook his head muttering, "Still can't believe how heavy it was."

"Waters, does the missing gold have anything to do with Colonel MacArthur?" asked the colonel softly.

"I don't know, Colonel. It's just one of the mysteries surrounding the war in the Philippines."

Roy said, "MacArthur didn't get along with many people, did he? Look at his derogatory remarks about Admiral Hart, General Brereton and his entire Air Force general staff, and General Drake. You do know he has a track record of never taking blame and always taking credit of others' work?"

"Those words would have caused a duel in the old days," Tom answered, dryly. He paused for a moment and thoughtfully added "General Marshal ordered MacArthur to bring out his staff. Where are the rest of them?"

"Why did MacArthur leave so many of his staff behind?" echoed Waters. "He was ordered to bring out his complete staff.

Tom's wrinkled brow did not hide many freckles. "You know, I just can't see how he thought he was going to get away with chucking Rainbow 5 aside and dropping the air operations without word of it getting back to the War Department or the Chief Of Staff," Tom said. "But he sure tried to get back to it when the Japanese Army ran through his troops like green poop through a goose. Then to lie about it—three times, wasn't it?"

The Colonel cleared his throat and growled angrily. "Well, we have got to nail down why there was about a ten hour delay before he tried to take positive action. Not much to go on according to the headquarters timeline. FEAF—General Brereton's Fighter Group did get into action, but that's about all." Colonel Mac said.

"We may never find out exactly what happened but there are all of his inner circle staff officers that might provide some answers or direction." His voice trailed off as he paused.

"Did any of the GHQ Comm Center officers or soldiers get out? We really need to talk with them. Their radio logs have critical information we could use." Sergeant Waters raised his hand for the Colonel to acknowledge.

"Waters?" he asked.

"Sirs, do you suppose the Comm Centers at the Presidio San Francisco and CG Schofield Barracks, Honolulu would have copies of transmissions between MacArthur's army groups?" Waters thought about something else. "Colonel, can you get permission to check out the Air Force files at General Arnold's GHQ at Bolling Field? There may be a lot of stuff, there."

"Ohhh, I don't know but that's pretty good thinking," the Colonel said. "Check that out. Might be some important intercept messages—Oh yes, I need to check with the secret radio people also. SIS-6 and CAST monitored everything."

Tom stirred, stretching his arms to clear back muscle cramps. "Colonel, if MacArthur moved his GHQ to Malinta Tunnel on Corregidor, his Comm Chief would have TWX'd status of code books, copies of messages, and radio logs. That's easy enough to check."

Clint looked up from his folder of notes and quietly asked. "Have you all picked up on the MacArthur Protective Society? I mean, look at all the charges by his inner circle charging others of misdeeds. Nothing against MacArthur at all by those guys—'cept Major General Brereton."

"They aren't exactly yes-men, are they? Because under severe pressure, yes-men are inclined to ooze out of the light. They don't fall on swords like the inner circle." Roy stopped and scribbled a note and looked up.

"Do we have the Table of Organization of his USAFFE command showing all staff directorates and as many of their individual staff members as possible, yet? If not, General Marshall's G1 has a complete roster of officers and senior NCOs as of December 7th. We've got to find as many of those people as possible." He looked around grimly. "Most of them are dead or will be prisoners in a short time. Sergeant, you get on G1 and see what you can develop."

"Okay Colonel, will do as soon as we break."

The Colonel stood and turned to his blackboard, "Lookee here." Picking up a fresh stick of chalk he wrote

> Rainbow 5 to Beach Defense without including FEAF.

> Lying to senior officers three times.

> Failure to carry out two Presidential commands.

> Accepting orders from a foreign government.

He drew a line under item 4 and said, "Those are the given ones that defense probably won't challenge and may try to deal. Let's try and get a copy of his Beach Defense War Plan. Now these . . ."

> Making an impeachable statement as rationale for non-action.

> Missing gold.

"These two may be a little hard to prove."

Pointing to number 6 on the list, "Certainly, trying to identify the soldiers who picked up part of the Queson government gold shipment from the submarine is going to be difficult. The Aussies and our CID have made no headway in their investigation." He picked up his coffee cup and sipped appreciately. Placing it back in the saucer, he continued. "CID say the paper work was legal, signed by MacArthur's Chief of Staff, Brigadier General Richard K. Sutherland. He claims to have no knowledge of the gold shipment or the paper he admits must have been slipped in for his signature."

Tom leaned forward. "Okay but how about Queson not batting an eye when the bank officials said the gold shipment was short more than five hundred thousand dollars?"

"Sure, we have purely circumstantial evidence—rumors—really hearsay, that this is MacArthur's payoff money. For this one, we need some hard facts we can use. Now, any more basic charges to add to this list?" asked the Colonel.

"Could we charge him with treason for not taking action immediately following word of the Pearl Harbor attack?" Staff Sergeant Waters asked hesitantly.

Roy looked at him and smiled. "We probably will once we get our ducks in a row."

"Ya know, I just bet there is a whole file drawer of communications between General Arnold and General Brereton with some very interesting data," said Clint.

Colonel Mac sat down again and became formal. "Listen gentlemen, and hear me. MacArthur is a very powerful man." He paused and looked at Millington, Worthington, and Waters, individually. "He was Chief of Staff of the Army; he has friends in high places; and he is not paying for his defense counsel.

"If we want to throw the book at him, several charges come to mind; however, then we dilute the strength of our offense. I believe we can find two very serious nailed down charges and include the others as part of the testimony we must extract from friendly and hostile witnesses. Almost all of MacArthur's staff is very protective and therefore hostile. You saw when they arrived here. They practically drew swords and surrounded him."

"Let's see," Worthington drawled, "Queson is in Australia now. Do you suppose we could subpoena the President-in-Exile as a witness? One of the reports we have indicates that General Sutherland threatened to leave Queson's group behind if he did not sign off on the $500,000 and $38,000 expenses, before he would manifest them on the flight to Australia."

The Colonel and Millington looked at him thoughtfully. "If we come down the line and find he would be useful, we certainly could give it a try. Good idea, Clint," said the Colonel.

Staff Sergeant Waters had been taking notes and waited until conversation trailed off. "Excuse me, Colonel. Did you happen to pick up on the fact that CG FEAF Comm Center files and NCO's are not mentioned in all this material? I bet there is a gold mine of evidence there."

A surprised silence followed as three pairs of eyes took in Waters and chewed on his comment.

"Speaking of CG's, why do you suppose Brigadier General Drake, Quartermaster General, didn't come back with MacArthur?" posed Tom, quietly. "I mean, he is responsible for all the regular and war supplies, isn't he?"

Roy sighed. "You're absolutely right, Tom. We'll try to find out about him, too. Right. Sergeant Waters? And see if you can locate any of those Air Force communications personnel. Let's see what we can pull out of them."

"I'm on it, Colonel." Waters grinned as he picked up his chair and walked back out to his desk.

MacIntyre nodded and looked at Millington. "Okay, Tom, let's put together our witness list. We need to pass that along to Van der Wendt right away.

"Try these out for size: Brigadier General Sutherland, Chief of Staff; Lieutenant Colonel Huff, MacArthur's Junior Aide; Colonel Willoughby, Intelligence; Major General Brereton, CG FEAF and the 19th Bombardment Group; unaccounted for: Brigadier General Drake, Quartermaster General; unaccounted for: Colonel Casey, Engineering; unaccounted for: Colonel Jones, Communications; and several John Does, at the moment."

He paused while Tom continued to write. "You know," he said grimly, "we don't know how many more are going to get out. It looks like Bataan is going to fall any day now." He thought for a moment. "Most of these people will be hostile witnesses. The friendly witnesses are trapped behind the lines."

Tom nodded and sighed.

CHAPTER FOUR

Eric Van der Wendt was thoroughly enjoying his dinner on John Engelson who obviously picked his restaurants with care. They had come to some conclusions. Studying Colonel MacIntyre's list of witnesses had been instructive. Most of the prosecution witnesses would have to be declared hostile to the Army questioning. On the other hand, Defense in turn, would declare Major General Brereton a hostile witness because he had preferred the charge of treason against MacArthur.

The primary problem was whittling away at that ten-hour "dead" time before MacArthur allegedly took action.

"Eric, have you been able to find out any more information about the missing Filipino gold?" John's eyes flicked between Eric's face and his own plate of sole, as he asked.

Eric placed his stem glass of chardonnay carefully on the table and patted his mouth with a napkin. He shook his head before answering. "No, and I think we are as far away from an answer to that as Roy and company are. CID is really embarrassed but they haven't a clue, so far."

John nodded. "Keep on them, Eric." He took another bite of sole, savoring the white sauce. "Have you been able to develop some witnesses of our own?"

He shook his head once again. "No, that is pretty grim. I talked with Colonel Eisenhower, finally." Eric sipped more chardonnay and held his stem glass. "He really tried to avoid me. I had to ambush him in the officers' latrine before he would even talk to me." He carefully placed his nearly empty stem glass on the table and looked at John's face. "Ike said he would not be a good witness for the defense, then excused himself."

"That is astounding. Eisenhower appeared to enjoy being his Chief of Staff out there."

Eric chuckled and broke into a loud laugh. "Ike's comment about serving as MacArthur's Chief of Staff in the Philippines, was that he learned about theatrics from Mac." His eyes flicked back and forth as he considered options. "So, Sutherland and Willoughby are his only help."

"And Huff," John said.

"Huff doesn't count, I'm afraid," said Eric. "The Army Gray Line will discount his testimony, even though Huff is an Annapolis graduate."

John sighed and studied the ceiling for a moment. "Well, enjoy dinner while you can. Preliminaries begin tomorrow."

Eric nodded agreement and went back to his chicken cacciatore.

CHAPTER FIVE

Barry Ford, Washington Star-News Editor-in-Chief, was a dandy. He took great pride in his grooming, preferring 3-piece suits, and never the same suit or at least the color combinations two days in a row. For instance, today he arrived in his office dressed in a light green gabardine suit, white handkerchief tucked into his coat breast pocket, white shirt and tan tie. His tan fedora surrounded with a narrow, pale yellow band set off his suit nicely. He took great pleasure in selecting suits off the rack that fit perfectly. His five foot, ten inch slim body caught the eye of several lovely ladies.

Barry arrived in his office at his usual time, flipped his hat onto the hatrack, unbuttoned and removed his coat and slipped the coat onto a wooden coat hanger; and waited for delivery of his first cup of coffee from the third floor. The waitress, in a tight skirt, delivered his coffee and smiled a come on smile. Barry smiled but wasn't biting. He slipped his finger into the coffee cup handle and alternately sipped coffee and puffed on his cigar as he watched her rhumba her way back to the elevator, ever hopeful.

Nice.

Barry settled in his chair and began his day reading the publisher's daily interoffice memos and the latest war news. The memos were color-coded: White was run of the mill information; Green was a personal note to the recipient; Red meant we have trouble, can you take care of it?; and Blue was take immediate action. This was a blue memo. He pulled it from the stack and laid the others aside.

They can wait.

The blue memo had several attachments fastened to it. He unclipped the attachments and laid them aside for the moment to read the memo first.

Hmmm, looks like the Army wants press coverage at some sort of hearing.

Now he put the blue memo down, pulled off the attached sheets and looked at both sides of what appeared to be some kind of U.S. Army order and a pass. Thoughtfully, he read both the Army instructions and the pass.

About the only time the Army wants press coverage is to introduce a new war machine of some sort. Whatever it is, this looks like a big, fat, juicy scandal. Very unusual.

Mr. Ford looked at his reporters through the glass separator into the newsroom, frowning.

Who would be the best choice for this job?

Just then, Gregory Pines stood up looking down on the story rolled into his typewriter. He stretched his arms over his head, rubbed his nearly numb butt, and sat back down, shaking his hands and wiggling his fingers to loosen them from long typing on his L.C. Smith typewriter. He looked out the window for a second and got back to clacking away on his story.

Mr. Ford chuckled and heaved himself out of his overworked chair. Opening his door, he called out, "Hey, Pines," stuck his cigar back into his teeth, chomped down on it, and beckoned him in when Pines looked up from his typewriter.

Mr. Ford pivoted and went back to his chair. Pines sighed.

What the hell does the boss want?

Greg got up from his chair, pulled his brown suit jacket from the back of his chair, shrugged it on and checked his sagging jacket pockets. He walked into Mr. Ford's office, shutting the door.

"What's up, boss?" He asked, pulling his ever-present notepad and pencil from his jacket patch pocket.

Ford tossed the memo across the desk at Pines. "Read it and weep, Greg. You're going to witness an Army hearing and maybe a court-martial and write it up as a great story."

Pines curled his lips back like he tasted awful cough medicine and glanced at the memo. Then he read it again, slowly. Frowning at it, his brow wrinkled in thought, he said, "I don't see a date on this, Barry. When does it start and who is it?"

"Tomorrow, and I thought that was curious, too." He grinned. "You want to give me your Senator baseball tickets if this hearing and court-martial go into the beginning of baseball season? I'll see that some worthy person gets to see them play."

Pines turned red in the face and yelled out. "Dammit all to hell, Chief, I traded assignments, promised the world, and juggled my schedule just so I could see those first four home games, the season openers. Can't you get someone else to take this assignment?"

"No, Pines." Mr. Ford's face turned frosty with an angry look on his face, "you got the call. Now get going," he growled. You do not argue successfully with Mr. Ford, especially when you yell at him.

Pines left Barry's office, slammed around his desk for a couple of minutes, growling about the injustice of it all, finished his story and pulled the dust cover over his L.C. Smith typewriter. He looked around the newsroom and spotted a young man walking along the far aisle.

"Copyboy," he shouted, waving sheets of paper. The copyboy veered from his path to Gregory's desk.

"This is for Rewrite, Art," said Gregory, nodding toward the Rewrite Desk. With his story taken, he swung his jacket over his shoulder and sauntered out of the newsroom.

CHAPTER SIX

The function of an Army Board of Inquiry can be likened to a civilian grand jury investigation: to determine if the recommended charges have enough merit to send the charged individual forward to a court-martial. To put it another way, to determine if there is enough evidence of a wrongdoing to charge an offender under Army Regulations or the Articles of War.
The board consists of several officers. The selected room is arranged with military precision.

The Trial Judge Advocate *is a military law specialist. He is, or they are, in effect, judge and jury. Sometimes, several officers will sit with the Trial Judge Advocate. All must be equal in rank with the accused, or higher rank.*

The President of the Board *sits at the center of a table on an elevated platform with other members of the Board to his left and right. The Board faces the antagonists, witnesses, and galleries, to hear testimony and eventually render the decision to dismiss or forward any or all charges and specifications to a court-martial.*

The Defense Counsel, *also a Judge Advocate, other counsels, assistants, and defendant sit on his right front, forward of the visitors' gallery, at a pair of tables pushed together, with armchairs. These tables are prepared with notepads, pencils, tumblers, and water pitchers filled with iced water.*

The Army's Prosecutor, *also a Judge Advocate, and assistants representing the United States Army sit on his left front, forward of the press gallery, at a pair of tables pushed together, with armchairs. These tables are also prepared with notepads, pencils, tumblers, and water pitchers filled with iced water.*

The Witness Chair *consists of a single chair and small table, slightly below the Trial Judge Advocate, on the right side of the Trial Judge Advocate facing the courtroom. The table contains glass tumblers and iced water pitchers. All people being questioned or giving testimony sit in this chair.*

The Recorder and his assistants, *usually two or three, sit at small tables stacked with steno pads and pencils, to the Trial Judge Advocate's left, facing the Witness Chair.*

The <u>Clerk of the Court</u> is located to the right of the Trial Judge Advocate. This individual is responsible for logging and maintaining all exhibits involved in the proceedings.

A <u>podium</u>—or lectern—is positioned immediately between the two Judge Advocates' tables and slightly forward of them, generally facing the Witness Chair. The podium contained glass tumblers and iced water pitchers.

The <u>Sergeant-At-Arms</u>, standing to the left side of the Trial Judge Advocate, acts as the Court Bailiff. His staff of Military Police is stationed at all doors to prevent unauthorized entry or exit.

CHAPTER SEVEN

0845, February 23, 1942
Building B-6 Conference Room 3
Fort Belvoir, Virginia

Gregory Pines visited Fort Belvoir every fall to watch the great First Army football team stomp their opponents into the turf. Gregory passed by Building B-6 on the way to the football field every time he came to a game. It was easy to find a place to park under the bare trees and carefully lock his 1934 green Dodge Coupe doors and rumble seat. He crossed the street to Building B-6's Main Entrance.

He smiled and nodded to the two Army Military Policemen watching him as he approached. One of them was very short and chunky, the other tall and skinny. Greg grinned, reminded of the comic strip, "Mutt and Jeff".

Several sawhorses and ropes tied to the sawhorses formed a cattle chute to the wooden stairs. MP Mutt stuck his nightstick across Greg's path. Gregory stopped, surprised, and looked down at Mutt.

"Just a moment, mac. This is off limits to unauthorized personnel. You gotta pass? You gotta have a pass to get in," demanded MP Jeff, holding out his hand.
"Uh, yeah." Greg said, looking up at Jeff.
"The pass and some identification, please." demanded MP Mutt.

This has never happened before. 'Course, I haven't been here since before Pearl Harbor. Probably just increased war security.

"Yeah, sure. What's this all about?" He asked, frowning at them.
"Sorry, sir. No one is authorized past this point unless they have a pass or are on this list," explained MP Mutt apologetically as he carefully inspected the civilian.

Gregory fumbled for his wallet and handed over his Army invitation and his Washington Star-News identification card. MP Jeff held up a clipboard while they both scanned down a list and stopped looking.

"Uh, yes sir, you're on the list—that is, an unnamed reporter from Washington Star-News is on the list, so I guess that's you," said MP Mutt.

The Corporal scratched out 'unnamed reporter' and wrote 'Gregory Pines' above the line, and handed Gregory his letter and card. "Don't lose these, sir. You need 'em every time you go in. Go up the stairs and into the building to the first cross corridor and turn right, Conference Room 3 is on the left two doors down the corridor." MP Mutt spoke and MP Jeff nodded.

Gregory's lips moved, silently repeating their instructions, nodded, and trotted up the wooden staircase stuffing his wallet in his left hip pocket at the same time. He looked around to get a sense of the place. He could feel the tension. Both officers and enlisted men were frowning or had unhappy looks on their face.

This had to be pretty important if MP's made sure only the approved people entered the building. Leastways, these soldiers seemed to think so.

Greg Pines made sure his press pass was shoved firmly into the tan band on the brim of his straw hat. Soldiers and civilians were thumping along the wooden floor in both directions hurrying about their business. A big easel against the far wall pointed the way to Conference Room 3. Pines walked along the hall, absorbing the old Army photographs and posters hanging on the wall. He joined the line of people waiting to enter the conference room. MP's were searching everyone.

One MP motioned with his hand for Greg to move forward. "Sorry sir. We are looking for wire recorders, cameras, and weapons of any kind. We have to pat you down."
Gregory raised his arms while they thoroughly searched him. The MP pulled out his two bulging tobacco pouches and looked inside one, which contained a pipe and tobacco and stuffed it back in its pocket.

He opened the second one and looked up suspiciously with hard eyes. "What's this, Mr. Pines?"
Greg chuckled, "Those are my writing tools and supplies." The MP looked again, poking his finger into things inside the pouch to see them better, relaxed a bit and nodded, closed the pouch and handed it back.

"Thank you, sir," he said. "We have to search you every time you go through this door in either direction." At that last, Greg turned with raised eyebrows, "Why?" He asked as he dropped his pouch in his jacket patch pocket.

The MP, bored silly repeating this to all the newsmen, pointed to his other patch pockets filled with stenographer notepads. "Those can't leave the room, sir. It will all be explained in great detail in a few minutes."

Greg paused inside the muggy room to remove his straw hat and wipe his forehead with a large white handkerchief already wet from previous wipes and stuffed it back in his handkerchief pocket. Greg's straight black hair, trimmed above his shirt collar was wet with perspiration. His light blue seersucker suit was wrinkled and damp across the back of his coat, and his shirt collar was soaked. Saturated with perspiration, limp from the high humidity, he wished he could loosen his blue striped tie.

His brown eyes darted around the conference room-turned-courtroom sizing up his competition from other newspapers and wire services. There were no civilians in the visitor gallery across the aisle. That side was loaded with a lot of Army brass.

They certainly have a lot of interest in this hearing.

Gregory combed his hair back with his fingers as he looked at the available chairs. All of the chairs were varnished oak with straight backs and without arms.

Just the ticket to numb your butt and bruise your shoulder blades.

He decided upon one near the back of the room. Greg was more than a little wilted in this humidity, wiggling around as he tried to settle comfortably—sitting up straight—in the chair. Giving it up as a bad try, he eased down slouching in the chair with his ankles crossed in front of him, fresh notepad in hand on his lap.

Flipped the hard cover open, he checked the time on his wristwatch, and began jotting background notes about the room and people in it. Greg recognized most of the news journalists and wire service reporters.

He wished he had a table or student chair with an arm desk to write his impressions of the main characters in this heavy drama. His notebook paper was already damp from his sweaty wrist; writing with a pencil was getting difficult and a fountain pen would be impossible. He pulled out a handkerchief and wrapped it under his wrist to keep the dampness from getting on his papers.

Since this hearing wouldn't start for a while, he pulled his tool pouch from his right patch pocket and opened the pouch to check his supplies again, just for something to do. Extra pencils, a little hand pencil sharpener, an art gum eraser, a few paper clips, nickels, dimes, and quarters for phone calls, a couple rubber bands, a wad of string, assorted thumb tacks on a small piece of cardboard, and a six inch ruler completed the ensemble. Two more blank shorthand notepads were in his other patch pocket. He was set.

Gregory checked out the room wall by wall. He came to the conclusion this large room was used for theatrical productions because it had a three-foot high stage with curtains. Behind the center chair, in front of maroon drapes, an American flag and an Army flag stood guard over all.

Gregory thought he was in a great position to see and hear the officers of the court, the accused's staff of lawyers, and the accused. U.S. Army and Army Air Force officers, and various allies, were being seated now. He hadn't recognized any of the officers; however, he saw uniforms of the British Empire, Free French, and Filipino Armies. Of course, all witnesses were in another room where they could not see or hear the proceedings.

CHAPTER EIGHT

0900, 23 February 1942
Conference Room 3, First Floor
Building B-6
Fort Belvoir, Virginia

Three technical specialists, one equivalent to a Master Sergeant, the other two equivalent to Technical Sergeants, talked quietly, as they strolled in and took their seats at the Recorders' desks.

A colonel in a well-tailored uniform entered the Courtroom and walked to the Court Recorders' area and spent a moment talking in hushed voices with the three specialists. They looked at the Regulator clock on the back wall to jot down the time on their pads.

The Colonel turned around to face the audience and cleared his throat to attract attention. He tugged at his jacket and Sam Brown belts. Quiet conversations, coughing and shuffling died down as people turned to him.

"Good morning, gentlemen. I am Colonel Robert Obrey of the Army Judge Advocate General Corps. For the benefit of the press, in this Article 70 hearing, I am the Trial Judge Advocate functioning as judge and jury. On any question of Army law, I have the final say."

He stopped for a moment to rub his nose and inspect his shoes, collecting his thoughts, and continued, raising his head to face the audience. "The purpose of this hearing is to determine if there is sufficient evidence to convene a general court-martial on the person so charged."

The colonel cleared his throat. "This is an unusual hearing because it is secret. You shall not discuss or write anything outside of this courtroom." Sounds of dismay came from the Press Corps. "You all," pointing to everyone in the courtroom, "shall be sworn to the official secrecy act of the United States of America."

He turned to look directly at the Press Corps. "You reporters, artists, and journalists: you may write or sketch drawings during each session to your hearts' content but you cannot remove your notes, sketches, or pictures from this hearing room, nor shall you discuss this with anyone outside this room until permitted by the War Cabinet, Attorney General, and the President."

More sounds of distress rose from the press section. "Anyone who cannot abide by these rules will be summarily thrown in jail for the duration of the war for violating the official secrecy act. If you cannot accept this ruling, please leave now."

The colonel looked at the military officers in the visitor's gallery. "This applies equally to everyone in the visitors section." People looked back and forth at each other, waiting for someone to move. Nobody budged.

This was BIG!

Colonel Obrey raised his right hand and said, "Very well, please stand, raise your right hand, and repeat after me, using your own name . . .

> *I, Robert Obrey, (there was a flurry of names mumbled) do solemnly swear or affirm to keep secret, not disclosing the contents of this Article 70 hearing to anyone, all that I read, see, write, or hear at this hearing. So help me, God."*

Looking around again, he said, "Good. You may put your hands down and be seated now. Before we begin, an MP is bringing that oath to you for your signature. If you will not sign it, leave this room now and do not return. Reporters will turn in all their notebooks to the MP's every time they leave this room for any reason. When you return, they will be returned." He watched as the MP began getting signatures on the oath.

Colonel Obrey left the courtroom through the side entrance.

CHAPTER NINE

0930, 23 February 1942
Conference Room 3, First Floor
Building B-6
Fort Belvoir, Virginia

The side door by the stage opened. A colonel, followed by a captain, first lieutenant, and a staff sergeant who brought large boxes of material on a rubber-wheeled cart walked into the room, glanced at the visitor section, smiled, nodding to faces here and there, and took their seats. The sergeant sat down on a bench behind the officers. The officers, helped by the staff sergeant, shuffled the boxes around, on and under the desk to their liking.

The double doors at the rear opened. A sibilance of sound and moaning rippled toward the front. A colonel and two civilians—the only civilians, besides the press—in the courtroom, followed by two grim MP's, marched to the Defense Table. The MP's about-faced and marched back to stand against the rear wall.

In a classic double take, recognition dawned in the audience. Whispered comments bounced back and forth.

> *Is that General MacArthur? Is he the defendant?*
> *My God, it is MacArthur! Why is he wearing those civilian clothes?*
> *What is he doing before this Board of Inquiry?*
> *They're doing a Seventy on Mac?*
> *I thought all people in the military service were required to wear their uniforms at all times.*
> *I read that MacArthur had been transferred to Australia.*

Greg Pines copied these whispered comments into his notebook as fast as he could, then he described MacArthur.

MacArthur wore a single-breasted, dark gray, 3-piece silk suit, white shirt, maroon tie, and carried a dark, wooden walking cane. His face was pale, looking somewhat sickly. Even so, he held his head high, slightly tilted, looking straight ahead, as was his wont. He had marched in ramrod straight, characteristically aloof and not smiling.

CHAPTER TEN

0945, 23 February 1942
Conference Room 3, First Floor
Building B-6
Fort Belvoir, Virginia

The Sergeant-at-Arms and his guard detail of MP's marched to the back of the Conference Room, shut and latched the double doors. Both window shades were pulled down. Having insured the latch was secure, the Sergeant-at-Arms pivoted and called out, "All rise!"

The buck sergeant wore his black MP armband over a khaki shirt. His khaki trousers were pressed with a very sharp crease down the front. A 1911 M1A1 Colt .45 caliber semi-automatic pistol was clipped in a spit shined black leather holster on a guard belt with two extra ammunition clips attached. His shoes were likewise spit shined. He wore the new bucket style khaki helmet with MP painted in white on its sides. The other 4 MP's were similarly attired and looked just as formidable as the Sergeant-at-Arms.

Chairs scraped across the wooden floor as everyone rose while the Trial Judge Advocate, Colonel Obrey, filed in through the side door and climbed the steps to the stage. A gaggle of coughs and clearing of throats ensued, and then quieted as the Colonel stood waiting. A gavel appeared in his hand, which tapped the table once.

He spoke sternly. "This United States Army Article 70 Board of Inquiry hearing is now in session," he said, in a quiet but strained mid-western twang. The Court Recorders carefully noted the exact time in each of their stenographer pads.

Technical Specialist 7 Ernst Tillotson, Senior Recorder stood. "Members of this Hearing, please assemble in front of me for the Oath." He waited as they stood in front of him.

"Raise your right hand. You—say your name—do swear or affirm that you will, well and truly, examine and inquire, according to the evidence, into the matter now before you without partiality, favor, affection, prejudice, or hope of reward. So help you, God."

There were murmurs of I do from each member.

Tillotson looked at each of them. "Then you may return to your seats." T/S-7 Tillotson pivoted, saluted Colonel and said: "Colonel, the Members of this hearing are sworn" and returned to his seat.

Colonel Obrey stood again and looked at the recorders. "Technical Specialist Seven Tillotson, front and center." Tillotson stood and marched across the floor, turned, and saluted. "Reporting as ordered, Colonel."

"Raise your right hand, Master Sergeant." He waited a second as Tillotson did as ordered.

> *"You—say your name—do swear or affirm that you will, according to your best abilities, record the proceedings of this hearing and the evidence to be given to the case in hearing. So help you, God."*

"I do."

"Post!"

T/S-7 Tillotson saluted Colonel Obrey and marched back to his seat.

The Colonel studied the accused, visitors and reporters. He took a deep breath, and began. "The information you learn in this hearing would cause grievous damage to the United States of America by rendering aid and comfort to the enemy. You members of the press corps have been invited here to record this event on your own terms for posterity.

"Even so, there are times when highly classified documents, sources, and statements may be discussed. In that event, the board will clear this hearing room or retire to secure offices to discuss the matter. There will be times when this board must adjourn until witnesses appearing before another Board of Inquiry or Court-martial or the 27th Congressional Joint Committee investigating the Japanese attacks in the Pacific, are released from those hearings and can appear here." He gazed at the audience for a moment and looked at MacArthur for the first time. He tapped the gavel once. "You may be seated," and sat down himself. There was another rustle as everyone in the courtroom settled amid another fit of coughing.

Two Military Policemen stationed themselves in front of the closed rear doors. Two others were along each sidewall. The

MacArthur's Pacific Appeasement, December 8, 1941
Part II
U.S. Army Article 70 Board of Inquiry

Sergeant-at-Arms marched forward and stood at Parade Rest close to the stage edge in order to respond to Colonel Obrey's needs.

Gently tapping his gavel for attention, Colonel Obrey began. "For your general information," he said, "at 1500 hours, December 17, 1941, Eastern War Time, then Lieutenant General Douglas A. MacArthur was abruptly relieved of duty as Commander-in-Chief of the U. S. Army Forces of the Far Eastern Area, headquartered in Manila, U. S. Commonwealth of the Philippine Isles, by Franklin Delano Roosevelt, the President of the United States and Commander-in-Chief of all U.S. military and naval forces.

Greg Pines broke his first pencil with this announcement. The press corps and visitors were in an uproar. Colonel Obrey quietly tapped with his gavel and continued.

"General MacArthur was reduced to his permanent rank of Colonel, Infantry, USA, and ordered to Fort Belvoir to stand before an Article 70 Army Board of Inquiry into the Philippine disaster. Further, Colonel MacArthur and those of his General Staff who came out from Manila with him, are under house arrest—incommunicado—at least until the conclusion of this Article 70 hearing." There were more shocked murmurs from the visitors' gallery.

My God, what disaster?
What has he done?

Colonel Obrey looked at a sheet of paper in his hand. He looked down at the prosecution table. "Colonel MacIntyre, is the prosecution ready?"

The senior member and his three assistants rose coming to attention. "Yes, Colonel Obrey. For the record, I am Colonel Leroy Q. MacIntyre, assigned to the Army Judge Advocate General's office, detailed to this Board of Inquiry as senior Trial Counsel. I am assisted by Captain Thomas E. Millington, Infantry, detailed to this hearing as Assistant Trial Counsel, First Lieutenant Clinton Worthington, Army Air Force, detailed to this hearing as Investigator, and Staff Sergeant Ryan Waters, detailed to this hearing as Clerk and Junior Investigator. Sir, we are ready to proceed."

"Very well, Colonel." He looked over to the defense table. "Colonel Van der Wendt, Is Defense ready to proceed?"

MacArthur's Pacific Appeasement, December 8, 1941
Part II
U.S. Army Article 70 Board of Inquiry

"Yes sir, Colonel." The colonel and civilian rose, also coming to attention. "For the record, I am Colonel Eric Van der Wendt, Coast Artillery, Seconded to the Judge Advocate General Corps, detailed by the Army Judge Advocate General as Defense Counsel for the accused." Van der Wendt looked to his left. "Mr. John Engelson, Esquire, of Engelson, Engelson, and Engelson Law Offices, in Arlington, Virginia, certified to practice before Army courts-martial, has been retained for the accused and will be the lead counsel for defense."

"Very well, Colonel." Colonel Obrey was silent for a moment as he studied MacArthur in his civilian clothes. MacArthur ignored the Colonel. "Is the defendant ready to proceed, Mr. Engelson?"

John Engelson, a porcine gentleman wearing round glasses on his shiny, round face, stood up again, buttoning his three-button brown coat as he looked at Colonel Obrey. "Yes, Colonel. Mr. MacArthur is ready to proceed."

Colonel Obrey's eyebrows came together above the bridge of his nose. He stared coldly at the Defense for a moment. His gavel banged loudly. "Will you or Colonel MacArthur explain why he is in civilian attire and not in Class A uniform as ordered by the convening authority?" asked Colonel Obrey, icily.

Mr. Engelson eyes flicked between Colonel Obrey and Colonel MacIntyre before answering. His hand dropped to the table in front of him. He picked up a short stack of paper and walked to the Recorders.

"Mr. MacArthur has resigned his Army commission," he said pivoting, "and gives as the reason the fact he was relieved of his command, impugning his honor and combat ability. This is a mimeograph copy of his letter of resignation being handed the Chief of G-1 now by a member of my staff." He handed copies of the letter to the Court Recorders for distribution, the Clerk of the Court for Colonel Obrey, and several to Colonel MacIntyre before returning to his place.

Colonel Obrey looked up from the letter and glared at Mr. Engelson and Colonel MacArthur, and studied MacArthur for a period of time. He said softly,
"Colonel MacArthur, that dog won't hunt."

Mr. Engelson's eyebrows tilted at the redneck remark. "Colonel, Mr. MacArthur is aware that a witch hunt is in progress and he is to be another scape goat. He is not going to be ignored or pilloried like Lieutenant General Short and Admiral Kimmel. He is a private citizen now and that means he cannot be reduced in rank or lose his seniority number, if found guilty."

Mr. Engelson watched as the Colonel leaned back and stared at MacArthur for a moment, then took a deep breath and let it out. "Mr. Engelson, whether MacArthur is a witch or scape goat remains to be seen. He is being investigated for offenses allegedly committed by Lieutenant General Douglas Arthur MacArthur while he was on active duty in the United States Army in the United States Commonwealth of the Philippine Isles as Commander-in-Chief of the United States Army Forces, Far East. If the evidence presented here is strong enough to presume a court-martial is required to determine innocence or guilt, charges and specifications will be forwarded to the convening authority." Colonel Obrey picked up the water pitcher and filled a glass with iced water. After taking a sip, he set the glass down, cleared his throat, and continued.

"He may wish to think he is a civilian all he wants but he is still subject to the United States Army Articles of War." MacArthur's mouth twitched almost to a grimace as he stared back. Obrey broke eye contact and looked to the Prosecution Judge Advocate.

Greg wrote down that Engelson appeared satisfied with the last remark. Greg, all ears and writing as fast as he could, was dumbfounded by the accusations being made against MacArthur.

At this rate, he's going to Leavenworth or face a firing squad.

"Colonel MacIntyre, read the orders, promulgating this hearing."
The Colonel stood, picked up a brief, cleared his throat, sipped some water, and began reading aloud.

"An Article 70 Board of Inquiry was ordered by the Army Chief of Staff, General George Catlin Marshall, at the direction of the Commander-in-Chief, President Franklin Delano Roosevelt, on December 17, 1941. The purpose of the Board of Inquiry is to investigate how the Imperial Japanese Air Force and Imperial Japanese Navy Air Armadas under Imperial Japanese Army commander General Homma were able to destroy the United States Army Air Force in the Philippines and land Japanese Army troops without effective counter measures by then Lieutenant General Douglas Arthur MacArthur."

Colonel MacIntyre looked up to Colonel Obrey and nodded his head as if to say 'that is all', and sat down.

"Colonel MacIntyre, read the proposed charges and specifications into the record,." ordered Colonel Obrey.

The Colonel stood and began reading.

CHARGE I. VIOLATION OF THE 75TH ARTICLE OF WAR, MISBEHAVIOR BEFORE THE ENEMY.
SPECIFICATION (1):

In that then Lieutenant General Douglas Arthur MacArthur feloniously agreed with Philippine Isles President Manuel Queson, United States Commonwealth of the Philippines, on or about December 1, 1941, not to anger the Japanese by attacking Japanese forces or retaliating from any attacks elsewhere in the Pacific by Japanese forces, causing them to attack the Philippines. To wit, "Hostilities with the Japanese Empire begin only after the first bomb from a Japanese warplane or shell from a Japanese warship explodes on Philippine soil."

SPECIFICATION (2):

The accused, then Lieutenant General Douglas Arthur MacArthur, feloniously denied a request of Air Force Major General Brereton, under his command, to implement Rainbow Five; and the accused ignored warnings from his general staff and from the Navy.

SPECIFICATION (3):

In that then Lieutenant General Douglas Arthur MacArthur feloniously forbade Major General Brereton from flying a large formation of Boeing B-17 heavy bombers on a bombing mission to destroy or damage Japanese warships and troopships in their sea ports and destroy or damage Japanese warplanes, runways, hangers, and ancillary equipment on Formosan soil, this to the scandal and disgrace of the military service.

CHARGE II: VIOLATION OF THE 64TH ARTICLE OF WAR, ASSAULTING OR WILLFULLY DISOBEYING SUPERIOR OFFICER.
SPECIFICATION:

In that the accused, then Lieutenant General Douglas

Arthur MacArthur willfully and feloniously failed to implement Rainbow Five Phase Two upon notification of Japanese attack on Pearl Harbor. To wit: the accused failed to alert Army and Air Force units to take appropriate defensive posture upon notification of Japanese attack on Pearl Harbor.

CHARGE III. VIOLATION OF THE 83RD ARTICLE OF WAR, MILITARY PROPERTY — WILLFUL OR NEGLIGENT LOSS, DAMAGE OR WRONGFUL DISPOSITION.
SPECIFICATION (1):

By then Lieutenant General Douglas Arthur MacArthur's wrongful, felonious and willful disobedience to a lawful order on or about December 8th, 1941, the Army Air Force could not destroy the Japanese air fleet on the ground in Formosa that bombarded military and civilian targets in the Philippines. In particular, nearly all Army Air Force bombers and pursuit planes were destroyed on the ground; Army bases, Navy bases and stations, and Navy ships were severely damaged or destroyed. Many military and naval personnel and civilians were killed outright or wounded.

SPECIFICATION (2):

By a wrongful, felonious and willful disobedience to a lawful order on or about December 8th, 1941, Lieutenant General Douglas Arthur MacArthur's order, the Army Air Force did not destroy the Japanese landing fleet at their anchorage in Formosa, thus allowing them to land unhampered by defensive forces.

SPECIFICATION (3):

By then Lieutenant General Douglas MacArthur's wrongful, felonious and willful disobedience of a lawful order, the Army Air Force B-17 bombers and P-40 pursuit planes, lost on the ground, on or about December 8th, 1941, were unable to provide cover or offensive action in accordance with Rainbow 5 in support of allied forces in Singapore and the Dutch East Indies, and indirectly caused the loss of His Britannic Majesty's battleship HMS Prince of Wales and battlecruiser HMS Repulse on or about December 9th, 1941, and the ABDA fleet at great loss of life."

CHARGE IV. VIOLATION OF THE 95TH ARTICLE OF WAR, CONDUCT UNBECOMING AN OFFICER
SPECIFICATION (1):

Then Lieutenant General Douglas Arthur MacArthur lied to General Gerow, the Deputy Chief of Staff for War Planning of the U.S. Army, on or about December 3rd, 1941, when asked if he had executed Rainbow Five Phase One.

SPECIFICATION (2):

Then Lieutenant General Douglas Arthur MacArthur lied to General George Catlin Marshall, the Chief of Staff of the U.S. Army on or about December 8th, 1941, when asked if he had executed Rainbow Five Phase Two.

Colonel MacIntyre carefully placed the charges and specification sheets on his table and looked at Colonel Obrey and Mr. Engleson.

"Colonel, the United States Army charges that General MacArthur acted treasonably by twice disobeying a direct order to act, lied misrepresenting the state of his forces, and lied about the damage suffered by the Japanese aerial attack on December 8, 1941, Manila time."

Colonel Obrey poured more iced water from the pitcher watching the chunks of ice tumbling into his water glass. Colonel MacIntyre paused, watching Colonel Obrey taking another sip of water. Then he continued. "Under consideration before the Board of Inquiry are suspicion of treason, disobedience of direct orders, making false official statements, and malfeasance while he was Commander-in-Chief, U.S. Army Forces Far East in the Philippines." Colonel MacIntyre looked at Colonel Obrey and sat down.

Colonel MacArthur had tilted his head back, glaring down his nose at Colonel Obrey, and appeared ready to stand and speak. John Engelson put his hand on MacArthur's arm, shook his head, and murmured into MacArthur's ear. Nodding, MacArthur, shaking in anger, slowly relaxed and did not speak.

Colonel Obrey licked his lips a couple of times. He looked around, not seeing who or what he wanted.

"Sergeant-at-Arms—It is very humid in here. Turn on all the fans and make sure they are oscillating back and forth to circulate the air.

We'll just have to put up with their noise," he ordered. The Sergeant-at-Arms and one of the other Military Policemen hurriedly walked around the conference room turning on fans.

MacArthur sat stiffly upright; arms folded across his chest, staring straight ahead and did not appear to have listened to the reading of the charges against him.

Colonel MacIntyre stopped and placed the orders containing the charges on his table. "Colonel Obrey," he said. Obrey pointed his gavel at the colonel.

"You have something to add, Colonel MacIntyre?"

"Yes, sir. The United States Army reserves the right to bring forth additional charges."

"Colonel, I believe you said you were ready to present your case. Is that true?"

"Yes, Colonel, we were given 30 days to begin this hearing. We are still waiting for significant information to be flown in from Australia. That is taking much longer than we expected," he said.

"What is the nature of this investigation, Colonel?" Obrey asked.

"Colonel, it is not in the best interest of the Army nor the accused to present that information at this time, sir," he said.

Mr. Engelson almost leaped from his seat. "Colonel, charges have been read. Any additional charges cannot be added to this court-martial."

Colonel MacIntyre stood again and cleared his throat. "Colonel Obrey?"

Colonel Obrey pointed his gavel at Mr. Engelson. "Sir, this is a hearing, not a court-martial. There is a significant difference."

Mr. Engelson's face turned pink while Colonel Obrey was chastising him. "Colonel, I apologize for my error in wording. It is, as you said, a hearing," and sat down.

The Colonel now looked at Colonel MacIntyre and nodded.

"Colonel, there is an ongoing investigation in Australia to determine how more than five hundred thousand dollars of Philippine Treasury gold bars disappeared after the gold was delivered to U.S. Army trucks from the U.S. Navy submarine that brought four million dollars in gold bars from the Philippine Treasury, and where it is now."

"And what, pray tell, does that investigation have to do with my client, Colonel MacIntyre?" cooed Mr. Engelson.

Colonel MacIntyre, uncomfortable with his statement, glanced at Mr. Engelson. "There has been a suggestion the gold bars are not missing but paid to Colonel MacArthur by President Queson . . ."

Mr. Engelson erupted from his chair shouting. "What a cheap shot, how scurrilous an attack . . ."

A pounding gavel stopped him, as Colonel Obrey stood and glared at Colonel MacIntyre. Colonel Obrey was still banging to restore order. When the courtroom settled down, he turned to Colonel MacIntyre with red face and menacing voice, "You, sir, explain yourself. That was a contemptible statement."

"Colonel Obrey," exclaimed Colonel MacIntyre, and turned so he could see Colonel MacArthur and Mr. Engelson and spoke, picking his words with care.

"Sir, the operative word here is 'suggestion'. This is why we did not want to bring this out at this time but you insisted."

He paused nervously, filled his own glass with iced water, and sipped some of that ice water. "If this is a tempest in a teapot, nothing would have ever been said. However, if an evidentiary trail leads to Colonel MacArthur, we would be obliged to add a charge of bribery. The only known fact at this time is that of the four million dollars in gold and silver that arrived in Sydney, something over five hundred thousand dollars disappeared—the same amount that President Queson allegedly paid to Colonel MacArthur." He sat down.

Colonel Obrey cleared his throat. "Mr. Engelson, we do prefer one hearing instead of two or three or four. In the event additional charges can be preferred before Colonel MacIntyre completes his case, they will be accepted, granting you and Colonel MacArthur time to study them."

Mr. Engelson angrily sat, thought about it, leaned over and began whispering with MacArthur. MacArthur shook his head and shrugged.

"Colonel MacArthur, how do you plead?" Asked Colonel Obrey. John Engelson stood up and looked around the court, thumbs hooked in his armpits. "MISTER MacArthur pleads not guilty to all charges and specifications. He asks that you address him by his title. It is Mister, not Colonel."

Colonel Obrey leaned back, considering the attorney thoughtfully. "Colonel MacArthur is the subject of this inquiry, Mister Engelson. He will be addressed in that manner," he answered icily.

"I understand, Colonel, but my client will only respond when addressed as Mister."

"Mr. Engelson, if that occurs, I will hold you and Colonel MacArthur in contempt: if necessary, you both will be escorted to Fort Belvoir Stockade to reconsider your actions. I will give you fifteen minutes to determine your course of action." He said, angrily. The gavel smacked down hard, breaking the handle. "This court is in recess for fifteen minutes."

"All rise."

Colonel Obrey stood and stalked from the courtroom. Colonel MacIntyre and his assistants hurried after him, as did Colonel Van der Wendt. There was a strong sound of feet trying to be quiet as people headed to the door, most asking for directions to the latrine.

John Engelson leaned back in his chair, not bothering to follow, smiled at and whispered to MacArthur. Engelson was very tall, about 6' 3", rather stout and bald as a cucumber. Brilliant green eyes bulged slightly in his round face.

Gregory sat on his 1934 Dodge coupe running board and tossed peanuts to the squirrels. He wondered what was going to happen to MacArthur.

If the information that MacIntyre was presenting was truly fact, it looked like he was a candidate for the firing squad. Would FDR approve that?

He moodily watched the pigeons argue noisily with the squirrels over feeding rights. Two sparrows were sparring how best to break a peanut half into smaller pieces so they could feast.

What has Engelson got to counter these charges? Got to be very powerful medicine in his bag of tricks.

Sweat trickled down his nose in the early afternoon heat. Greg wondered if squirrels perspired. He had never seen one pant. When birds were too hot they held their beaks open—to let the hot air out, he guessed.

I wish I could talk to the boss. He could give me some guidance on whether this is another attempt to hide the true Washington guilt or not.

Another pigeon fluttered down and beat the squirrel with its wings until the squirrel gave up and scampered off. Greg only had a few peanuts left. Scattering them on the ground for those folks to argue over, he got up and ambled back to the courtroom.

CHAPTER ELEVEN

1050, 23 February 1942
Colonel Obrey's Office
Building B-6
Fort Belvoir, Virginia

Colonel Obrey's Clerk pulled the office door shut.

"Now then," said Obrey, "what are we going to do about this?" He thought for a minute. "Well, for starters, where's my clerk?" he asked, looking around for his clerk.

"Right here, Colonel."

"Get on the horn to G-1. See if they have received MacArthur's letter of resignation. Tell them to continue his status as "waiting reassignment to a new command" and to return his letter of resignation, unaccepted: it's wartime, by God. If there is any problem, let me talk to G-1."

"What if they've already received his letter, Colonel?"

Colonel Obrey stared at the Clerk. "What did I just say?"

"Right away, sir," and he stepped into the next room to call.

"Lord, the brass of Mac. But gentlemen, we will address him as Colonel until his status is confirmed."

Gregory began outlining while the court officers were out. He always did this whenever he had the time. Otherwise, when he got back to his desk at the Star-News, the story of the moment needed extra organizing time.

I don't have enough information for conceptualization yet, but this was going to be one hell of a story.

He bent over his notebook again and wrote: 'This Round goes to MacArthur—and the proceedings haven't really started yet'. He chewed on the pencil for a second and continued writing. 'If the Trial Judge Advocate gets angry and loses control, Engelson will have no problem getting a new hearing if Mac is found guilty.'

MacArthur's Pacific Appeasement, December 8, 1941
Part II
U.S. Army Article 70 Board of Inquiry

Question: if MacArthur hearing goes against him, is he automatically guilty, or does that wait for the outcome of a general court-martial?

Gregory checked his wristwatch and found he had plenty of time to smoke a short pipeful. He stood and stretched, feeling his jacket peel away from the chair varnish. Stuffing his notepad in his jacket pocket, he was stopped at the door by the MP's. Realizing what he had done, he returned to his seat and left his notepad and writing supplies on his chair.

Sheepishly, he submitted to a grinning MP's search and hurried out of the room, looking for a payphone to call his editor. It was outside and there already was a line waiting to use the only pay phone. He always had nickels as phone change in his writing supplies pouch.

He pulled his tobacco pouch and stuffed his pipe as he waited his turn. He struck the long wooden match with his thumbnail and held the match over his pipe. Puffing the Rum and Maple pipe tobacco contentedly, he looked around the fort enjoying the scenery. Dogwood, daffodils, and grape hyacinths were in bloom; bees were demanding their tribute. Sentries armed with rifles marched back and forth at their posts along the road. Several squads of soldiers marched about, doing the manual of arms with their rifles.
He felt moisture building on his whiskers.

Too bad the air isn't moving.

In the short time since the hearing started, the temperature had really jumped.

Would you look at that haze building up across the valley? I don't think those eight floor fans are going to do the job. Why the hell didn't I bring my palmetto fan?

His armpits began to drip.

Slowly moving toward the pay phone, Gregory listened to the excited conversation around him. Apparently no one else had known the stunning charges against MacArthur. Most of the other reporters there had been in the War to End All Wars and knew that things got out of control sometimes and the Commander ate it because he was commanding. But this was different. Mac was going to be hung out to dry.

Finally, his turn at the pay phone to drop a nickel. "Listen fast, Barry. Got to go inside in just a minute. This is going to be a powerful story when it breaks."

"How long do you think it will take, Greg?" asked Barry.

Greg hesitated as he thought. "I'm not sure. They haven't done a heck of a lot of anything, yet." He looked over his shoulder and saw people filing back inside the building. "Hey Barry, no more time, court is going back in session. Call you later." Gregory tapped out his pipe dottle onto the ground as he raced for the door.

An MP stopped him at the double doors. "Sir, all reporters have been moved to that area," he said, pointing to a group of men settling into chairs behind the Prosecution. "If you will gather your material from this box, I will move your chair over there."

Gregory groaned and muttered under his breath.

That was not a good place to see and hear everything.

He smiled stiffly, grabbed up the envelope with his name on it and carried it over where the MP moved his chair. "Thank you, Soldier," and eased into his chair.

"That's okay, sir," and he walked back to the doors to resume his post.

Greg pulled out his notepad and pencil, adjusting the chair around so he was somewhat comfortable.

I wonder if they have crossed swords in the past?

CHAPTER TWELVE

1115, 23 February 1942
Conference Room #3
Building B-6
Fort Belvoir, Virginia

The Sergeant-at-Arms entered. "All rise." Everyone stood quietly and waited. He locked the double doors, and marched up to stand next to Colonel Obrey.

Colonel Obrey entered and sat down. All three Recorders jotted the time on their steno pads and waited for the first words. The Colonel picked up the broken gavel by its head and tapped lightly two times. "Court is back in session at this time." He paused, looking down at the Defense Table. "Mr. Engelson, which is it to be, sir?"

Mr. Engelson spoke from his chair. "Yes, thank you, Colonel Obrey. Colonel MacArthur will respond to his military title."

Colonel Obrey looked directly at MacArthur. "We will address you as Colonel, Colonel MacArthur. When we reconvene following noon recess you will be in the Class A uniform as prescribed and promulgated by the First Army command." He looked at Mr. Engelson, daring him to reply. Instead, he sank in his chair without comment. Colonel Obrey nodded once, satisfied. "Mr. Engelson, you may proceed with your opening remarks for the Defense."

Mr. Engelson stood and fiddled with his tie. "I have no remarks at this time; however, I reserve the right to make them later."

Colonel Obrey raised his eyebrows and looked directly at MacArthur to make sure that was his call. MacArthur did not address the Court or in any manner affirm or deny Mr. Engelson's statement.

"Very well. So noted." He turned to the Trial Counsel. "Colonel Macintyre, are you ready to proceed for the Army?"

"Yes, sir, I am."

"Then proceed, Colonel," waving his arm toward him.

Colonel Obrey relaxed and leaned back in his chair to pay particular attention as Colonel MacIntyre began his plan of attack. Colonel MacIntyre stood by the Trial Counsel Table facing Colonel Obrey with a stack of 3x5 cards and glanced at the first one.

(Both Trial Counsel and Defense Counsel are permitted to sit at their desk, stand by their desk, or use the podium as they choose.)

"Colonel Obrey and Members of this Board of Inquiry, the Army intends to prove that Lieutenant General MacArthur abandoned War Plan Rainbow 5 in favor of a plan he believed was better: he named it: 'War Plan Beach Defense'. As you will see, even the name Beach Defense is indicative of his intention to abandon all parts of Rainbow 5. General MacArthur explained in radiophone conversations and broad language letters why he desired to abandon Rainbow 5 in favor of his new plan.

"We will prove General MacArthur did not include the Army Air Force action of over flying Formosa or to later bomb Japanese airfields and ships in harbors. He kept this out of the dialogs with the War Department and General Marshall because he had no intention of bombing the Japanese forces. He never contemplated an offensive war, only a defensive war."
He paused for a moment, ostensibly to look at his current 3x5 card. In reality, he really wanted Colonel Obrey to consider his last statement.

"When rumors filtered back to the War Department that FEAF would not overfly Formosa for any reason, they radio telephoned MacArthur about the plan. He avoided directly answering the question. On November 27, by message and radiotelephone, the War Department ordered General MacArthur to execute the initial phase of Rainbow 5. He replied that everything was under control and his army was ready, once again avoiding directly answering the question 'Have you executed Rainbow 5 Phase One?'"

The colonel stopped momentarily for a breath, then continued. "The War Department and Chief of Staff had every reason to believe that the famous warrior General Douglas Arthur MacArthur would carry out his orders, especially in wartime." He pointed at MacArthur as he continued. "It never entered their minds in Washington that General MacArthur would avoid the exact truth, dishonoring all that he stood for.

"So," he paused for effect, "we will prove that General MacArthur willfully disobeyed the order of the President, his

Commander-In-Chief, to execute the remainder of an international agreement, Rainbow 5. That order was messaged and again radio telephoned 35 minutes after the Japanese attack began at Pearl Harbor, while the attack will still underway. He did nothing—NOTHING," he voiced, strenuously. Colonel MacIntyre looked around to see what impression that last loud word made.

"Major General Brereton's 19th Heavy Bombardment Group stood ready to take off and bomb military targets on Formosa before an hour had passed in the Japanese air attack. He was ordered by Lieutenant General MacArthur's Chief of Staff, Brigadier General Richard K. Sutherland, to stand down."

Colonel MacIntyre pulled a couple more 3x5 cards up and glanced at their contents. "This sorry state of affairs continued until after the Japanese attacked Baguio. At this point, General MacArthur suggested to General Brereton that he should mount his reconnaissance flight over Formosa. By the time the B17 was ready to roll out of its revment and take off, Japanese fighters began to strafe and bomb Clark Field eliminating fifteen of eighteen B17s and the six P40s still on the ground."

Colonel MacIntyre stood quietly looking Colonel Obrey and glancing at MacArthur. Then, he began anew. "What actually happened on December eighth in the Philippines may never be untangled to everyone's satisfaction. In the heat of battle, when suddenly bombs are bursting and machine gunners shooting at everyone, even soldiers living at peace, are shattered by the immediate need of hiding from unexpected destruction.

"When positions are overrun, the administrative side of war is often lost as papers are scattered about or burned. While we may be short of sworn testimony on paper, we do have several witnesses from the War and Navy Departments and the Philippines who will respond to the ten hour gap question when Douglas MacArthur was Lieutenant General, commanding."

Colonel Macintyre glanced at his top card and turned it face down on his desk.

"Let us examine this officer. Colonel Douglas Arthur MacArthur won the Medal of Honor in France in 1918 for bravery above and beyond in combat. He went on the become the Chief of Staff of the United States Army.

He retired from the Army in 1935, and at the request of Incoming Philippine President Manual Queson, General MacArthur

Field Marshal began serving as Philippine President Manual Queson's Military Advisor in 1935 as Field Marshal.

Please note this did not include command of the U.S. Philippine Department of the Army. His appointment as Field Marshall of the Philippine Army under President Queson, serving a foreign government, was with permission of the War Department.

Records of that period show he continued to draw his Army salary of $7,500 per year and also was paid $33,000 per year by the Philippine government to train, staff and arm the Philippine Army at modern warfare operating levels.

"If, by the end of 1942, the Field Marshall had accomplished his goal, he would receive an additional $250,000 bonus, or nearly $500,000, altogether. In 1937, the Field Marshall determined the combined Philippine / U.S. Army budget was way too low and increased the budget to $105,000 per year. This influenced his bonus, which then increased to $500,000, plus his $231,000 salary for the 7 years."

"Colonel Obrey," interrupted Engleson, seated at his desk, "do we have to air Mr. MacArthur's personal wealth for all to see? I don't see where this is going." Mr. Engelson looked at the Colonel and waited as Colonel MacIntyre listened.

Colonel MacIntyre turned back to Colonel Obrey. "Goes to show that Field Marshall Douglas MacArthur was still at President Queson's beck and call, even though General MacArthur was recalled to active duty July 29, 1941. He continued to draw his salary from the Philippines in addition to his $7,500 General's salary." Colonel MacIntyre was not quite successful in keeping a grin from his face.

Obrey looked at both counsels and nodded. "I'll allow it. Continue, Colonel." Mr. Engelson puckered his lips, blew air, turned completely around dramatically, and sat down.

"Thank you, Colonel. We can prove that President Queson told Field Marshall aka Lieutenant General MacArthur . . . "

"Objection! That is a scurrilous attack on Mr. MacArthur; downright insulting by using 'aka' as though he were a criminal," fumed Engelson.

"Overruled. I want to see where this is going, Mr. Engleson. Continue, Colonel."

"Yes sir, we're just developing the background at the moment.

President Queson told Field Marshall aka Lieutenant General MacArthur that he did not want to make the Japanese military establishment nervous. He, President Queson, in 1941, believed a low profile without military action on the U.S. Army's part would keep the Philippines neutral and out of the war. We will prove—beyond any doubt—that is exactly what General MacArthur decided to do: avoid an offensive operation and ignore Rainbow Five Phase One and Two."

The courtroom was very quiet. This had the makings of a sacrilegious outcome—MacArthur being guilty of the Law of War. Pencils and pens were all that could be heard. Colonel Obrey listened intently as the Trial Judge Advocate began building his case to destroy MacArthur.

Colonel Van der Wendt looked like he would rather be somewhere other than at the Defense table. MacArthur himself was glaring at Colonel MacIntyre, trembling with rage. Mr. Engelson kept reaching out and patting MacArthur's arm and whispering in his ear.

Colonel MacIntyre paused, then stepped to the podium. He tapped his 3x5 cards, glanced at the top one and laid it aside.
"I now move forward to 1939 while Field Marshall MacArthur was still attempting to build the Philippine Army." He cleared his throat and took a sip of iced water. "During that period, he determined there were insufficient Filipinos in the Philippine Army to hold off an enemy and he did not believe there was enough time to train the Filipino soldiers in combat tactics anyway. Field Marshall MacArthur decided that Rainbow Five, that is, the revised War Plan Orange Three, would not work and wrote his own war plan called Beach Dee-fense," drawing out the last word. MacIntyre paused to sip some more water and let his words soak in. He glanced at the gallery and Engleson before continuing.

"Under the Beach Defense war plan, the Quartermaster General, Brigadier General Drake, would pre-position ammo, fuel, food, medicine, and other supplies to specified depots and bunkers near beaches that Japanese forces would use to invade the Philippines." MacIntyre paused here to let Colonel Obrey massage this thought. Then he continued.

"Of course, selecting the beaches was a tactical decision. This required the Quartermaster General to remove tons of already pre-positioned ammo, fuel, food, and medicine from behind the Bataan Peninsula fallback position according to Rainbow 5 plans, to new locations behind the selected beaches. Deliberately, MacArthur did not make the War Department aware of the supply movement from Bataan to Northern Luzon beach areas." Colonel MacIntyre paused to let people absorb that change in tactics. "Let War Plans believe what they want to believe."

"In another move, Field Marshall MacArthur did recommend that President Queson approach the U.S. government and ask that the Filipino Army be disbanded and the better units be attached to the U.S. Army in the Philippines as Scouts. President Manual Queson and U.S. Army Chief of Staff, General George C. Marshall concurring, this change of forces took place.

"On July 29, 1941, in a surprise change of orders, Field Marshall Douglas A. MacArthur was recalled to active duty in the United States Army as Lieutenant General, Commander in Chief, U.S. Army Forces, Far Eastern Area or CinC USAFFE, a new command headquartered in Manila, Philippines, at Fort Santiago. This change absorbed the former U.S. Philippine Department of the Army.

"His new status caused consternation in the Philippine Commonwealth government who expected Field Marshal MacArthur to build Philippine defenses. President Queson was dismayed and had a private discussion with his Field Marshall of the Philippine Army and now Lieutenant General MacArthur of the U.S. Army.

"Whatever the outcome of that discussion, it was never made public and does not appear in any surviving document. Even before Field Marshal MacArthur became Lieutenant General, USA, President Queson was beginning to have doubts about MacArthur." Colonel MacIntyre paused here to let that idea sink in.

"However, Philippine Field Marshal, now U.S. Lieutenant General MacArthur, continued to receive full pay in gold from the Philippine government.

"Because the U.S. Chief of Staff General George C. Marshall had approved his Beach Defense plan sight unseen, General MacArthur did not feel it necessary to provide the War Department with a copy of his war plan. We obtained a complete copy of his Beach Defense War Plan." He looked at his staff and nodded.

Capt. Millington and Staff Sergeant Waters stood and handed bulky packages to Colonel Obrey's Court Clerk and the Court Recorders. While they were so employed, Colonel MacIntyre held up one of the packages and said, "If it please the Board, the Army would like to enter this document as Army's Exhibit 1: Lieutenant General Douglas MacArthur's Beach Defense War Plan."

Mr. Engelson scrambled to his feet as a shocked Colonel Obrey reached for the thick document. He thumbed through it for several minutes, pausing momentarily here and there to study an entry, and finally put it down.

"So ordered, Colonel, Exhibit One."

"Colonel Obrey," complained Mr. Engelson, "this has nothing to do with the charges against my client. These are notes of a commander for his field commanders."

"Mr. Engelson, I believe I know the difference between a fully staffed war plan and a commander's field notes. This document is accepted into the record as MacArthur's Beach Defense War Plan," replied Colonel Obrey, testily.

Colonel MacIntyre was getting angrier as he addressed the Board. He looked at Mr. Engelson who was furiously writing notes as the colonel spoke. Lt. Worthington stood and walked over to MacIntyre and whispered in his ear while handing him a piece of paper. The colonel glanced at the paper and smiled at his fellow counselor.

MacArthur sat still, head tilted back as he looked down his nose at Colonel MacIntyre. He leaned over and spoke in low tones to Mr. Engleson. Colonel Van der Wendt leaned in to listen. Suddenly, both Engleson and Van der Wendt shook their heads vigorously no. MacArthur's voice now became almost understandable and definitely under a strain. Mr. Engleson looked up to Colonel Obrey.

"Colonel, may we have a ten minute recess outside the courtroom, please?"

Colonel Obrey looked at a disturbed Colonel MacArthur for a moment. "This hearing is in recess for fifteen minutes," he ordered.

"All Rise." ordered the Sergeant-At-Arms, motioning to his MP detachment.

As the galleries scrambled to their feet, the Defense Team was joined by the MP's and departed the hearing room.

1130, 23 February 1942
Conference Room #3
Building B-6
Fort Belvoir, Virginia

The rear double doors opened, two MPs led the way back to the Defense Table with Colonel MacArthur, Colonel Van der Wendt, and Mr. Engleson. They settled in their chairs as the MPs marched back to their positions at the rear double doors.

"All Rise."

Everyone arose and quietly waited until Colonel Obrey waited to his dais. "Be seated." Colonel Obrey looked at the Defense Table and addressed Mr. Engleson. "Is your client calmed down and under control now, sir?"

Mr. Engleson leaped to his feet. "Colonel, I apologize for Colonel MacArthur's unseemingly behavior. We are ready to continue, sir."

Colonel Obrey announced, "This hearing is back in session at 1130 hours.

"Colonel MacIntyre, let's get on with it," growled Obrey.

"Yes sir," smiled Colonel MacIntyre.

The Colonel slapped down the next card. "On November 27, 1941, coded urgent war warnings were transmitted to all commands in the Pacific from the Army Chief of Staff, General Marshall, and the Navy Chief of Naval Operations, Admiral Harold Stark, that stated the Empire of Japan was expected to strike somewhere in the Pacific in the very near future. The Philippines was considered a primary target." MacIntyre cleared his throat and looked to his bench.

Capt. Millington got up and handed him a sheet of paper, passing copies to Mr. Engelson, to the Clerk for Col. Obrey, and the Court Reporters.

Col. MacIntyre held up the sheet and said, "Army's Exhibit 2, Colonel Obrey. On November 28, 1941, General George C. Marshall called on the radiotelephone and asked Lieutenant General MacArthur what progress he was making in preparation for war, specifically with Rainbow Five. General MacArthur replied, and I quote,

'**EVERYTHING IS IN READINESS FOR A SUCCESSFUL DEFENSE.**'

Exhibit 2 is a copy of that conversation.

"What is very strange is that FEAF flew a photo-reconnaissance of Garaspi in and around Southern Formosa on November 20, 1941. The B17 pilot also reported seeing more than 100 of the new Mitsubishi twin-engine bombers, we know as

Betty's, lined up on two airfields. General MacArthur did not mention this critical information to General Marshall."

Colonel MacArthur started to stand, shaking his finger at Colonel MacIntyre. Growling, he began to speak before being pulled back down by Engelson and Van der Wendt. MacArthur thumped the table and remonstrated with his counsels. Mr. Engelson's loud whisper 'Shut Up!' was heard throughout the hearing room.

"Mr. Engelson, do we need to clear the hearing room again?" politely asked Colonel Obrey.

Obviously embarrassed by his client's behavior, Mr. Engelson suggested, "Colonel Obrey, I feel my client is very hungry. Might this be a good time to break for lunch? Not only that, Mr. Engelson's palm slapped his table. "This sheet is not proof, Colonel Obrey. It is a photocopy of a handwritten note alleging that General Marshall talked with General MacArthur. I object to this being entered into the record. It is not evidence." Mr. Engelson's head bounced around as he spoke heatedly, glasses flashing in the light of the auditorium.

Colonel Obrey sighed, looked at Mr. Engelson, and said: "I remind you, counselor, this is not a court-martial. This is a hearing to determine whether a court-martial will follow this hearing."

Mr. Englelson sat down, saying, "Thank you, sir."

Colonel Obrey considered the opposing teams for a moment, and wondering if MacArthur was going to be a real problem. But, breaking for lunch might give the defense team an opportunity to determine MacArthur's distress. He sighed. "Gentlemen, this is indeed a good time to break for lunch. This hearing will reconvene at 1400 hours." The colonel got up and headed for the stage door.

"All Rise," yelled the Sergeat-At-Arms. Everyone had started to rise when Obrey got up.

1400, 23 February 1942
Conference Room #3
Building B-6
Fort Belvoir, Virginia

Before time to start, the hearing room was already filled with eager observers of the astounding events unfolding.

"All Rise," the Sergeant-At-Arms commanded.

Everyone stood as Colonel Obrey entered the stage and took his seat. Looking at the assembled people, he called out "Be seated. This hearing is back in session at 1400 hours. Mr. Engleson, are you satisfied your client is prepared to continue.?"

Mr. Engelson stood and looked at Colonels Obrey and MacIntyre. "Yes sir, we are prepared."

Colonel MacIntyre, are you ready to continue?"

Standing at the podium, Colonel MacIntyre responded with a cheshire grin. "Yes, Colonel, we are prepared to continue."

"Then, proceed, Colonel," sweeping his arm with gavel extended.

Colonel MacIntyre pivoted sideways to look at MacArthur. "President Queson visited General MacArthur in his U.S. Army headquarters to ask him to make no moves that would force the Japanese to take action against the Philippine people. He didn't trust the Japanese war lords, a vengeful people."

The Colonel's voice grew ragged. "Lieutenant General Douglas A. MacArthur, the United States Commander-in-Chief of the U.S. Army Forces in the Far East," his voice shook now as he pointed an angry finger at MacArthur, "promised President Manual Queson he would take no action until hostilities commenced in the Philippines. That is, and this is another quotation out of General MacArthur's mouth:

'UNTIL A BOMB FALLS OUT OF A JAPANESE PLANE AND STRIKES PHILIPPINE SOIL'.

"That was a treasonous act against the interests of the United States of America by Lieutenant General Douglas MacArthur while serving in the United States Army in the Philippines, a Commonwealth of the United States."

Voices in the audience rose in shock and anger. The Colonel's gavel dropped twice, then pointed to the audience. "You will be quiet or I will clear the galleries." Voices stilled rapidly.

"You have no proof of that alleged statement," growled Engelson.

The Colonel picked up another sheet of paper. "We ask this be taken in as Army Exhibit 3, Colonel Obrey. This is a certified copy of the quotation as given by Major General Brereton who was present when General MacArthur uttered this to him."

MacArthur began to rise out of his chair, his knuckles rapping the desk for attention. He was pulled down by Mr. Engelson who quietly argued with his client. MacArthur was whispering furiously wanting to say something.

The gavel tapped several times before he got Mr. Engelson's attention. "Control your client, sir, so we may continue," Colonel Obrey said angrily.

"Yes, sir. I apologize for Mr. MacArthur."

Colonel Obrey tapped the gavel head solidly. "Mr. Engelson, MacArthur's title is Colonel, not Mister. I thought we have that clarified earlier."

Mr. Engelson halfway stood and wearily spoke: "I am so sorry, Colonel, yes, Colonel MacArthur. It slipped my mind."

Without comment, Obrey stared at Mr. Engelson for a moment, then waved his gavel at Colonel MacIntyre to continue. Colonel Obrey drank some cool water.

"On December 3, 1941 Manila time, the Army Chief of Staff, the Chief of Naval Operations concurring, wired General MacArthur and Admiral Hart, copy to General Brereton to execute Phase One Rainbow Five." Colonel MacIntyre looked at Colonel MacArthur and raised his arm to point at him. "Lieutenant General MacArthur was supposed to immediately sign the order for Major General Brereton to officially send an Army Air Force Boeing B-17D Flying Fortress to scout and photograph the Imperial Japanese Navy in their anchorages and Imperial Japanese Air Forces on their Formosan airbases.

"When he received the message to execute Rainbow Five Phase One, Major General Brereton moved seventeen B-17's to Del Monte Field on Mindanao out of range of Japanese aircraft. Preparing one B-17D for reconnaissance, he asked General MacArthur to sign the order to let the reconnaissance mission take off. General MacArthur refused to allow General Brereton's reconnaissance flight to take off in accordance with Phase One. And, in response to General Brereton's dispersal order, General MacArthur ordered all B-17's returned to Clark and grounded them there.

"Lieutenant General MacArthur refused to talk to Major General Brereton on the telephone or see him personally, nor would he countermand his order." He turned to his table and Capt. Millington handed him the next exhibit. "I now have in my hand a certified copy of a message received at CNO communications center moments after the Phase One Executive Order was transmitted to General MacArthur and Admiral Hart. I ask that it be entered as Army Exhibit 4."

Mr. Engelson glared at the colonel but made no motion to quash the exhibit.

"So ordered," responded Colonel Obrey.

"Meanwhile, also on December 3, 1941, in accordance with Rainbow Five, Admiral Hart sortied the Asiatic Fleet to the Dutch East Indies preparing to join with the combined fleet (ABDA) under a Dutch admiral.

Admiral Hart acknowledged the Phase One order and notified CNO his fleet was proceeding in accordance with the plan of leaving Manila Bay. He couriered a copy of that message to General MacArthur's headquarters and forwarded a copy of his Phase One Execution order to MacArthur's headquarters to make sure the Army headquarters had received the message of execution.

"General MacArthur was furious with Admiral Hart and the Navy in general for leaving him alone in the Philippines." The colonel paused for a sip of water. "Despite his uncomplimentary language toward Admiral Hart and the Navy, this was all in the Rainbow Five plan and the former Orange Three plan. The Navy's position was that the Philippines Isles were indefensible and the Navy did not intend to get caught at the Cavite Naval Base or in those anchorages."

"I remind the Court that upon commencement of hostilities in the Pacific, Phase Two of Rainbow Five would be executed. That is, eighteen B-17s of the Nineteenth Bombardment Group would be loaded with bombs and sent to Formosa to bomb Japanese ships and airfields based on reconnaissance information that should have been obtained on the overflight of Formosa on December 3, 1941."

"So noted, Colonel. Continue your opening statement."

Mr. Engelson jumped to his feet. "Colonel Obrey, this is not an opening statement, it is a series of accusations that . . ."

"Not true, Mr. Engelson. It . . ."

Mr. Engelson raised both arms at his side and brought them down violently and spoke angrily. "Mr. President, this is a kangaroo court . . ."

BANG went the gavel again.

"Mr. Engelson, control yourself and apologize to this board immediately or suffer the consequences." Colonel Obrey was barely containing himself as he rose half way and glared down at the Defense Counsel. "This is a Board of Inquiry, not a civilian court where they may be entertained by your hysteria."

Mr. Engelson swallowed, realizing he may have gone too far. "Sir, all I am trying to do is protect the interest of my client. So far, I have not heard an opening speech. It has been a series of unverified charges and responses without my being able to intervene and cross examine."

"Mr. Engelson, was that an obtuse apology to the court or a further insult on the integrity of this hearing?" He asked, sweetly. Engelson, realizing he was treading on very thin ice, hastily back peddled and bowed slightly from the waist. "Colonel, I offer my abject apologies to you. I am just concerned that my client receives a fair hearing."

"Oh, trust me, sir. Colonel MacArthur is receiving as fair a hearing as is possible under the circumstances." Engelson shrugged, turned to look at the rest of the courtroom and visitors, and sat down, apparently satisfied with the last remark.

Obrey glanced at the visitors and tapped his gavel, glaring at the visitors, quashing the whispering with a severe frown. He pointed his gavel at Colonel MacIntyre. "Continue, Colonel."

"Yes sir." Colonel MacIntyre pulled another card from the stack, glanced at it, and laid it aside.

"The time line becomes critical now. I will refer once to Hawaiian time and Washington time, compare those with Manila time, and thereafter, refer to events according to the Manila clock. Crossing the International Date Line creates a little confusion. December 7, 1941 in Hawaii at the initiation of the Japanese air attack is 0755 hours. In Washington, D.C., the time is December 7, 1455 hours. In Manila, the time is December 8, 0225 hours."

The colonel walked around the space and came back to his desk. "About 0227, Admiral Hart's Communications Center woke and notified the admiral they had just intercepted the following plain language message from Naval Air Station Ford Island, Pearl Harbor, Hawaii:

AIR RAID ON PEARL HARBOR THIS IS NOT DRILL

The Admiral instructed his communications officer to phone that message to MacArthur's headquarters and follow it up with a message along with the following message to his Asiatic Fleet, already scattering from the naval base at Cavite, near Manila:

JAPAN STARTED HOSTILITIES STOP GOVERN YOURSELVES ACCORDINGLY

He followed that with an amplifying message a few minutes later:

JAP AIR RAID ON PEARL HARBOR IN PROGRESS STOP A STATE OF WAR NOW EXISTS BETWEEN THE UNITED STATES OF AMERICA AND THE JAPANESE EMPIRE STOP EXECUTE UNRESTRICTED SUBMARINE WARFARE AGAINST ALL JAPANESE NAVY AND CIVIL MARITIME TARGETS

 I emphasize these messages were sent to MacArthur's headquarters as well as Hart's fleet."
Lt. Worthington handed him another sheet.
"This is a certified copy of both of those messages as received at CNO communications center, a few minutes after 0300. I ask that it be entered as Army Exhibit 5."
"So ordered."

"At 0400 hours, the Chief Of Staff messaged Generals MacArthur and Brereton to execute Phase Two. Brereton transmitted a message to MacArthur's headquarters, copying the War Department, stating that all units are ready for action, targets identified." He held up another sheet. Army Exhibit 6, a certified copy of that message originated from Army Headquarters on this fort."
"So ordered, Colonel," said Colonel Obrey, glancing at the Defense table.

"At 0430 hours Brigadier General Leonard T. Gerow, Deputy Chief of Staff for War Plans under General Marshall, called General MacArthur on the radio telephone and gave him verbal orders issued by General Marshall, the Chief of Staff, to CARRY OUT TASKS ASSIGNED RAINBOW FIVE. MacArthur assured General Gerow that his forces were on full alert and ready for action." Another sheet of paper waved in the air. "Army Exhibit 7, Colonel."

MacArthur's Pacific Appeasement, December 8, 1941
Part II
U.S. Army Article 70 Board of Inquiry

"At 0500 hours, General Brereton arrived at MacArthur's headquarters for permission to fly 18 B-17s on a bombing mission to Formosa. Brereton had already messaged and called MacArthur without having received Phase 2 orders or acknowledgement, to report his bombardment group was armed and ready to sortie to Formosa. MacArthur ignored him, refused to see him.

"At 0530 hours, MacArthur is again ordered by the War Department to put Rainbow Five into operation, carrying out tasks assigned in Rainbow Five. Additionally, MacArthur was directed to cooperate with the British and the Dutch to the utmost without jeopardizing the accomplishment of the primary mission to defend the Philippines. Army Exhibit 8, Mr. President."
"So ordered."

"Much later, when Major General Brereton again asked for an audience with General MacArthur, the Chief of Staff, Brigadier General Richard K. Sutherland, repeated Lieutenant General MacArthur's statement, to wit: 'the Philippines is not at war with Japan. There are no hostilities here and we will not take action until the first bomb is released from a Japanese plane and strikes Philippine soil'."

"At 0817 hours, the Japanese Air Force bombed Camp John Hays Hospital at Baguio. Still no action by General MacArthur after Japanese bombers have attacked and bombed Philippine soil."

"About 1130 hours, the new SCR-270B secret radar station at Iba Field reported a large number of aircraft over the China Sea heading in the direction of Manila."

"About 1200 hours, General MacArthur called General Brereton and told him to send his reconnaissance plane to Formosa. By the time the aircrew could be briefed, it was too late.

"At 1235 hours, the Japanese Air Force bombed Clark Field and Fort Stotsenberg. That is, more than ten hours after the attack at Pearl Harbor had commenced, the Japanese Air Force attacked Clark Field destroying most of the B-17s and fighter planes." Colonel Macintyre paused at this point to drink a sip of iced water to cool his dry throat. He sorted through his 3 by 5 cards to find his place again.

"To that point, Lieutenant General Douglas A. MacArthur had taken no action to defend the American Army, the military aircraft, and the Navy ships and bases they were supposed to support. He was still bound by his promise to Philippine President Queson . . ."

"Hearsay hearsay" Mr. Engelson bounded out of his chair and strode so close to Colonel MacIntyre that MacIntyre could smell bacon on his breath. "I object. There is no evidence to support that statement, Colonel."

Colonel MacIntyre turned to Obrey. "There is direct evidence linking Colonel MacArthur to the Philippine government. There is no evidence that Lieutenant General MacArthur ever severed or renounced his relationship with the Philippine government. This is malfeasance at its worse. It doesn't take an accountant to add up all the lives lost because he refused to take action—thousands of lives . . ."

"I object to this scurrilous attack on Mr. MacArthur." Mr. Engelson slammed his open palm down on his desk and practically hopped up and down.

Colonel Obrey looked at the Defense Counsel. "Mr. Engelson, his title is Colonel."

"Uh, sorry, sir. Won't happen again."

Colonel MacIntyre was breathing heavily and his chin jutted out as he leaned toward the Defense table. "You can object all you want, Engelson, but those are the facts and if I had my way, that son of a bitch . . ."

SLAM!

Colonel Obrey's shocked and angry voice boomed out at the Colonel. "You forget yourself, sir. This is a board of inquiry, not two cowboys at a shootout. Colonel, you will conduct yourself as an officer and gentleman."

Colonel MacIntyre continued breathing heavily and glared at Mr. Engelson. Bowing his head, he seemed to have himself under control in a moment. "Mr. Engelson, I apologize for my loud and rude voice. You did not deserve that." He abruptly sat down. Mr. Engelson nodded in amusement. Colonel MacArthur looked rather frostily at the Colonel.

SLAM!

"This court is in recess until tomorrow morning at 0930 hours. I will see all officers of this hearing in my office forthwith."

Colonel Obrey waited until Defense Counsel, and Recorders had crowded into his office. "Sergeant-at-Arms," he snarled with anger. "You place an MP at each end of this corridor and let no one enter. You stand outside this closed door. I don't care if it is the Chief of Staff himself, no one enters. Are your orders clear?"

The Sergeant-at-Arms, stiff-faced, standing at attention, saluted. "Yes sir, Colonel, my orders are perfectly clear. Absolutely no one enters this room." He pivoted, closed the door behind him and carried out his orders.

Colonel Obrey turned, his face red with anger, trunk thrust toward Colonel MacIntyre, in a soft, deadly voice said, "Colonel MacIntyre, before I hang your ass out to dry for that insult to Colonel MacArthur and his mother, I will give you one chance to explain your verbal insult." He waved his arm at the colonel, folded his arms on his chest, and glared at MacIntyre, his eyes burning holes in MacIntyre's face.

Colonel MacIntyre, livid with anger himself, said in a quivering voice filled with emotion, "Sir, I may be a private in the stockade in a few minutes but you gave me a chance to explain myself and I will." He wiped his mouth and glowered at everyone. "MacArthur is personally responsible for the death of thousands of our soldiers and sailors, Colonel." . . . .
Obrey opened his mouth to speak . . .

"No, goddammit, don't interrupt me, you gave me my say and I will say it! I tried to enlist a charge of murder. But how do you do that?" he said looking around. "He caused thousands of deaths SO FAR because he refused to stop the Japanese in Formosa. This is not conjecture. This is fact. What is the unknown factor is why that son of a bitch—YES—why that bastard did nothing for more than ten hours. Now, I could try him for the murder of one soldier and when found guilty, go on with the next and the next. Several years from now, the courts-martial would finally end. HE should be in the stockade for the rest of his life.

"Instead, we have to try him for treason and malfeasance, and if we get the information from Australia in time, bribery also." He exploded with a short burst of laughter.
"John Engleson hasn't a chance in hell of saving his sorry ass. I have all the proof I need for each charge and specification.
"Colonel, my job as prosecutor is try find him guilty AND, – I – WILL – PROVE – EVERY — CHARGE." Breathing heavily, he slumped against the wall and waited, head down.

Colonel Obrey looked at the opposite wall for a few seconds, around at the civilian attorney Engelson, and MacIntyre who had put his career on the line. He took a deep breath and let it out. "Colonel MacIntyre, do you have this out of your system now?" he asked softly.

"Yes sir, I do."

Then crisply, "good. I shouldn't have to say this, Colonel, but just to remind you, it is my job to listen to both sides of the equation so that I come to the correct decision in the case of Colonel Douglas A. MacArthur vs. the United States Army." He paused to let that sink in.

"As you said, your job is to prosecute to the best of your ability and facts available to you, not persecute. Do you think you can do that without further outbursts like we just heard, in court and in here?"

"Yes sir, I can."

"Good. When we reconvene, you WILL apologize to Colonel MacArthur for your unseeming outburst and insult. Do you understand that?"

"Yes sir, apologize to him."

"Colonel?" He said, his voice drawn out and rising.

"Sorry sir, yes sir, apologize to the accused, Colonel Douglas MacArthur."

"Better," Obrey nodded, "better." He looked around at the gathered. "This is a matter of record now. Let's adjourn. We reconvene at 0930 hours tomorrow."

"Atten hut!" Everyone snapped to attention. Colonel Obrey strode out, nodding at the Sergeant-at-Arms, "it is over."

CHAPTER THIRTEEN

0930, 24 February 1942
Conference Room #3
Building B-6
Fort Belvoir, Virginia

The Sergeant-At-Arms sucked in his breath. "All Rise." Everyone stood and waited while Colonel strode across the stage to his dais and picked up his gavel.

The gavel tapped twice and the courtroom quieted rapidly. "This Board of Inquiry is back in session at 0930 hours, 24 February 1942. Let the record show all members of this hearing and the accused are present. Colonel MacIntyre, are you ready to continue?"

Colonel MacIntyre faced Colonel Obrey and came to rigid attention. "Colonel, may I address this court?"

Colonel Obrey nodded and said, "very well."

Colonel MacIntyre about-faced, looked at Colonel MacArthur, and spoke. "Colonel MacArthur, I spoke intemperately yesterday, and shamefully involved your mother. I abjectly apologize for my remarks and pray that you accept my apology." He about-faced again, saluted Colonel Obrey, and returned to his seat.
Colonel MacArthur stared at him, frostily without uttering a sound.

After a moment, Colonel Obrey scratched his nose, gave MacArthur another second to respond and looked at Colonel MacIntyre. "Colonel MacIntyre, your comments are noted for the record. Are you ready to continue?"

Colonel Macintyre rose fiddling with his black tie. "Yes, Colonel. The Army calls Major General Lewis H. Brereton."
On Colonel Obrey's nod, the Army Sergeant-at-Arms disappeared through the rear double doors. Three minutes later, he returned with General Brereton who approached the witness chair.

Colonel MacIntyre stood and brought the bible to the witness, then raised his right hand. "General Brereton, place your left hand on the bible, raise your right hand,

"You swear or affirm that the evidence you shall give in the case now in hearing shall be the truth, the whole truth, and nothing but the truth, so help you God?"

"I so swear, Colonel."

"Be seated, general." General Brereton settled in the chair and leaned back, completely relaxed.

"State your name, rank, and organization for the record, sir," said Colonel MacIntyre who returned the bible to the table.

"I am Lewis Hyde Brereton, Major General, U.S. Army Air Force, formerly commanding general of the Far East Air Force, headquartered at Nielsen Field, Luzon, Philippines. My current assignment is detached, witness at this hearing."

"And you are aware of the purpose of this Article 70 hearing?" asked Colonel MacIntyre.

General Brereton nodded and responded affirmatively.

"When were you assigned duty as Commanding General, Far East Army Air Force, sir?"

"November 3, 1941. The War Department had determined the Philippines air defense posture was weak. General MacArthur wanted to beef up the air power. MacArthur personally asked for me to head his Air Force.

"Two, possibly three groups of heavy and medium bombers were to be positioned around the Philippine Archipelago, to be protected by a group of pursuit planes. Antiquated Seversky or Republic P-35A Guardsman and Boeing P-26 Peashooter already on the ground would be or had been turned over to the Philippine Army Air Corps. Curtis P-40B and P-40D Warhawk pursuit planes had arrived in January 1941. Boeing B-17C and D Flying Fortress heavy bombers had already arrived and more were expected. Douglas B-18 Bolo light bombers were scattered around the islands. The War Department was concerned about the Japanese buildup and wanted to counter their moves." He paused, flashing a look at the reporters. "Uh, there were other aircraft on the way."

Colonel Obrey leaned forward. "General, everyone has been sworn to secrecy. You may discuss your assets, freely."

"Oh. Thank you, sir. We were expecting a squadron of long range Consolidated B-24 Liberators for high altitude bombardment and medium range Douglas A-20A Invaders for low-level attack and ground support, but probably not until 1942."

"General, as of November 27, 1941, what were your assets in hand?"

"I had 39 Boeing B-17C/D and 2 B-17E heavy bombers and 30 obsolete P-35A's. The mix of 140 B and E model P-40's were not equipped with disposable belly tanks, so would not be able to escort the B-17's to Japan and back. There were 18 B-18 light bombers, too. Those Bolos were no longer used in combat bomber configuration. They were used as multi-engine pilot training, cargo, and passenger service. Most were located at Clark Field. Some were flown to different outlying fields, as far away as Del Monte, Mindanao, for pilot familiarization." He stopped and sipped some ice water, then continued.

"Only two fields, Clark and Del Monte were long enough to handle fully bomb-laden B-17s and the B-24s when they arrived. Most of the fields from Aparri without any facilities in the north where the B-24s were to be based, to Davao in the south on Mindanao were substandard alternative dirt fields with some facilities. They were somewhat dangerous in that, as aircraft arrived or departed, they made huge dust clouds. Really only emergency fields. That is, no fueling, living quarters, messing facilities, workshops or hangers. These fields would be upgraded to fighter and pursuit strips as time and funding permitted. Iba—now Iba was a good fighter field and was the location of our only fixed radar, the secret SCR-270B.

General Brereton ticked off the items as he mentioned them. "Ground support consisted of fuel bunkers and fueling trucks. Ammo dumps for several kinds of aerial bombs and machine gun ammunition. That's another thing: we were so short of .50 caliber machine gun ammunition that most of the guns in the combat ships had never been fired. There were aircraft machine shops only at Clark Field in case of problems."

Brereton reached over, filled his tumbler with iced water, and took a long drink.

"This is besides the standard supply dump of any camp. But also note I did not have enough air crews to man the bombers. There were too few in the entire United States Army Air Force. Better than half the B-17 pilots were just ferry pilots that returned to the States." He snorted. "That meant half our B-17's were spare parts, so to speak." He chuckled and said, "That's truer than you think. There were NO spare parts of any kind nor tools to handle the parts."

"A battalion of Coast Artillery soldiers manned a few .30 caliber and .50 caliber machine guns and 3-inch anti-aircraft guns around each field, plus M3 Stuart light tanks and half-tracks. This is in addition to the usual cooks, bakers, administrative personnel and aircraft mechanics who worked on all the aircraft."

He looked at the ceiling for a moment, and then continued. "The Navy had some assets, too, of course, over by Subic Bay. I don't know the numbers but there were Grumman F3F-2 pursuit jobs and a number of Brewster F2A-3 Buffalo pursuit planes. They were scattered around various Navy facilities. Oh yes, a number of Consolidated PBY-4 and PBY-5A Catalina patrol planes, 15 of them I recall, mostly down south. I don't know their status.

"Thank you, General. I take you now to Rainbow 5. Relate to the court your command's function in Rainbow 5."
General Brereton, shifted around in his chair, glared at Colonel MacArthur, sipped more water, and leaned back. "Admiral Hart's Asiatic Fleet and my 19th Bombardment Group bore the brunt of that war plan. All my heavy bomber crews were drilled on Rainbow 5 until they knew it by heart."

"Phase One was the high altitude photo reconnaissance of Formosa military and naval facilities. Phase Two was the saturation bombardment of Japanese airfields, aircraft and associated facilities, and in the seaports, heavy bombardment of all shipping, docks, and supplies. If we had any aircraft left, Army bases would also be bombed."
"Any aircraft left, General?"

"The Japs wouldn't take our bombardment lightly, Colonel; their fighters would be buzzing us like angry bees. But we knew that. Those B-17Ds are called Flying Fortresses for a reason. We would take down a lot of their fighters. Our task was to take out as much of the Imperial Japanese war machine as possible and return to base—if possible."
"I see. Now, General, let's move to December 3, 1941. Did you receive any special communiqué from the War Department that day?"
"Objection. Leading the witness."
"Withdrawn. What happened on December 3, 1941?"

"Well," he paused looking at the far wall, "on November 28, we received another War Warning from the War Department. This message was transferred to my GHQ communications center from Admiral Hart's Navy communications center. On December 3, I received a Priority message from the War Department to execute Rainbow 5 Phase One.

MacArthur's Pacific Appeasement, December 8, 1941
Part II
U.S. Army Article 70 Board of Inquiry

"I placed FEAF on alert, manning anti-aircraft guns and distributed all aircraft to my various fields. One Flying Fortress had been prepared, already been stripped of non-essential weight, fully fueled with a full load of ammo for all of the machine guns. Cameras were installed. The ship was waxed and buffed to get an extra bit of speed out of her. All we had to do was load the cameras with film and get the crew on board. This film would provide us with the latest information on the Japanese bases."

"Just a moment, General. You said latest information. Do I understand you to mean there was earlier information?"

General Brereton chuckled sheepishly. "Yes Colonel. I had a photoreconnaissance flight over Southern Formosa on November 20, 1941, as a dry run. That was to establish our necessary flight routes in and out." He pointed his finger to Colonel Obrey and shook it. "As a matter of fact, the Navy PBYs regularly cruised around Formosa watching the Jap's buildup.

"General, who all knew about this flight of FEAF?"

"It was a sneak flight. My staff, the flight crew, and the photo analysts, of course knew. Oh yes, General Sutherland, MacArthur's Chief of Staff, was kept in the loop, too. We kept it very quiet. Also, to our best knowledge, the Japs never saw us. At least, they did not climb to our altitude to check us out."

"Us?"

"Yes, Colonel. I was Plane Commander on the flight. We saw a lot of medium bombers that turned out to be Bettys on two airfields. The photo analysis people counted more than 100 Bettys on the film we took. The harbors didn't have too many ships there."

"Did you report this flight to General MacArthur?"

"No sir, I did not. He would be obliged to report this as an international incident if he knew about the flight," explained General Brereton. He took a drink of water and looked up at Colonel Obrey. "The main thing was, Colonel, this allowed us to develop flight routes to and from the various target areas. The Phase One flight would pin the new information on our table."

Brereton snapped his fingers. "I forgot to mention: we kept General Arnold and his staff in the loop. His Air Staff knew about the flight. They, that is, the Air Staff, was preparing large charts for us indicating where all the towns and villages are located on Formosa."

"I see." Colonel MacIntyre glanced around the courtroom to see how this played. MacArthur looked stunned.

"Anyway, Colonel, I reported by message to my superior, Lieutenant General MacArthur, we were ready to execute Phase One and requested permission to execute. I got no answer. At 0430 hours, I flew my L1 light aircraft to General MacArthur's headquarters to find out what was the delay. Not in his GHQ, I was driven over to his quarters. General Sutherland would not permit me to see General MacArthur."

"Why did General Sutherland deny you access to General MacArthur?"

"He said General MacArthur did not want . . ."

"Objection. Hearsay. He's putting words into General Sutherland's and General MacArthur's mouths."

"Colonel, we will have full corroboration with our next witness. Let him deny or affirm this event." Colonel Macintyre said.

"I'll allow it, Mr. Engelson, but Colonel, if your next witness cannot produce the evidence, this line of questioning will be removed."

"Thank you, sir."

"General Brereton, you say you did not have an audience with General MacArthur, is that correct?" probed Colonel MacIntyre.

"Yes."

"Did General Sutherland give any reason for this?"

"Sutherland said it was a suicide mission and no one would return. I tried to point out our mission was to stop the Japanese from attacking the Philippines. We expected some of our bombers would not return. But it was not a suicide mission anymore than soldiers under an artillery attack or charging through machine gun fire. I ordered General Sutherland to stand aside. I was going to see General MacArthur."

"What stopped you?"

"General Sutherland physically blocked my passage at the door into General MacArthur's private office in his quarters."

"I see. Did General Sutherland give you any reason for this behavior?"

"Yes, he said that 'The General had sent you his orders and he will not change them.'"

"Did General Sutherland give you any indication why General MacArthur had taken this stance?"

"Yes. General Sutherland told me that there is to be no hostile action until the first bomb from a Japanese plane falls on Philippine soil."

"That's it?"

"That's all. I went back to my headquarters and made sure all my aircraft were widely scattered. I knew that Japs were coming and wanted . . .

"Objection. Conjecture on the part of witness, facts not in evidence. He could not know that."

"Sustained. Rephrase, Counselor."

Colonel Macintyre returned to his table for more 3x5 cards and a drink of ice water. He turned back to General Brereton.

"After that refusal, what did you do?"

"I got back in my L1 and flew to Clark."

"Did you take any further action?"

"Yes, as I stated, I had all my aircraft scattered over the entire country."

"And why did you do that, General?"

General Brereton looked at the defense table. "If,—I said if, Mr. Engelson."

"Witness will not badger Counsel," asserted Colonel Obrey.

"Yes sir. If the Japanese were to attack, I wanted as much of my command to survive as possible."

"General Brereton, at any time during that struggle to execute your orders, did you see General MacArthur in the background or at a distance?"

"No."

"General, later, did you ever hear his voice while you were at his quarters?"

"No."

"Later, at his headquarters, did you see or hear General MacArthur?"

"No."

"Usually when the commanding general is present the demeanor of those soldiers around him appears busier than when he is not." General Brereton nodded agreement with a thin smile.

"Witness nodded in the affirmative. Were the personnel acting like General MacArthur was present?"

"Ah, I didn't pay that close attention, Colonel. I had other things on my mind."

"Did it occur to you that General MacArthur might not be in his headquarters, that General Sutherland knew he was somewhere else and didn't want others to know that? That is, he was protecting him?"

Mr. Engelson jumped out of his chair so hard it fell over backward. "Objection. Counselor is attempting to discredit General

MacArthur with a scurrilous attack on his honor and professionalism."

"Withdrawn. What happened next, General Brereton?"

"A courier delivered a written order signed by General MacArthur to recall all my aircraft to Clark Field. Further, I was to line them up in the center of the runway, wingtip to wingtip."

"General, was the order actually signed by MacArthur?"

"Yes, I recognized his signature."

"What happened next?"

"I called General MacArthur on the telephone to rescind his order. General Sutherland told me that MacArthur said President Queson did not want to present a hostile front if the Japanese came here. He wanted no war on his country's soil.

"Did you talk with MacArthur this time?"

"No, Sutherland said MacArthur was in conference, not to be disturbed, and told me to obey my orders."

"Then what?"

"I sent a message to the Air Department for General Arnold explaining what was going on. It was going over my superior's head but in my professional opinion, his action was a prelude to disaster."

"And?"

"About 0530 hours Manila time, the War Department radioed MacArthur specifically ordering him to carry out tasks assigned Rainbow 5. Additionally, it directed him to cooperate with the British and Dutch to the utmost without jeopardizing the accomplishment of his primary mission of defense of the Philippines. I ordered all my group commanders at Clark for briefing."

"Is there anything else you can add, General Brereton?"

"Yes, around 1200 hours, General MacArthur personally called me on the phone and ordered the reconnaissance aircraft readied for the mission but not to take off. Before we could get the other aircraft rolled off the runway, it was too late."

"Why was it too late to fly the mission, General?"

"Well, about 1235 hours Manila time, the Japs raided Clark and Iba Fields and wiped us out. After that, I wired the War Department preferring charges of treason against MacArthur."

"Were there repercussions because of the latter action, General?"

"Not directly, Colonel. I flew to Fort Santiago to let MacArthur know what I thought of him and to kick his ass. I did call him a traitor. Sutherland and Huff dragged me out of his office and shoved me out the door. So, I suppose there were repercussions.

"You suppose so?" asked Colonel MacIntyre with a big smile.

"Well, my command was disbanded. Then, a couple of days after the initial Jap landings at Aparri and Vigan, MacArthur called me into his office and explained my flight and ground troops were transferred to the Infantry because we had no aircraft to fight the Japs; and that the remaining B-17's at Del Monte Air Field and flight crews were to fly to Australia, leaving behind up to 4 aircraft." Almost all of the P-40s were destroyed on the ground or shot down by the Jap's new Mitsubishi fighter plane.

"I have no further questions, Mr. President. Your witness, Mr. Engelson." Colonel MacIntyre sat down with a trace of a smile as he scanned the audience who were studying him as well as Generals Brereton and MacArthur.

The gavel came down. "We'll break for the noon meal now reconvening at 1330 hours."

CHAPTER FOURTEEN

1330, 24 February 1942
Conference Room #3
Building B-6
Fort Belvoir, Virginia

Promptly at 1330 hours, the side door opened.

"All rise."

Colonel Obrey strode across the stage and took his seat.

"Be seated. This hearing is back in session at 1330 hours." He looked down at the general who was looking back at him. "General Brereton, you are still sworn."

"Yes sir."

Colonel Obrey looked at Mr. Engelson. "Mr. Engelson, you may cross examine."

"Thank you, sir." He studied General Brereton for a moment, more for the affect than thoughts of how to proceed. "Colonel Obrey, I request General Brereton be declared a hostile witness and that I have leeway in questioning him."

Colonel Obrey nodded and looked down at General Brereton. "General, you are instructed to answer all Mr. Engleson's questions truthfully and to the best of your knowledge and ability."

General Brereton's glasses flashed as he looked back up at Colonel Obrey again. "Yes sir, I will," he vowed.

General Brereton turned around and watched Mr. Engleson like a cat in a tree watches a barking dog below.

"General, what was your relationship with General MacArthur, your superior officer?"

"He was my commanding officer, sir, not superior officer!"

"I see. Did you play tennis with him?"

"No," he answered.

"Did he invite you to his quarters for dinner and drinks?" He rolled his hands, twirling his fingers. "That kind of relationship is what I mean."

Brereton nodded, his face showing—perhaps distaste. "General MacArthur was not one to socialize within the Army. He did socialize with senior government officials, people at the Country

Club, and the press. Otherwise, he was aloof. He kept his family here after ordering all other Army families back to the States. To my meager knowledge, he never played sports with anyone."

"I see. Would you agree he is a professional soldier?"

"Not any more!"

"Let the record show the witness meant no."

General Brereton sat up ramrod straight in his chair. "Sir, I said he is no longer a professional soldier."

Mr. Engelson turned to Colonel Obrey. "Sir, will you instruct the witness to answer in the affirmative or negative without editorializing?"

Colonel Obrey cleared his throat and put his hand up to his mouth to hide a smile. "General, your remarks are out of order. Please answer counsel's questions with yes or no unless he asks for amplifying information." However, Colonel Obrey did not strike that remark.

"Yes, sir, I will," answered General Brereton.

"Did you have much contact with him officially? By that, I mean conferences, dress parades, the sorts of things army commands do from day to day?"

General Brereton stared at MacArthur briefly and hunched over, elbows on knees, hands held together loosely.

"Let me put it this way. Several members of President Queson's inner staff and Queson himself attended my arrival on the China Clipper, November 3, 1941. Neither MacArthur nor Sutherland attended. My air command put on an aerial show as the Clipper was arriving. I saw him once before the December 8th debacle."

"Move to strike that last characterization, Colonel Obrey." demanded Mr. Engelson.

"So ordered. Recorders will ignore that remark. General Brereton, I remind you not to allow your personal feelings enter into your testimony."

"Yes sir, sorry," as he attempted to hide a grin with his hand.

Mr. Engelson sat down for a moment looking at his notes. Then stood again and addressed the court. "Colonel, we move to strike General Brereton's entire testimony, colored throughout by personal animosity toward my client. He obviously wants to hurt Colonel MacArthur." General Brereton nodded agreement with a tight smile.

Colonel MacIntyre stayed in his chair as he watched Obrey ponder the question. Not seeing an outright denial, he stood up and attracted his attention.

"Colonel Obrey, may I remind you that General Brereton is not only the Army's witness but he is the officer who preferred the charge of treason against the accused. He is understandably angry that his entire command was wiped out because of General MacArthur's lack of action, which caused undue death and destruction by the Japanese air armada." He looked at General MacArthur for a moment, and continued softly. "We have not heard yet from the Japanese since General King surrendered the Bataan force."

"Objection," bellowed Mr. Engelson. "He is introducing facts not in evidence and attempting to influence your decision by this attack."

Colonel Obrey said: "Motion to strike denied. However," looking down at the Reporters, "strike his last sentence from the record. Colonel, do not try that again."

"Sorry, sir." He looked properly chastised and Obrey looked at him suspiciously for a moment before looking toward Mr. Engelson. "Do you wish to continue, Mr. Engelson?"

"No further questions for this person, Colonel." He waved his arm at General Brereton in disgust.

Colonel Obrey struggled to keep a smile from his face, sucking in his cheeks in the process. He looked at General Brereton. "You may step down, General."

General Brereton eased out of the witness chair and strode from the courtroom, glaring at MacArthur as he passed.

"Call your next witness, Colonel."

"The Army calls Brigadier General Sutherland." Colonel Obrey pointed his gavel at the Sergeant-at-Arms who marched out.

Colonel MacIntyre sat down and checked his 3x5 cards for the next series of questions. The door opened and General Sutherland strode down the aisle, hesitating next to MacArthur just for a second to nod his head before continuing to the witness chair.

Colonel MacIntyre stood and brought the bible to the witness, and raised his right hand. "General Sutherland, place your left hand on the bible and raise your right hand:

"You swear or affirm that the evidence you shall give in the case now in hearing shall be the truth, the whole truth, and nothing but the truth, so help you God?"

"I so swear, Colonel."

"Be seated, General," returning the bible to its place on the table and sat down. General Sutherland sat in the chair carefully arranging the crease in his trousers and the drape of his coat.

Colonel MacIntyre stood. "For the record General, will you state your name, rank and assignment?"

"Yes Colonel, I am Richard Kerens Sutherland, Brigadier General, Infantry, seconded to Lieutenant General Douglas A. MacArthur's command as Chief of Staff," smiling reassuringly to Colonel MacArthur who nodded back. "I am currently waiting reassignment."

The non-verbal exchange between MacArthur and Sutherland did not escape MacIntyre's eyes. He turned to the Colonel Obrey. "Colonel Obrey, General Sutherland was and is very close to Colonel MacArthur. I request he be declared a hostile witness and that I have leeway in questioning him."

Obrey too had observed the exchange between General Sutherland and Colonel MacArthur. "I'll allow that. General Sutherland, you are directed to answer all questions submitted by Colonel MacIntyre." Sutherland responded crisply. "Certainly, Colonel."

Colonel MacIntyre checked his 3x5 cards again and looked at General Sutherland. "General, when the Japanese began their attack on Pearl Harbor at 0225 hours December 8, where were you?"

"I was in my quarters asleep."

"For the record, General: where were your quarters?"

"I lived in a hotel about ten minutes away by car from General MacArthur's residence in the Manila Hotel Penthouse, Colonel."

"When did you learn of the attack, General?"

"Ohhh, it was about two hours later when the headquarters command duty officer called to say some of the men were listening to a San Francisco radio station announcing that Pearl Harbor had been bombed by the Japanese."

And what time was that, General Sutherland?"

"About two hours after the attack began, Colonel." His voice suggested annoyance and dissatisfaction of being questioned by a lower ranking officer.

"General, most people when confronted with such an astounding report would certainly have remembered the time more accurately. Will you be more specific?"

"Oh, I don't remember exactly, just about two hours, Colonel."

"Let the record show that the Command Duty Officer called General Sutherland at 0338 hours to report the attack. That's an hour and thirteen minutes after the attack on Hawaii began."

"Objection. That is hearsay." Mr. Engelson was highly agitated.

Colonel MacIntyre turned to Engelson. "No, Mr. Engelson, it is not. The C.D.O. next called the CAST duty officer and commented he had just reported to General Sutherland. That's the source of our information on this time frame."

Bang when the gavel. "Objection overruled. We will recess for ten minutes while counsels, the accused and I reconvene in my office."

"All rise."

Not quite silent, the visitors were whispering amongst themselves about the testimony they had just heard. As soon as Colonel Obrey left the stage, they departed for the latrine and outdoors.

CHAPTER FIFTEEN

"Sergeant," said Colonel Obrey, "secure the area. No one is to enter while we are in conference."

"Yes, sir." He pulled the door closed behind him.

Now, Colonel Obrey did a very strange thing. He backed himself into a corner, beckoned with his hands for everyone to come in close, and spoke in a low voice barely above a whisper. "Can everyone hear me well enough to understand what I am about to say?"

Everyone nodded or murmured in the affirmative, puzzled by this action.

"Colonel MacIntyre just referred to CAST as his witness, at least as the source of log time," Colonel Obrey said, enunciating carefully. "Mr. Engelson, as difficult as it is to understand, you may not challenge anything about CAST. They brought all their records out. This unit is so very secret only a handful of people even know of its existence; it was the first unit to be evacuated from the Philippines after the Japanese invaded the Philippines. And, Colonel MacIntyre, you will refrain from using CAST as a source unless your point is critical and there is no other proof to be found." He looked at John Engelson and the Colonel. "I trust I have made myself clear, gentlemen?"

Mr. Engelson placed his left hand on his hip and the other flourished in the air. "How do I know that Colonel MacIntyre won't use false information in the name of CAST?"

"Because for each referral, he will hand me a certified copy of the deposition or message that only I will see and retain. Please remember, do not ask for any sort of identification of this group."

"All right, Colonel. We'll see how it goes."

"Thank you, Mr. Engelson. Now if we're all through here, we can reconvene in the courtroom."

Colonel Obrey peered down at General Sutherland in the Witness Chair. "You are still under oath, General."

"Yes sir."

Obrey looked at MacIntyre. "Colonel, please continue."

Colonel MacIntyre moved to the podium and leaned over the podium toward General Sutherland. "We know Admiral Hart received the Pearl Harbor report and responded to it within ten minutes of the commencement of the Japanese air attack. Why did it take over an hour—an hour and thirteen minutes to be exact, before you UN-officially heard about the attack from a San Francisco radio station the troops were listening to?"

Expressing annoyance, General Sutherland said, "I was asleep, Colonel. I have no idea why I was not informed of the attack earlier."

MacIntyre studied Sutherland's face for a moment. "I see. Did you later discuss this delayed air raid information with the Command Duty Officer?"

"I do not recall that I did. Things got rather busy after that."

"Did you discuss this with the Staff Communications Officer?"

"No, I did not," he replied snappishly.

"General Sutherland, please explain why the Communications Center and Radio Rooms were closed," demanded Colonel MacIntyre.

General Sutherland looked at him like an idiot. "It was Sunday night. They are always closed from eighteen hundred hours Saturday night until Monday morning at oh eight hundred hours. Everyone knows that," he said disgustedly.

Colonel MacIntyre referred to his 3x5 cards. "On December 4th Manila time, you received Rainbow 5 Phase One Order. As Chief of Staff, don't you think it would have been advisable to keep communications open to watch for urgent war traffic?"

General Sutherland glanced furtively at Colonel MacArthur. He opened his mouth to speak and thought better of it. Then, "the subject never came up."

Colonel MacIntyre stared at him in disbelief. "I see. Well, what did you do with that information about the bombing attack, General?"

"I dressed and went to General MacArthur's quarters and woke him to tell him of the attack on Hawaii and ask what action we should take. He asked if there was any official message on that. I told him no."

"An official message. Why was that so important?"

"I suppose he didn't want us to go off half-cocked without official messages to confirm the attack."

Colonel MacIntyre looked at him coldly: "Just how was he to receive an official message if the Communications Center and Radio Rooms were shut down?"

General Sutherland hunkered down in his chair and shook his head.
'Tell me, would it not have been quicker to telephone General MacArthur by several minutes? You said you lived about ten minutes away by car."

"Yes. However, The General's standing order was to have the telephone lines switched off between Taps and Reveille."

"So, with two war warnings, emphasizing the Japanese might strike the Philippines, you were still operating on peace time operations—through rose colored glasses, so to speak?"

"This is outrageous, Colonel Obrey." Breathing heavily, responded Mister Engelson. "No facts are in evidence to support Colonel MacIntyre's slanderous statements and," his hands making quotation marks above his head, "the insulting reference to rose-colored glasses. I object to this entire line of questioning."

Colonel Obrey studied Colonel MacIntyre. "Strike the reference to rose-colored glasses. Colorful statements are not called for, Colonel."

The gallery exploded into laughter. Colonel Obrey looked at the Gallery in mingled amusement and annoyance and quietly tapped his gavel twice until the noise subsided.

"Sorry, Colonel," answered Colonel MacIntyre, and turned to General Sutherland once again.

"What happened then?" asked Colonel MacIntyre.

"He told me to let him know when an official message arrived and went back to sleep."

"Did you take any further action, General Sutherland?"

"Oh no. The General makes those decisions, Colonel."

Col. MacIntyre consulted his 3x5 cards again, keeping a weather eye on MacArthur.

"All right. What did you do after General MacArthur went back to sleep?"

"I switched on the telephone lines, called the duty officer and told him to call me at The General's Quarters the moment any important message was received."

"Yes, and then what?"

"Well, I waited at The General's Quarters while he slept, Colonel."

"I see. Tell me: who was in charge at GHQ since both you and General MacArthur were in his Penthouse Quarters?" MacIntyre studied Sutherland for a moment, letting it draw out.

"That would be the Command Duty Officer, which would be the case at any time one of us was not present.

"At what time was 'Call to Arms' announced throughout the command?"

"I beg your pardon?"

"Call to Arms, when was Call to Arms announced or TWX'd throughout the command?"

"Oh, uh—I don't know. I was not at GHQ at the time."

"Well, who would have the authority to issue 'Call to Arms', General?"

"The General, of course. I suppose I did, too."

"Would the Command Duty Officer have that authority?"

"Oh no. Colonel. The General would not let a junior officer make that decision."

"Do you know if 'Call to Arms' was ever issued?" the Colonel asked.

"Ahhh, no I don't, as a matter of fact. Things got very tense, you know."

"Indeed," MacIntyre said, ironically. He looked around, frowning, and looked to his cards again.

"General Sutherland, let's move forward in time to about 0430 hours."

Sutherland nodded.

"Were you still in General MacArthur's Quarters?"

"Oh yes. I was catnapping," flicking a glance at MacArthur.

"Go on, General."

"Well, I jotted the time when the phone rang. It was General Gerow, Army Chief of War Plans and he wanted The General, right now. He sounded very excited."

"Did he talk to you at all?"

"Oh no, Colonel, he just wanted The General just as fast as I could get him on the phone. I told the General to hang on and went into The General's bedroom and woke him up."

"What happened next?"

"The General came out in his old West Point bathrobe and sat down with the phone on his lap." Sutherland took a drink of water. His hand trembled slightly.

"Did you hear any part of that conversation?"

"Well, I heard everything that The General said."

"Good. What did he say?"

He glanced at Colonel MacArthur who was frowning at him. "Well, I don't remember all of it, you understand but the gist of it was our troops are ready to repel the Japanese."

"Then what, General Sutherland."

"Umm, The General got dressed and we went to his office at 1 Calle Victoria. You know, GHQ."

This son of a bitch is humoring me.

"Now, General Sutherland, shortly after you arrived at GHQ about 0500 hours, General Brereton appeared and wanted to see General MacArthur."

"Yes, that's right. You see, Brereton is a milquetoast kind of officer; sometimes he did a lot of whining. The General did not care to talk with him."

"That's a strange turn of events. MacArthur specifically asked for him, and yet after just one month—he doesn't like him?"

"That is correct, Colonel."

"According to General Brereton's sworn testimony, you would not allow him to enter General MacArthur's office."

Sutherland chuckled. "That's right. I threw him out. The General didn't need him in there at this time."

"So, *Brigadier* General Sutherland, on your own authority as Senior Aide de Camp, you denied *Major* General Brereton the right to access to his senior officer?"

"Colonel MacIntyre, I was Chief of Staff. The General had told me he didn't want to be disturbed. So that means no one gets in to see him."

"I see. Who was General MacArthur confiding in—that is, was he in conference with someone?

"About 0530 hours, General Marshall called and you put his call through to General MacArthur. Is that about right?"

"Well, not until I cleared it with The General first."

"And what was that conversation about, General?"

"The General didn't say, Colonel."

Colonel MacIntyre appealed to Colonel Obrey. "Colonel, would you remind the witness he is to answer all questions put to him?"

Colonel Obrey cleared his throat and leaned toward General Sutherland. "General, you are to answer all questions put to you. You are under oath to tell the truth."

"Yes, sir, Mr. President." His face had turned a dark red.

"General," asked the Colonel, "what was that conversation about?"

"Well," rather drawn out, "The General was rather angry at being ordered around by someone his junior. He said he wasn't going to order the 19th Bombardment Group out to certain death. He believed the B17s were no match for the Japanese fighter planes."

Colonel MacIntyre walked over to his desk and held out his hand to Captain Millington, whispering instructions as he did so. Millington leaned over the file box and pulled out a folder. Checking it, he handed it up to Colonel MacIntyre who also checked it and turned back to his witness. General Sutherland watched him apprehensively.

"General, you did indicate the B17s were no match for the Japanese fighter planes, didn't you?"

"Yes," Sutherland answered, wondering where this was leading.

"How did you know this or where did you obtain that information, General?" MacIntyre asked gently, with arched eyebrows.

"Ah, well you see, we had a special source of information that was brought to us."

The gavel tapped twice.

Colonel Obrey stood. "Sergeant-at-Arms, please clear the courtroom and lock the door from the outside. All members of this hearing are to remain. Members of the press and visitors, consider this an extended break until tomorrow morning at 0900 hours."

"Yes sir, Colonel. He nodded at two of his MP's and pointed to the locked door. "Open both doors wide with usual security procedures." They moved to obey the Sergeant-at-Arms. People began gathering their hats and coats, standing to leave.

"While the gallery is being cleared, gentlemen, this might be an excellent time to use the latrine. This hearing will reconvene in ten minutes." With that, Colonel Obrey hurried to the latrine in his office.

"All rise," called out the Clerk.

The gavel tapped once. "This hearing is back in session. Colonel MacIntyre, you have the floor. General Sutherland, you are still a sworn hostile witness and will answer all questions put to you, is that understood?"

"Yes sir, it is."

"Be seated." A much quieter rustle than with the gallery present.

"General Sutherland," asked Colonel MacIntyre, "what is the title of your special source?"

"Oh, I can't reveal that, Colonel. Even the title is classified Secret. General Sutherland's face looked rather smug as he announced that.

Colonel MacIntyre looked at his sheet of paper. "My secret information states that you, General MacArthur, and Admiral Hart were the gentlemen who received almost daily briefings from the CAST duty officer involving highly classified information about the Japanese military and government messages. Do you agree with this paper?" holding it out where General Sutherland could read it, then Colonel Obrey, Mr. Engleson, and Colonel Van der Wendt, in turn as Colonel MacIntyre walked it around to each.

"I am sorry but I cannot make a copy of this. It has to return, as is, to Arlington Hall." (An obtuse reference to an early National Security Office location.)

"Now, General Sutherland, what did you know that convinced you or General MacArthur that this new fighter would slay all our B17's?"

"CAST showed translations of IJAF performance data of their new Mitsubishi fighter we now call the ZERO. It was secret and being battle tested in the Philippines air battle."

"Was this information passed to General Brereton?" asked MacIntyre.

"Oh no, Colonel. We could not do that. You may not even be aware how important CAST is…"

Colonel Obrey interrupted Sutherland, sounding irritated. "General, do not be so condescending. That smacks of conduct unbecoming. Are you clear on that?" he snarled.

"General," asked MacIntyre, "you could not even paraphrase that information and swear General Brereton to secrecy? This was vital information for fighters and pursuit planes, as well as the B-17s. All you had to do was say something like 'Read this as gospel but don't ask.'"

"No sir, we could not."

Colonel MacIntyre bowed his head in anger to bring himself back in control.

"Move along, Colonel. You chewed on this long enough." But Colonel Obrey obviously didn't like what he just heard. "Never mind. We will break for the day and continue tomorrow morning." Tap went the gavel.

"All rise."

0900, 25 February 1942
Conference Room #3
Building B-6
Fort Belvoir, Virginia

"This hearing is back in session at 0905. General Sutherland, you are still sworn as a hostile witness. Colonel MacIntyre? You may continue at this time."

"Thank you, Colonel. General, recalling the closed session, your statement does not jibe with earlier testimony. Didn't that photoreconnaissance flight on November 20th convince you the B17s could handle themselves?"

General Sutherland snapped upright, shocked. "How did you find out about that flight, Colonel? I did not inform the War Department."

"*You* didn't?" MacIntyre asked, sarcastically.

"Well, The General didn't know. Brereton wanted to test the waters, so to speak, and he wanted someone to know about the test flight." He ran his finger around the inside of his collar.

"So, he wasn't such a milquetoast after all, was he, General?" Sutherland slouched a little lower in his chair. "How many fighters escorted the B17 to and from Formosa?"

General Sutherland glared at Colonel MacIntyre. "The B17 flew alone at its service ceiling. There was no need for fighter protection."

"Indeed. There were no drop tanks in the Philippines, anyway." Said Colonel MacIntyre, idly.

The Colonel paused for a moment, looking at Lieutenant Worthington who nodded concurrence. "General Sutherland, what time did General MacArthur arrive at GHQ?"

"I don't recall the exact time, Colonel."

"Well, approximately what time would you say?"

"Oh, I was pretty busy on the Pacific Ocean map and don't recall when he appeared."

MacIntyre turned to Colonel Obrey. "I would like to introduce a map of General MacArthur's GHQ in the Intramuros to point out certain features of his headquarters."

Obrey pointed his gavel at Engelson and raised his eyebrows.

"No objection at this time," he responded.

Staff Sergeant Waters leaned over and pulled out the easel tripod and positioned it so a chart could be seen by everyone. Then he placed a floor plan of GHQ on the easel and returned to his bench. "Let's see if we can rebuild this time element, General Sutherland."

Mr. Engelson stood. "Colonel Obrey, what has this to do with anything? It sounds like the Colonel is stalling again. Move to strike this line of questioning."

Colonel MacIntyre showed a toothy smile to Engelson. "I believe it is important to establish certain elements into the tragic events that began early on December 8, 1941. Where I am leading will be apparent within a few questions, Colonel."

Colonel Obrey studied both counselors for a moment, "Overruled. Continue, Colonel."

"Do you agree General that the attack on Hawaii commenced at 0225 hours, Manila time?"

'That's what I understand, Colonel." His response was arrogant or flippant in tone.

"Where were you at 0225 hours, General?" MacIntyre pushed at Sutherland.

"As I said previously, I was asleep in quarters. I usually sleep at night, you know." His speech was sarcastic and impatient with MacIntyre.

"I see. The Asiatic Fleet Communication Center apprised their duty officer who woke Admiral Hart in his quarters at 0230 hours . . . "

"Colonel, I fail to see what this line of questioning will clear up. Can we get on with it?" complained Mr. Engelson.

Colonel MacIntyre looked at Colonel Obrey with wide-eyed innocence. "Colonel Obrey, General Sutherland is a declared hostile witness. It is really necessary to draw out each item in order to get at the truth of the matter. His responses will be truthful or he perjures himself."

"I'll allow it. Get on with it, Colonel. Don't drag this out unnecessarily."

"Yes sir. Thank you, sir." He turned back to General Sutherland. "Immediately on receiving the air raid message, Admiral Hart transmitted a message to his command, copying GHQ USAFFE, FEAF, and CNO."

"Yes, yes. We all have heard that, Colonel." His demeanor was falsely bored.

"General, can you explain why it took you until 0340 hours to notify General MacArthur of the attack? That is one hour and fifteen minutes after the attack began. Surely this was information of great urgency—didn't you understand that?"

"Ahh, yes, Colonel. Very important." He began tapping his fingers on his knees. "Um, Well, you see, our Command Duty Officer called me and said his troops, listening to a San Francisco radio station, heard the announcer break in and announce the attack on Pearl Harbor."

Colonel MacIntyre nodded, hands on hips. "I heard that, too, General. Now tell me, wasn't your communications center manned during the night hours, especially in that time of urgency about war in the Pacific? We know you would have had at least one enemy contact report message from Admiral Hart, which should have been received about 0315 hours."

"Oh, I don't know about that, Colonel. It would have been encrypted, transmitted, decrypted. That takes quite a while." He said, falsely yawning.

"Admiral Hart instructed his communications duty officer to send it in the clear. The Japs knew Pearl Harbor had been struck." There were stifled snorts of laughter around the courtroom from the visitor's gallery. Sutherland's pressed his lips tightly together.

"You have not answered the question, General. Was the USAFFE Comm Center manned or closed?"

"Colonel, regular procedure is to close the Comm Center overnight from 1800 hours until 0800 hours, seven days a week. I presume that was the case on Monday morning, December 8."

"Move along, Colonel."

"Yes, Colonel Obrey."

"So, in spite of the November 28 War Warning, it was business as usual at GHQ, despite information derived from your special source. When your command duty officer called, what did you do?"

"I dressed and drove over to the hotel where The General lived and woke him in bed."

"Why didn't you call with this urgent information?"

"The General turns off his phone when he goes to bed."

"You have a key to his quarters?"

"Yes, and so does Colonel Huff, his Junior Aide."

MacIntyre nodded. "What did General MacArthur—strike that—what was General MacArthur's response to your urgent report?"

General Sutherland shifted around in the Witness chair. He appeared uncomfortable and ran his finger around his collar. "Well, I'm not sure what he said."

"Colonel Obrey, instruct this witness to answer the question, please."

"General Sutherland," Obrey spoke very softly. "You are ordered to answer all questions truthfully and fully. If it later appears you have lied or avoided the truth, you will be tried for Conduct Unbecoming and Perjury. Do I make myself clear, General?"

"Yes, sir, sorry." He stopped a turn toward MacArthur, realizing that would be counter-productive. He sighed and looked at the floor for a brief moment, collecting his thoughts.

"Colonel, General MacArthur said, as I recall, 'then the Philippines hasn't been struck' or words to that effect. He thanked me and went back to sleep."

"The Philippines hasn't been struck." Colonel MacIntyre looked at Colonel Obrey and repeated the sentence. "The Philippines hasn't been struck." He tapped his stack of 3x5 cards a few times as emphasis.

"Let's move forward. What time did General MacArthur appear at 1 Calle Victoria, his headquarters?"

"As I said, Colonel, I don't exactly know."

"Then at 0430 hours, where were you?"

"I told you, Colonel, I was in the Map Room at headquarters."

"No, you said you were still in his quarters. Was General MacArthur present with you? Shall I have the Reporters read back your previous answer?"

General Sutherland hesitated not sure where this was leading but wished he were somewhere else. He shifted uneasily around in his seat again. "I don't recall."

"At 0430 hours, General Gerow in the War Department called on the RCA radio telephone and talked with General MacArthur IN HIS QUARTERS. Does that refresh your memory, General?"

"Yes."

"Do you know the nature of that call?"

"No, Colonel. I was not in quarters with The General, but Sid—Colonel Huff was there with him."

"Earlier in your sworn testimony, you stated you were in General MacArthur's quarters at 0430 hours. Which is it, General?"

The gavel tapped. Colonel MacIntyre looked up in shock. "Let's take a fifteen minute recess at this time. General Sutherland, you are still in the witness chair when we reconvene."

"Yes sir."

Dammit all to hell, I had him on the ropes.

Colonel MacIntyre was upset. Colonel Obrey had broken the string to the trap door he was setting.

"All rise." The sound of people springing to their feet and then quiet as Colonel Obrey almost ran out. He was in a great hurry to find the latrine. Then, the gallery inhabitants made a concerted drive to the door.

MacIntyre, red-faced with anger, dropped into his seat at the table. "I had him. Damn Obrey for breaking that. I had him on the ropes." He leaned down, chin in his hands. Tom leaned in and whispered.

"Listen, Colonel, Sutherland is sitting there sweating right now. When we reconvene, why not back off to review something, then charge ahead?"

MacIntyre stared at Captain Millington thoughtfully. "Yeah, that might be the trick." He straightened up and stared at General Sutherland who did not want to meet his eyes. He was rubbing his hands on his carefully creased trousers.

Ah ha! His hands are wet. What the hell is he hiding?

"All rise. Court is back in session."

Colonel Obrey looked down at General Sutherland. "You are still under oath, General." He waved his gavel at MacIntyre. "Continue, Colonel."

"General, a little review here is necessary to place things in proper perspective."

"Major General Brereton was Commanding General of the Army Air Force Far East under General MacArthur. The FEAF Comm Center, manned twenty-four hours a day, had gotten the message from Admiral Hart and General Brereton issued his Call To Arms, bringing his entire command to full alert on or about 0300 hours.

Since that time, General Brereton had been clamoring for permission to launch his bombers against Japanese targets on Formosa in accordance with Rainbow 5 Phase Two. Not getting any response from you," pointing his fingers at Sutherland to emphasize that, "he came from his headquarters at Neilson Field to GHQ about

0500 hours to find out what was going on. What do you recall of that meeting?"

"You mean with Brereton?" Sutherland asked.

"Yes, General, with Major General Brereton." The Colonel's tone was gritty for the less than respectful tone of General Sutherland's voice.

"We talked and I sent him back to Neilsen."

"What did you talk about, General?"

"Only that The General did not want to see him."

"His senior commander, and General MacArthur refused to see him?"

"Yes, Brereton had his orders and MacArthur was too busy to see him. Besides, the Japanese had not attacked the Philippines, so there was no great urgency."

Colonel Obrey leaned over his table glaring at General Sutherland. "Brigadier General Sutherland, I remind you the proper address is Major General Brereton or General Brereton."

"Sorry, sir."

"Did General Brereton try to enter General MacArthur's private office?" asked Colonel MacIntyre.

"Yes, I tried to order him away and finally had to block that by pulling him away from the door. Even so, he managed to bull his way in with both Huff and I holding him," he smirked. "His attitude was unbecoming a general officer."

"And your physical display was becoming, pushing a senior officer around?" He asked, sarcastically. The Colonel thought for a moment. "General Sutherland, where was General MacArthur at this time?"

"Why, he was in his office, of course."

"When did General MacArthur arrive at GHQ, General?"

"Oh, must have been just after 0430 hours."

"Then, at 0530 hours, you received another RCA radio telephone call from the War Department to speak directly with General MacArthur. Is that correct?"

"As I recall, that sounds about right."

"General Sutherland, I submit that General MacArthur did not arrive at GHQ until sometime between General Brereton's arrival at the Penthouse after 0500 hours and the War Department phone call about 0530 hours."

"Colonel, I am The General's Chief of Staff. I know what he wants and when he wants it. Do not impugn his honor with trashy questions."

Colonel MacIntyre smiled and continued. "Was General MacArthur in his office when General Brereton arrived at 0500 hours? Please answer with yes or no, and I remind you, you are under oath."

General Sutherland glowered at Colonel MacIntyre and did not answer immediately.

"Colonel Obrey?"

"General Sutherland, you will answer that question."

"I don't remember if he was in his office or not."

Colonel Obrey glared down at General Sutherland. "General, you are close to contempt. Answer the question."

"General, I don't know." Colonel Obrey leaned back in amazement. "That is incredible. As you just testified, you were his Chief of Staff. And you didn't know where he was?"

"No, sir."

"Colonel MacIntyre, subject to the results at the completion of this hearing, General Sutherland is in contempt of court and he will be subject of an Article 70 court of investigation on whether he is lying or ignorant."

General Sutherland looked stricken and his usual ruddy complexion turned grey.

Mr. Engelson jumped up. "My God man, he is trying to tell the truth of the matter. I object on the grounds this is further dishonoring my client as well as General Sutherland."

Colonel Obrey looked to Mr. Engelson. "The motion of defense counsel is overruled."

"Colonel, I have no further questions for this witness, but reserve the right to recall him later."

"Very well. Your witness, Mr. Engelson."

"I have no questions for this witness at this time, Colonel."

Colonel Obrey hefted his gavel. "This is a good a place as any to adjourn for the noon meal. We will reconvene at 1400 hours." He tapped the gavel once.

"All rise." Through the sliding of chairs and shuffling of feet, the Colonel departed for lunch.

CHAPTER SIXTEEN

1000, 25 February 1942
Malinta Tunnel, Lateral 7
Corregidor
The Philippines

General Wainwright's Chief of Staff, formerly General MacArthur's G1, stood in the dim light deep in Lateral 7, Malinta Tunnel on Corregidor, watching a corporal and three privates set up a conference table. The corporal lifted a Coleman lantern and shook it, satisfied with the gurgling gas. Glancing at the general, he placed it quietly on the table, released the pump valve and pumped twelve strong strokes, pressurizing the fuel tank.

He took a long match from his shirt pocket, struck it and after the flare died down, checked the mantle. It was good. He confidently twisted the gas knob and listened for its sputtering hiss to start. He pushed the blazing match through the hole to a point just below the mantle. There was a muted explosion of yellow flame followed by the mantle creeping into a bright, white hot color.
"General, where do you want the Coleman, sir?"

Without a word, the general pointed to a hook on the wall. Nodding, the corporal hung the lantern on a wall hook. The Coleman lantern hissed and sputtered, hanging from its hook in the concrete wall.

"That will be all, Corporal. Post."
"Yessir, General. Come on, you guys." They turned and shuffled out of the corridor.

Five exhausted, haggard senior General Staff officers of the United States Army Forces, Far Eastern Command straggled in one-by-one and grimly looked at each other.
"Be seated, Gentlemen." They silently plopped into the chairs and waited.

Lieutenant General Wainwright's Chief of Staff looked at the other five through dry, bloodshot eyes. "There is no mistake: everyone here is in agreement with this statement?" He swallowed trying to wet his throat. "I repeat, Skinny agrees with this statement but believes he cannot sign it himself." He paused scratching an irritated armpit. "Let me read this slowly, one more time.

"We, the General Staff abandoned by General MacArthur when he was ordered home, want it known that we did not learn of the order nor his departure until the day after he was flown out on two of the last flyable Flying Fortresses. We wish to emphasize we each were in our offices next to our EE-5 phones, as were our Sergeants Major or First Sergeants.

"Those of us left behind had frequently disagreed with decisions the Commanding General ordered, and went on record to that effect. It is our considered opinion that one of us must return to Fort Belvoir, Virginia to insure the events of December 8th and following, are offered to counter any negative statements that General MacArthur may give.

"Handwritten this day and attested by signature of the following staff officers."

The general sighed and laid the paper on the desk. He signed and printed his name, organization, serial number, and date. Looking around, he slid the paper to his right. That officer bowed his head in prayer for a moment, grimaced and following the Chief of Staff, signed and passed to the next officer and the next until the instrument came back to the Chief of Staff.

With the signed instrument back in his hand, he looked around the table and slowly stated the obvious: "one of you must go. Is there a volunteer?" The five other officers shook their head, declining the offer.

"I expected that of you all. Therefore, as I must stay with Skinny, I have prepared five straws for you to draw. The officer drawing the short straw will depart on the Aussie PBY as soon as it is dark." He turned around and arranged the straws so the tops were even in his cupped hands. He turned around and offered it in the center of the table. They hesitated, not wanting to be the first to draw nor pick the short straw.

The Chief of Staff growling, ragged voice tore at them, "Draw, dammit!" he ordered
Hands reached out, then stabbingly jerked a straw out of his hands. They all looked at their own straw and the others.

"General Drake," ordered the Chief of Staff, "gather what you can in one small bag. I will meet you at the PBY to change the passenger manifest." He looked around grimly. "Perhaps you other gentlemen would like to write a short letter to your family. I am sure Drake will call on each of them."

He reached behind his chair for a flask and shook it.

Not much Maker's Mark left.

"Gentlemen, there's enough for a couple of sips around the table." So saying, he stood and waited as the rest tiredly scrambled to their feet. He held the silvery flask high and spoke:

"The United States of America and The United States Army." Taking a small sip, he passed it to his right. He picked up the letter, looked at them, and walked away while the rest enjoyed the last of the Maker's Mark bourbon the Chief preferred.

An hour after sundown, the Chief of Staff appeared at the landing. The Aussie PBY's right engine was ticking over slowly as the manifested passengers waited to board. He walked up to the MP Colonel who controlled the manifest. The colonel saluted, which was returned crisply.

"Let me have the manifest, Jake." Jake handed it over silently, curious as what the Chief of Staff was doing here. The Chief removed his fountain pen and its cap. "Jake, these names are in order of priority, aren't they?"

"That's right, General, least priority is on the bottom."
The general scratched the last name on the list and entered Brigadier General Drake's name and serial number, and then signed approving the change.
"General, I gotta ask: Does Skinny know about this?"
"Yes, he does, Colonel. Any other questions?"
"No, general."

"Then, I suggest you board your passengers now." He turned away as Jake began to call out names and walked over to Drake. Returning his salute, he said, as he gave him the instrument: "I understand this is a distasteful and sad duty that has been foisted upon you. But, as we agreed, it has to be done or that bastard will get away with it again."

They shook hands and waited as each passenger was handed a parachute and life jacket before boarding through the bubble hatch. As his turn came, he turned to the Chief of Staff. He put his left arm on the Chief's shoulder; likewise, the Chief did too.

"Good luck, General, see you after the war." They stared intently, yet sadly at each other for a long moment.

Then General Drake removed the manifest from the clipboard and handed the empty clipboard to the MP colonel. Glancing at the Chief of Staff, he folded it several times, tucked it into his left shirt pocket and buttoned it. Tears rolled down his face as he patted the pocket to make sure it was really secure.

Fuck!

Never looking back, Drake ducked through the waist bubble hatch boarding the PBY.

An Aussie sailor pushed the PBY away from the dock and hopped through the bubble hatch. The left engine started as the bubble slid shut. As the seaplane cleared the dock, it turned gracefully until it lined up with the watery sea-lane. A flashing green lamp in the distance showed the end of the sea-lane and at the same time granted permission to take off. The twin engines boosted to take off power and disappeared into the darkness. The Chief of Staff turned and walked back up the hill.

CHAPTER SEVENTEEN

1135, 25 February 1942
Washington Star-News
Washington, D.C.

Greg was antsy.

He wanted to talk to his boss because he thought he had figured out a way to prepare for the story without giving away secrets. In a short time, Greg was out the door, snapping open his umbrella as the rain bounced off the sidewalk allowing wet concrete perfume to tickle his nose.

At his car, Greg played close-the-umbrella-while-getting-into-the-car game, shaking off and closing his umbrella. Arriving at the Washington Star-News building, he discovered the editor had just departed for lunch.

Good, Mr. Ford has gone to lunch. He's going to bust a gut when I tell him I'm not going to tell him anything.

"Copyboy!"

This time Fred, a skinny underfed teenager, came to his desk. Greg reached into his pocket and pulled out a couple of bills.

"Get me a ham sandwich, potato salad and some coffee, Fred. I need it right away."

"Right away, Mr. Pines." He nodded. And he trotted off to the elevator.

Greg sat down at his desk without removing his coat or hat. Removing the typewriter dust cover, he rubbed his hands together briskly, pulled a fresh sheet of typing paper from a desk drawer, rolled it into his typewriter, lining it up as he did, and began typing a note summarizing yesterday's events without saying a word—because he didn't want to go to prison until the war was over.

```
       Mr. Ford:
       The Article 70 hearing began on time on
the first day and continues with precision timing.
A Colonel Obrey is the trial judge advocate acting
as judge and jury at this hearing to determine if
```

the charges will be dropped or go forward to a court-martial. Colonel Macintyre, Capt. Millington and 1st Lt. Worthington, head the prosecution team; and Colonel Van der Wendt is second chair to Mr. John Engelson as defense counsels for the accused. Col. Macintyre has begun to present the government's case.

This is a very serious case that could call for life in prison, if not death. I am shocked and depressed by what I have heard. I need some photographs for background material. Would you have the morgue deliver photographs to my desk of all of the members of the hearing, plus Generals MacArthur, Wainwright, Gerow, Brereton, Admiral Hart and Philippine President Queson, please.

GP

Greg folded the sheet of paper, slipped it into an envelope, licked the flap, sealed the envelope, and scrawled "Barry" on the outside of the envelope. Greg was worried. He could be stepping into a very large pile of cow manure leaving that note for his boss. Sighing, he walked over to Barry's office and slid it under the door. Then he headed for the elevator. Fred met him at the elevator and gave him his lunch in a paper bag. "Thanks Fred, keep the change."

Greg drove back to Fort Belvoir and parked. He thought about his story as he ate his lunch. Finally, he locked his car and hurried to the payphone. "Barry, did you get my note?"

"Yes, the morgue is working on your request. Did you tell me something very important?"

Greg grinned. His boss was no slouch. "I can't answer that. I don't want to spend the rest of the war in a psycho ward."

"I've also ordered up brief biogs on each of those photos to help you along. How much longer will the trial last, Greg?"

"I don't know. The Prosecutor is really tearing into one witness right now, and I've got to go so other reporters can call in. I'll drop off innocuous notes in the early morning hours for you."

"Okay, Greg. Don't get in trouble. No one is even hinting at a big story, so we won't either.

"Okay boss. Bye." And pulled down the line hook to disconnect.

Greg handed the receiver to the next guy and strolled away to stretch his legs and butt while he thought this over.

Sutherland seems to be getting knocked down a few notches. I wonder if he will crack?

He smoked his pipe as he reviewed the testimony so far this morning.

No doubt MacIntyre will slice Sutherland into little pieces before he is done with him.

Sergeant Waters backed into Colonel MacIntyre's office with a large wicker basket that smelled of delicious flavors. "My wife didn't want us to starve, sirs, so she made a large bowl of chile con carne with side bowls of chopped onions and shredded cheddar cheese—even Sen Sen." They all looked at his offering in happy surprise.

"Did she also think of bowls and spoons or forks for us?" Asked Capt. Millington, lifting the napkin and looking with his eyes and nose.

"Yes sir. She's bright that way." Waters grinned as he unrolled a clean dishtowel with tableware. "Even included some oyster crackers, too." In a moment, all four were busy demolishing the chile con carne.

Satisfied grunts and sighs followed. MacIntyre looked at Waters. "That was great. Please thank Susan for us."

Sergeant Waters beamed with pleasure. "I certainly will sir. Susan'll know when she sees the empty bowls."

"Oh well, back to business. Sergeant, any follow up from Sydney?"

He grimaced. "No, Colonel, not so far." He paused as he thought.

"You know, sir, I heard that MacArthur's Quartermaster General somehow got out and is trying to get back to Washington."

All three officers had his attention. "His name is Drake, Brigadier General Drake, Colonel."

MacIntyre spread his hands flat on the desk and stood, looking down on the Sergeant. "Sergeant Waters, subpoena Brigadier General Drake and get him on the next plane home."

"Yes sir, thought that might be the case." Waters smiled as he left for his desk.

CHAPTER NINETEEN

1400, 25 February 1942
Conference Room #3
Building B-6
Fort Belvoir, Virginia

"All rise."

Everyone stood and waited as Colonel Obrey marched in and sat. He had a new gavel. He tapped it once. "Court is reconvened at this time. Be seated."

A fit of coughing and sneezing began as everyone found a seat and moved around to get comfortable.

"Mr. Engelson," who immediately stood. "When we adjourned, you declared you had no questions of General Sutherland at that time. Do you wish to recall him now?"

"No, Colonel. Thank you," and sat down by General MacArthur and Colonel Van Wendt.

"Colonel MacIntyre, call your next witness."

"Yes sir. The Army calls Lieutenant Colonel Sidney Huff."

Colonel MacIntyre looked Huff in the eye and raised his right hand while thrusting the bible in front of Lt. Col. Huff. "Place your left hand on the bible, raise your right hand:

> *"You swear or affirm that the evidence you shall give in the case now in hearing shall be the truth, the whole truth, and nothing but the truth, so help you God?"*

"I do swear, sir."

"Be seated. For the record, please state your name, rank, and current duty station."

"Yes, sir, Colonel. I am Sidney Huff, Lieutenant Colonel, Infantry, seconded to General MacArthur as his Aide-de-Camp."

"You are still Colonel Douglas MacArthur's Aide?" he asked peering at Huff's lapel devices.

Huff drew himself up. "Yes sir, I am his Aide," he responded proudly, with a smile on his face.

"Then, Colonel, you are out of uniform. Your lapel devices indicate you are dog robbing a Lieutenant General, not a Colonel. Please correct that at your earliest convenience."

Huff's face was crestfallen as he nodded compliance.

"When did General MacArthur ask for your services as his Aide, Colonel?"

"Actually, not until just before the war broke out. I started learning the job on December 1, 1941."

"How did that occur?"

"I had a heart attack while I was a Commander in the Navy at Manila in the Marsman Building, and was medically retired from the Navy—in Manila, by my choice. As Field Marshall, MacArthur recruited me into his Philippine staff to help build the Philippine PT Boat Navy.

"We were supposed to build up a Coastal Patrol Force of 48 PT boats to patrol and protect the Philippine Isles from warring nations and pirates. We purchased two from the Brits and began building our force with local materials. The first one was just commissioned when I had my heart attack. I continued in that function in the Philippine Army after The General was recalled to active duty. General MacArthur asked me to join his U.S. Army general staff on November 30th. He swore me in as a Lieutenant Colonel, Infantry, on December 1st."

"Were you or are you close to Colonel MacArthur?"

"Oh yes, Colonel. Even more than his Aide, I am still part of his inner family."

"What was, and is, your function as his Aide."

"I live in Quarters to respond to his needs, if that's what you mean."

"What else."

"I watched over Mrs. MacArthur and young Arthur, sort of protector and babysitter. Ran errands. I kept his calendar, made phone calls and answered the phone for The General. Sometimes I woke him in the morning unless he specifically said not to disturb him. Stood at his shoulder at formal gatherings to announce the name of the next person or couple approaching the receiving line."

"Doesn't leave much time for a personal life, does it?" MacIntyre asked sympathetically.

"Colonel, here we go again, chatting down memory lane. Where are we going with this?" complained Mr. Engelson.

"Colonel, I'm just trying to establish all of his job functions serving General MacArthur."

"I'll allow it. However, this better lead to something, Colonel MacIntyre."

"Yes sir, it will."

He turned back to Sid Huff.

"Let's go now to the early hours of December 8, 1941, Colonel. Where were you—say, beginning just before midnight on December 7."

All present could see that Lt. Col. Huff tensed with that innocuous question.

"I went to bed right after The General and Mrs. MacArthur retired. That was about 2230 hours."

"Is there a phone in your room?"

"Oh, yes sir, but under strict rules of the House, the telephone lines are switched off when the MacArthur's go to bed."

"So General MacArthur is practically cut off from the outside world when he is sleeping. When did you learn of the attack on Pearl Harbor, Colonel?"

Huff swallowed and rubbed his hands on his pants. "Why, it was when General Sutherland arrived."

"What time was that?"

"Uh, I don't remember exactly." Colonel MacIntyre frowned at him and Colonel Obrey cleared his throat. Huff looked at both in near fright.

"Honestly, I really don't know. General Sutherland has his own key to the door and he rushed right by me and shut the door to The General's bedroom."

"Colonel, when I was a dog robber, I had a journal in my shirt or inside pocket in which I kept close tabs on my general and each entry was preceded with the time to the minute. Most of that information went into his diary at the end of the day. Don't you and didn't you keep track of General MacArthur that way?" asked MacIntyre.

"Well yes sir. But my journal was left behind when we rushed for the plane."

"You left your journal behind?" he asked incredulously.

"Oh yes sir. The General ordered us to take one small bag and forbade us from including any of our papers: that included my journal." He paused for a moment and added brightly, "But I started a new one as soon as we arrived in Sydney, Australia."

"Colonel Obrey, I want this witness declared a hostile witness. I believe he is stonewalling." Colonel MacIntyre was upset.

The Colonel leaned over the desk and looked down upon Lieutenant Colonel Huff. "Colonel Huff, you are a witness for the prosecution and required to answer every question truly and faithfully. As an Annapolis graduate, you are on your honor and duty bound to make the truth of this matter."

Colonel Huff looked upon the Colonel with fear on his face. "I'm trying, your honor. Truly, I am."

Colonel Obrey waved his gavel at Colonel MacIntyre. "Proceed with this hostile witness, Colonel."

"What was the last entry in your journal, Colonel Huff? And what was that entry about?"

"It was right after General Marshall relieved The General of his command. He told me to return to the Manila Hotel and help Jean, Au Chew, and Arthur pack one small bag for each of them." He thought for a second. "Me too, of course."

"I see." He turned away for a second then, "Oh, by the way, what time was that entry, Colonel Huff?"

"0947 hours, December 18th, Colonel." There were some quiet snickers from the gallery.

Colonel Obrey had frost in his voice. "Colonel Huff, let me understand you. You have no idea what time General Sutherland broke in on General MacArthur to announce that war had started but you remembered your entry to escape the Philippines. Is that correct?"

"That's right, Colonel."

Colonel Obrey stared suspiciously at Lt. Col. Huff for a few moments. He looked at Colonel MacIntyre. "You may continue."

"Colonel Huff, you were in quarters with General MacArthur the night of the 7th and early morning hours of the 8th. Is that true?"

"Oh yes sir. And I accompanied him to GHQ, too."

"And what time would that be?"

Huff had a puzzled look on his face. "I don't rightly remember, Colonel. It was in my journal, though."

"Colonel, were there any other interruptions to the regular household routines?"

"Why yes. After I switched the telephone lines on when General Sutherland arrived, General Gerow from War Plans in the War Department called The General."

"Do you know what time that was, Colonel."

"No sir, I do not."

"Let the record show that General Gerow's testimony stated the call was about 0430 hours and that he had talked with General MacArthur in his quarters—two hours after the attack began."

"Colonel Huff, was there anything else of note while you still were in General MacArthur's quarters in the Manila Hotel?"

"I think so. General Brereton tried to talk with The General but General Sutherland blocked the way."

"Why did he do that?" MacIntyre watched Colonel Obrey puzzling over this latest piece of information.

"General Sutherland told General Brereton he already had his orders. There was no use in bothering The General. Besides, flying to Formosa would be a suicide mission for all the fliers."

General MacArthur struggled to stand, pointing at Colonel Obrey. He was physically pulled down by Van Wendt and Engelson. A fierce whispered argument ensued with MacArthur arguing with Engelson, until gaveled down by an irritated Colonel Obrey.

"I see. What did General Brereton want, do you know?"

"Oh yes, General Brereton was livid. He was supposed to have launched his bombing attack on Formosa right after the attack on Pearl Harbor. According to General Sutherland, The General left orders that Brereton's command was to stand down."

A strong thud or booming sound came from the Defense desk. MacArthur was pounding his fist on the table despite his Defense teams attempts to stop him. His face was contorted in red anger.

"Court is in recess for fifteen minutes. Mr. Engelson, you will control your client or I will."

"Sorry Colonel. We do need a few minutes to cool down."

"All rise."

The gavel tapped on the table twice. "Be seated. This court is back in session. Colonel Huff, you are still under oath." Colonel Obrey looked like he had heard enough unpleasant things for the day.

"Yes sir," replied Huff.

"Do you know what time General Brereton appeared at the Manila Hotel, Colonel Huff?"

Huff looked at the ceiling in thought "I don't recall," he answered. "However, it was not too long after General Gerow called that General Brereton knocked on the outer door."

"General Gerow's testimony states he called at 0430 hours."

"All right. The General, General Sutherland, and I departed for GHQ soon after General Brereton left in anger. He was really upset," he chuckled. "I thought he was going to hit General Sutherland."

"Hmmm, yes! So, the three of you arrived at GHQ right around 0530 hours, is that correct?" queried MacIntyre.

Huff shrugged and considered his answer. "I suppose so."

"Did the War Department message to put the War Plan, that is Rainbow 5, into effect arrive before or after General MacArthur arrived at GHQ?"

He wrinkled his brow. "I don't know, Colonel. I was at my desk outside The General's War Room."

"Didn't you normally sign for all incoming messages directed at General MacArthur?" He asked, incredulously.

"Oh yes. Most of the time. General Sutherland signs for highly classified documents, though."

"This particular War Department message arrived just after 0530 hours. Does that help your memory?"

"I believe I was away at the Officers' Mess having breakfast at that time, Colonel." Colonel MacIntyre turned away in exasperation.

Capt. Millington, watching the exchanges, couldn't decide whether Huff was as stupid as he sounded or very good at covering for MacArthur.

Colonel MacIntyre rubbed his nose and checked his next card. "Colonel Huff, do you remember the Japanese Air Force raid at Baguio on Camp John Hays Army Hospital?" He asked.

"Yes sir."

"Do you recall the time of that first air raid?"

"Um, it seems to me it was about 0815 hours, sir. But that wasn't the first attack."

MacIntyre tried to hide his surprise. "Oh? Could you be more specific about the first attack?"

"Yes sir, we heard reports of air raids on small villages all the way up the north coast of Luzon, Colonel. I thought you knew about that."

Hell no, first I've heard about those raids.

"Hmmm, let me check my papers." Colonel MacIntyre pushed his stack of papers around without looking at them. Engelson was just getting the subterfuge when Huff spoke up.

"Yes, it was around dawn when reports were telephoned in from outlying villages."

"That would have been 0600 hours give or take fifteen minutes, would you say?"

"Uh, right. The Japs were machine gunning all those villagers."

"Military targets, Colonel Huff?"

"Oh no sir. Just natives living along the North Coast. But they did bomb the auxiliary air field at Aparri up on the northwest coast."

"Would you say that hostilities in the Philippines commenced when those Japanese planes machine gunned the villagers, Colonel Huff?"

"Oh—well," Huff ran his finger around the sinde of his collar. "The General always said hostilities would commence when the first bomb fell from a plane and exploded on Philippine soil. So, I guess machine guns do not count, do they, Colonel?" He responded.

"No, I guess not. What about them bombing the Aparri air field? Weren't those the first bombs on Philippine soil?" he queried gently.

Huff had a puzzled look on his face. "I suppose so, but remember there was nothing there, just a bulldozed dusty, dirt air strip."

"Do you recall General Brereton telephoning and talking with General Sutherland just before 0900 hours?"

"It was 0850 hours, Colonel. General Brereton wanted to speak to General MacArthur and General Sutherland would not permit that. He said that The General was in conference. I guess General Brereton wanted to load up the B17s and mount the flight to Formosa…

"Objection," called out Mr. Engelson. "Hearsay and facts not in evidence. Can't put words in the General's mouth."

"Sustained," said Colonel Obrey.

"Did you hear any part of that conversation, Colonel Huff?" asked Colonel MacIntyre.

"Yes sir. I heard General Sutherland tell General Brereton that there would be no raids on Formosa for the present."

Mac just looked at Huff for a moment, his eyebrows raised in amazement. "For the present, you said? No raids for the present?"

"Oh yes sir. General Brereton was really angry with General Sutherland. He called back three more times trying to talk with General MacArthur. Finally, General Sutherland told him the B17s were not authorized to carry bombs at this time." Huff sat back, satisfied with his response.

Colonel MacIntyre turned to Colonel Obrey. "Colonel, I have no further questions for Lieutenant Colonel Huff at this time." Colonel Obrey, still looking at Huff with a puzzled expression, pulled his eyes back to MacIntyre and nodded.

"Your witness, Mr. Engelson."

Engelson stood and walked to the lectern. "Colonel Huff, in your testimony, you stated that General Sutherland said General MacArthur did such and so or ordered this or that."

"Could Counsel be a little more specific?" asked Colonel MacIntyre. Engelson nodded. "Strike that, let me restate. Colonel Huff, from your testimony just given, did General Sutherland sometimes give orders without General MacArthur's knowledge?"

Lt.Col. Huff sat up, straightening his tie and tunic. "Well, yes, after all, he is or was Chief of Staff, for crying out loud!"

"Let me ask another question, Colonel Huff. You were General MacArthur's Junior Aide for only a few days before he was relieved of command, is that correct?"

Huff sighed. "Yes sir, only seven days."

"Who taught you your duties as Junior Aide, Colonel Huff?" Mr. Engelson's voice was soft and gentle.

"Why, General Sutherland did. He was happy to have someone helping out."

"No further questions." Mr. Engelson was smiling as he sat down.

"Colonel Obrey, the Army recalls General Sutherland to the stand."

"Colonel, I'm not sure if he is still in the building. If not, can you call your next witness?"

"The Quartermaster General, Brigadier General Drake is our next witness, Mr. President. I believe he is in the witness holding room."

Colonel MacArthur looked up, a startled look on his face, and then bent over and immediately began whispering to Mr. Engelson.

"Sergeant-at-Arms, General Sutherland. If not, the Quartermaster."

"Yes sir." He disappeared and moments later reappeared with General Sutherland.

"General Sutherland, you are still under oath and a hostile witness."

"Yes, sir." General Sutherland looked at Colonel MacIntyre with apparent lack of cordiality.

"General, Colonel Huff has testified you taught him his duties as Junior Aide to General MacArthur. Is that correct?"

Sutherland shifted around in the chair and rested his elbows on his knees. "Yes, this is true."

"He further testified you often gave orders that had not previously been authorized by General MacArthur. Is that correct?"

General Sutherland looked startled by the implications of this question. "Colonel, as Chief of Staff to General MacArthur, it was my business to know exactly what the General wanted at any given time and on any subject," glaring at MacIntyre. "So, the answer to your question is, yes, there were times and uncounted subjects that I delivered an order, verbal or written, without previous agreement by General MacArthur." He responded, tersely.

Unruffled by Sutherland's demeanor, MacIntyre asked, "These were innocuous orders or orders that had some meat in them, General? Can you give us a few examples so we may understand the relationship you had with General MacArthur?"

"Umm, that's interesting," relaxing a little. "Every so often a field exercise was not going precisely the way The General would have approved, so I made changes to the orders; that sort of thing. He always saw the orders later."

"Did he ever complain you had taken too much on your own?"

"Oh no sir. We had perfect understanding between us."

"Wonderful, isn't it, to have that close a relationship?" Sarcastically. "Let's go back to your testimony that you refused to permit General Brereton to see General MacArthur."

"Yes?" Sutherland tightened up.

"Was this one of the times you took it upon yourself to issue an order that General MacArthur had not previously written?"

Sutherland obviously squirmed when he realized he was stuck. "Colonel, The General himself issued that order." He bowed his head and avoided looking at MacArthur.

Colonel MacIntyre watched MacArthur carefully when he asked that question. MacArthur frowned angrily and began whispering to Engelson. "I have no further questions, Mr. President."

"Your witness, Mr. Engelson." Colonel Obrey watched the close whispering between Engelson and MacArthur.

"Mr. Engelson?" Engelson and MacArthur continued their whispered consultation. Mr. Engleson acknowledged Colonel Obrey's call by raising an index finger.

Colonel Obrey waited a moment, then called out: "Mr. Engelson, your witness." This time, Colonel Obrey snapped it out somewhat hostile.

"I have no questions for this witness."

"You are excused, General." General Sutherland averted his face as he walked by the Defense table.

"Colonel MacIntyre, call your next witness." Ordered Colonel Obrey.

"The Army calls Brigadier General Charles Drake to the stand."

The Sergeant-at-Arms departed and returned shortly with a short man, bald except for a fringe around his ears. Physically, General Drake was exhausted and malnourished. His uniform had been washed and pressed but showed obvious field wear and stains of war.

He slowly limped up to the witness stand and stood at attention waiting for Colonel MacIntyre to swear him.

Colonel MacIntyre thrust the bible at this witness. "Place your left hand on the bible and raise your right hand.

"You swear or affirm that the evidence you shall give in the case now in hearing shall be the truth, the whole truth, and nothing but the truth, so help you God?"

"I so swear, Colonel."

"Be seated. Please state your name, rank, and assignment for the record."

"I am Charles Drake, Brigadier General, Quartermaster Corps, formerly assigned to USAFFE as Quartermaster General, currently waiting reassignment."

"Thank you, General. When were you assigned Quartermaster General for USAFFE?"

General Drake looked at the ceiling and formed his answer. "I arrived in the Philippines in August 1939 and immediately took on those duties in the Philippine Department under General Grunert, sir."

"Are you familiar with War Plan Orange 3 or Rainbow 5? And, let me assure you, these subjects have been openly discussed in this proceeding." Amplified Colonel MacIntyre.

The general relaxed. "Yes sir. I was involved in WPO3."

"Oh? What was your responsibility in that respect, General?" Asked MacIntyre, leaning on the forward edge of his table.

"I assisted Colonel Casey and his Engineers setting up the various dumps and depots located off the Philippine Railroad lines on Bataan Peninsula. They had to be scattered enough and camouflaged so that an enemy action would not recognize any of the dumps."

"I see. Would you tell the Court what material you stored and where you located these dumps?"

"In detail, Colonel?"

"No, we want to establish . . . "

"Objection, leading the witness." Called Mr. Engelson.

"Sustained. Try again, Colonel."

"General Drake, reviewing WPO3, where were your dumps located?"

"Oh, I see what you mean. According to WPO3, a defensive line was established at the neck of the Bataan Peninsula. Sufficient supplies to support the Army for six months had to be moved behind that line. That is, Food, Fuel, Medicine, Field Hospitals and Aid Stations, Ammunition, Repair parts, Uniforms, just about everything an army needs, Colonel."

"I see. Did that take long, sir?"

"Oh yes. We had just finished by the summer of 1941; nearly two years to build, camouflage, and get everything in place if it would be needed. It was a good piece of work," he said, with pride.

"Indeed. You are to be congratulated."

General Drake nodded, smiling.

Colonel MacIntyre shuffled through his 3x5 cards and looked at the General Drake. "Let's move forward to August 1941. Did anything of significance happen then?" He queried, softly.

General Drake was silent, his head down as he cleared his throat several times. Then, with wet eyes, he looked at Colonel MacArthur. "Yes sir. That was when General MacArthur implemented his Beach Defense War Plan. I was to move all the War Supplies then stored in Bataan into his pre-positioned points along the Luzon north coast. We didn't complete the re-supply until late November 1941."

"I see. General, can you tell me about the remaining war supplies on Bataan that you had set up in accordance with WPO3?"

"Yes sir. None left. Stripped clean for Beach Defense."

"Nothing left on Bataan, is that correct?"

"That's what I said, Colonel," peevishly.

"Let's move forward now to December 15, 1941. Tell me about that day."

"That's the day General MacArthur decided his Beach Defense was not working and ordered WPO3 activated."

"How did that affect you, Colonel?"

"I had to remove all the dumps back into their Bataan locations."

"Did you complete that mission?"

"No sir. It would have taken fourteen days to move all the material to Bataan. The Philippine Government refused to let me use their railroad to move supplies into Bataan and I pleaded with General MacArthur to intercede with President Queson. Not only that, they would not let us take any of the military food supplies. They said they were needed for the people."

"Who said that?"

"The President."

"You mean President Queson?"

"Yes sir."

"Did you report this to GHQ?"

"Yes sir, immediately."

"And, to whom did you address this problem, General?"

"That would be the Chief of Staff, General Sutherland, sir."

MacIntyre turned to look at MacArthur as he asked his next question. "What was his response?"

"Use trucks." Spoken bitterly!

"How did that go?" MacIntyre asked gently.

"Colonel," General Drake cried out. "Casey's Engineers were already blowing the bridges to slow down the Japs. Our trucks went nowhere."

"How much of the war supplies got back to Bataan?"

"Only a handful of trucks, sir, and what could be carried on the backs of soldiers retreating into Bataan. The Army in Bataan was forced to go on half rations a couple of days later due to lack of food. The hospitals and Aid stations had almost no medicines. Ammo was in short supply." He paused for a moment and with choked voice said, "I did the best I could. I just could not get around the Philippine government not allowing or assisting in moving those supplies to Bataan." Drake was obviously dejected.

Colonel MacIntyre turned and looked at Colonel MacArthur for a long moment. "I have no further questions of this witness, sir."

Colonel Obrey deadpanned, "Cross examine, Mr. Engelson?"

Mr. Engelson pulled at his lips for a moment as he slowly stood. "General Drake, you were not part of General MacArthur's major staff were you?"

"Oh yes sir, I was. However, I was left behind when General MacArthur left with his inner circle."

"I have no further questions for this witness."

"Redirect, Colonel?" Nodding to MacIntyre in the affirmative.

"General Drake, General Marshall ordered out the entire staff . . ."

"Objection. Facts not in evidence.

"Sustained."

Colonel MacIntyre looked at his toes for a moment, and then nodded. "Colonel, just how did you escape to Australia?"

"An Aussie Consolidated PBY put in to Corregidor and I commandeered a space on the flight to Brisbane, sir"

"Was this authorized?"

"Skinny looked the other way, Colonel."

"Objection. Facts not in evidence."

"Sustained. Stick to the facts, Colonel."

"So, you did not have a set of orders to board that PBY?"

"No, Colonel. VOCG. (Voice Order by the Commanding General.) General Wainwright's Chief of Staff put me on that plane."

"Objection. Facts not in evidence."

Millington handed the Colonel MacIntyre a sheet of paper who held it up and presented it to Colonel Obrey. "I request this certified photocopy of the plane's manifest be entered as Army Exhibit 10. This shows the Chief of Staff's handwriting, which can be verified locally, scratching out one name and inserting Brigadier General Charles Drake's name and serial number as the last man on the manifest."

Meanwhile, Capt. Millington was handing a copy of the manifest to Mr. Engelson.

Colonel Obrey studied the photocopy a moment. "I'll accept this." He turned to the Clerk, handing the photocopy to him. "Army's exhibit ten".

"Yes sir."

"General," asked Colonel MacIntyre, "what happened upon arrival in Australia?"

General Drake leaned forward again. "Well, we passengers were shunted to an Army barracks while we were being processed. I was finally shipped to Sydney where I waited for transportation until your subpoena arrived."

Colonel MacIntyre turned add addressed Colonel Obrey. However, his statement was of interest to everyone there. "General Drake arrived in Australia after General MacArthur and his close advisors had departed for Fort Belvoir. He only arrived here yesterday," said Colonel MacIntyre.

"General Drake, why are you here?" Asked Colonel MacIntyre.

General Drake hesitated a moment, licking his lips. "We staff members discussed a particular aspect of General MacArthur's departure, and brought it to General Wainwright's Chief of Staff's attention. He agreed that given the opportunity to get out, one of us should go. I got the short straw."

"You actually got the short straw, General?" Drake looked sad as he said, "Yes, that is true."

"While being able to escape capture is one thing, what was the true purpose of leaving your comrades in arms, General?" Hoarse and eyes red from lack of sleep, Drake looked at MacArthur as he spoke.

"Everyone on staff wanted to make sure a," he paused here searching for the correct word or phrase, "a balanced—yes, a balanced report of what happened on and after December 8, 1941, was made known to the authorities in the War Department."

Colonel MacIntyre looked at Captain Millington for a moment, looking for encouragement and assurance. Millington gave a tentative smile and pushed his hands toward MacIntyre. Colonel MacIntyre turned to the General and asked, "you say a balanced report. Can you be more specific, sir?" He prodded.

"It is General MacArthur's nature to take credit of someone else's idea and conversely, he makes no mistakes. Mistakes are always . . . "

"Objection. This is a scurrilous attack on my client. There are no facts in evidence to ever prove such a charge. I move General Drake's testimony be stricken from the record."

General Drake turned to face MacArthur and Engelson. "Oh, yes sir. There is plenty of evidence going back to the World War. If something he plans goes awry, it is always somebody else who erred, never ever MacArthur. For example, he blamed me for being unable to bring the supplies back to Bataan. I had no warning at all. There was not enough time to reload and transport those supplies back to the peninsula." He sipped some water and turned back to the Colonel.

"Was there any other reason, General?"

He nodded slowly. "General, you have to speak your answers," said Colonel Obrey.

"Sorry, sir. The answer is yes; there was another reason. Every one of the senior staff officers left behind did not get along with General MacArthur because they disagreed with many of his decisions. We believed, rightly or wrongly, he didn't want us around to refute any statement he made."

"No further questions, Colonel Obrey."

"Recross, Colonel Obrey?" Asked Mr. Engelson.

"Proceed, Mr. Engelson."

"General, you say you drew the short straw to make sure that my client told the truth. Isn't that Conduct Unbecoming?"

"Objection. The witness is not on trial here."

"Sustained. Try again, Counselor."

"Isn't what you are doing, at the very least, spiteful?"

"It had to be done, sir. Otherwise, General MacArthur will talk his way out of his predicament." There were quiet chuckles from some of the audience who were familiar with his well know propensity of long monologues on any subject.

"And this exposè is just your word against my client, is that not correct?" He asked in a voice dripping with sarcasm.

General Drake did not answer. He reached up, unbuttoned his right breast pocket, and removed a many-folded piece of paper. As he carefully unfolded it, smoothing each crease, he spoke.

"No, Mr. Engelson, that is not correct. This paper is a statement made and signed by all the staff officers left behind when MacArthur escaped with his cronies."

Mr. Engelson reached for the paper, which Drake held away from him. General Drake stood, walked a few steps to Colonel Obrey and handed him the unfolded sheet of paper and returned to the witness chair. The Colonel carefully read the document.

Colonel Obrey looked at Mr. Engelson, MacArthur, and Colonel MacIntyre. "Approach." All the counselors scrambled to approach the Colonel.

"This is a very interesting document. You may look without touching. And, mind, it is not yet entered into the record."

Colonel MacIntyre saw what appeared to be a handwritten petition with several signatures. "Colonel, I suggest several photocopies be made for study by the Army and Defense. For my part, I want to study it carefully to determine if the Army needs or want the document in evidence."

Mr. Engelson said, "I agree with Colonel MacIntyre that it begs study."

Colonel Obrey nodded his head, "Very well, this is the twenty-fifth, as he looked at his calendar. He looked at Colonel MacIntyre and said "You and I have to appear before a House panel for the next three days. We will reconvene on March 2nd at 0900 hours. This will also allow time to photocopy and authenticate the document, and permit both sides to study it.—Back away, gentlemen." The attorneys returned to their tables.

"This hearing is in recess March Second at 0900." Colonel Obrey tapped the gavel once and stood.

"All rise."

CHAPTER TWENTY

1700, 25 February 1942
Washington Star-News
Washington, D.C.

Gregory Pines eased into his parking place at the Washington Star-News. Hurrying through the lobby to the elevators, he noticed two young men in dark blue business suits looking at every one. No dummy, he ducked into an elevator next to the starter.

"Quick Tony, I gotta get upstairs right now."

"Okay, Mr. Pines." He nodded at the elevator operator. "Take him straight up to the fourth floor now, Fred." The door shut in the face of the two blue suits and Fred started the elevator.

"Fred, go to the Sixth Floor, stop for a second, then drop to the Fifth, let me out on the Fourth. Then drop to the Third and Main floor."

"Got it. Think that will fool 'em, Mr. Pines?"

"I don't know but at least it will give me a couple minutes head start."

He rushed into Barry's office and sat on the floor in the far corner. If the blue suits came into Barry's office they couldn't see him without going around his desk.

"Barry, either the cops or . . . "

"Special agents of the FBI, Greg." Barry bustled importantly with papers on his desk head down to hide his lips. "I should not have asked for Biogs on all those people. They questioned me for about twenty minutes. Told em you were working on a feature story about the Pacific War and our latest hero, General MacArthur. That about right?" Barry said with a grin on his face.

"Oh, man oh man, this is going to be tough. I'm not supposed to say ANYTHING about this hearing. I'm just trying to marshal all my material when the trial does end."

"Yeah? How's it going, Greg?"

"It's just awful. I'm going to grab some more steno pads when I go back. I'm already on the third one."

"Wow, you're taking a lot of notes—uh oh, here they come."

Two Special Agents of the FBI walked into Barry's office without invitation. One of them looked a little short tempered. "Where is Mr. Pines?" He demanded!

"Didja check the cafeteria on the Sixth Floor? He usually eats there," Barry said, playing dummy.

"We checked." With a grim voice.

"How about Accounting on the Fifth Floor? He may be there about his expense reports."

"We checked there, too." With an exasperated snap.

Barry looked around them at Greg's desk. "Hmmm. He's not at his desk right now. Why do you think he is in the building?"

"We saw him come in."

Barry got up casually and stepped in front of Greg, shielding him from the Suits. Looking out the window he commented, "Yep, his car is in its parking spot, so he must be around somewhere. Did you check the Morgue on the Third Floor?"

The suits looked at each other. Barry smiled. "He goes there a lot when he is working on a story."

They nodded in unison. "If he comes back in here, please have him contact me at this number. We have some questions to ask him." He handed Barry his card and they left.

Barry watched the elevator arrow drop to the Third Floor, then to the Main Floor. He picked up his phone and dialed a three-digit number, and waited.

"Fred, this is Barry. Did one of those FBI guys just get out of the elevator?" He listened to Fred, then, "okay, let me know when they both leave, please."

"You can get up now, Greg. You go back to your desk and I'll join you there, just in case they check back."

Greg went back to his desk and began sorting through the material from the morgue. He wasn't satisfied with some of the photos and most of the Biogs were out of date. He labeled a file folder "Army Brass", stuffed it with the material and filed it alphabetically in his filing drawer.

Looks like some of that stuff has been around since the War to End All Wars.

Barry pulled up a chair and began pumping him trying to find out what the trial was all about. Meanwhile, Greg was going through accumulated papers on his in-basket. Most went into his waste can.

"Barry, about the only thing I can tell you with a clear conscious is that this hearing is very big. The person in question is both hated and loved; I can tell you this: they ought to hang the bastard on what we have heard so far."

"Gregory Pines?" An imperial voice asked.

Barry and Greg twisted around. The Suits were back!

"That's my name, Greg Pines. Who wants to know?"

Both opened and held out little wallets with a gold badge and identification card.

"FBI, huh? Who are you investigating? You know my sources are confidential."

"Please come with us. We have to ask you some questions.

Greg leaned back and looked up at them. "Fire away but I don't have much time." He looked at his watch. "As a matter of fact, you have about ten minutes before I leave."

"That won't do. You will please come with us."

Barry spoke up. "Are you charging Greg with anything?"

"Not your concern, sir. Mr. Pines, will you come with us, willingly or not?"

"Not unless you have a warrant for my arrest or subpoena."

"We have the War Powers Act to back us up, Mr. Pines."

Barry stood and glared at the Special Agents. "And I, gentlemen, am the editor of this newspaper. If you take him, John Edgar Hoover is not going to like our large banner headline that will read FBI TAKES REPORTER AWAY. And in lower bold type, I will tell the world you how bullied him and would not tell him what the charges he faces." He looked from face to face. "What do you think of them apples?" Glaring at them.

Greg watched their expressions change from contempt for him to concern about what Barry might do to their career.

"We will be back, Mr. Pines. Don't leave town."

"I come and go to Fort Belvoir for an Army hearing I am attending. But I will be home tonight."

Barry and Greg watched them march in lock step to the elevator and stand facing the elevator door until it slid open. With precision, they stepped inside and about faced. They were still glaring across the newsroom as the door slid shut.

Barry and Greg giggled and broke into hysterical laughter that had them holding onto each other to keep from falling off their chairs. Other people in the newsroom looked at them, not knowing whether they should smile, laugh, or ignore the whole thing.

"Boss, I am going home to clear my head. I don't want to miss anything. This is too big of a story. Oh, we don't start again until March Second. The Hearing judge has to appear before a House Panel on something else."

"Okay Greg. If I don't hear from you, I will track you down where ever they have taken you."

CHAPTER TWENTY-ONE

0930, 2 March 1942
Conference Room #3
Building B-6
Fort Belvoir, Virginia

Before Greg sat down, he removed his jacket and put it on the back of his chair. His shirt was sopping wet from the extra high humidity and strong rainstorm outside. Sitting down, he looked around and froze. The Blue Suits were standing against the wall behind him with smirks on their faces as they stared at him.

Crap!

"All rise." Everyone stood and waited as Colonel Obrey walked in and sat. There was the usual scraping and shuffling of feet as people stood at somewhat attention.

Colonel Obrey held a new gavel in his hands and looked around the courtroom. He tapped the gavel on his desk once. "This hearing is reconvened at this time. Be seated."

Mr. Engelson and Colonel MacIntyre remained standing.

Colonel Obrey beckoned to them and announced, "Counsel approach."

When all the lawyers were assembled in front of him, he looked at Colonel MacIntyre. "What do you think of the document, Colonel?"

The Colonel frowned. "My staff took the photocopy to the War Department to G1 (General Staff Administration) to compare file signatures very carefully. They concluded those were true signatures and therefore, it was a true statement. General MacArthur was known for that kind of leadership."

"I see," replied Colonel Obrey.

"As far as the Army is concerned, this document tends to make General Drake a reliable witness by carrying out the wishes of senior officers who cannot be present. Therefore, except for making it part of the evidence at hand, we see no reason to add a new specification to Conduct Unbecoming," explained MacIntyre.

Colonel Obrey nodded. "Mr. Engelson? Do you have a comment to make?"

"Yes, sir. We will accept the document as part of the evidence at hand, provided no further charges or specifications are drawn based on it."

"One thing more, Colonel," said MacIntyre. "We may have a problem at G1. We swore them to secrecy but I don't know how long those gossips will hold still."

"I will take care of that when we break."

"Thank you, sir."

"Very well. Step back, gentlemen."

"Mr. Engelson, proceed. General Drake, you are still under oath."

General Drake nodded from the witness chair, expectantly.

John Engelson looked at General Drake and shook his head. He knew you never ask a question for which you do not know the answer ahead of time, usually well researched.

Yet, this is uncharted territory. Any question I ask is liable to explode in my face and further damage MacArthur.

"I have no questions of this witness." Engelson stated.

Colonel MacIntyre was disappointed because he had hoped Engelson would open new territory to explore. However, he understood Engelson's hesitancy.

Colonel Obrey was also disgruntled. He was hoping to hear more from General Drake.

"Colonel, call your next witness, please."

Colonel MacIntyre stood. "Colonel, the Army recalls General Gerow to the stand."

"Objection. Counsel had two shots at the General and did not indicate he would recall him later."

"General Drake's testimony raises more questions. Following General Gerow's further testimony, I will recall General Sutherland to the stand to clarify one issue. Depending upon his testimony, it may be necessary to recall General Drake, Colonel."

Mr. Engelson stared at Colonel MacIntyre frostily, then his eyes popped wide as he figured out where MacIntyre was going.

General Gerow was irritated at being called for the third time. "I do presume this was necessary, Colonel." Edginess in his voice.

"Yes, General, just a few moments more please. You are still under oath, sir." General Gerow nodded.

"Let's go back to December 17, 1941."

"Yes?"

"Were you present when General Marshall recalled General MacArthur?"

"Objection. Facts not in evidence. We do not know if General Marshall…"

"That's why Colonel MacArthur is sitting here, Mr. Engelson." A loud gaffaw burst from the gallery.

"Overruled. I will allow that. Answer the question, General." Rapping quietly with his gavel, he gazed sternly at the gallery, and shook his head.

"General Gerow. Were you present?" Queried MacIntyre.

"Yes."

"Just you and General Marshall?" He pursued.

"No sir, Secretary of War Stinson was sitting next to me."

"Do you recall what General Marshall said to General MacArthur?"

"Objection…."

"Mister Engelson, I cannot call General Marshall or the Secretary. They are the source of this hearing. However, General Gerow had several dealings with General MacArthur at General Marshall's orders." His voice was clipped and loud.

"Overruled. Continue, Colonel MacIntyre."

"General?"

"I could repeat General Marshall's words verbatim, if you wish."

"A summary will suffice, sir."

"After ensuring that MacArthur could hear him clearly, he told MacArthur he was relieved and to fly out to the United States with his staff that day. General Wainwright was promoted to Lieutenant General and handed the reins to USAFFE. General MacArthur had to be threatened with irons before he acquiesced. That's about it, Colonel."

"Did General Marshall say which staff members were to come with MacArthur?"

Colonel Obrey looked to Mr. Engelson to see if he would object. He did not.

"His exact words, as I recall, were, 'Bring your staff out with you, especially Brereton.' Yes, those were his words." He nodded as he spoke.

"I see." MacIntyre sat down in his chair. He paused for a moment and looked at MacArthur. "Other than mentioning Brereton, he did not specify who to bring or leave behind, is that right?"

"That is correct, Colonel MacIntyre."

"Thank you, General." Looking up at Colonel Obrey with a tight smile, "I have no further questions, sir."

"Mr. Engelson, your witness."

He stood and shook his head. "No questions, sir."

"General Gerow, you are excused. Thank you for your forbearance in this matter."

General Gerow stood, straightened his blouse, nodded to Colonel Obrey and MacIntyre, and stared with disdain at Colonel MacArthur as he marched out of the hearing room.

Colonel MacIntyre stood.

"The Army calls Colonel Willoughby to the stand, Colonel Obrey."

Moments later, the double doors opened and Colonel Willoughby strode through, squaring his shoulders and twisting his neck to straighten his collar. He reached out slightly and touched General MacArthur as he passed.

Colonel MacIntyre, standing with the bible noted this with narrowed eyes. He thrust out the bible and Willoughby automatically placed his left hand on it, raising his right hand.

"Do you swear to tell the truth, the whole truth and nothing but the truth in the matter before this hearing?"

"I do." He replied quietly.

"Please state your name, rank, and assignment for the record."

"Charles A. Willoughby, Colonel, Infantry, awaiting new assignment."

"What was your last assignment, Colonel?" Asked Colonel MacIntyre.

Willoughby put a forefinger to his lips and tapped as he considered his answer. "I was G2 (Intelligence) in General MacArthur's USAFFE command, sir."

Colonel MacIntyre could see he was being very cautious and going to think out his answer to each question. "Colonel, I'd like to take you back to early November 1941."

"Yes?"

"Did you receive or were you receiving information the Japanese were on the verge of war?"

Colonel MacIntyre pointed his finger at Mr. Engelson, and asked Colonel Willoughby: "I know you had regular sources of information. I ask you, without naming your source, did you have irregular sources of information."

The gavel tapped. "Colonel, are we entering never-never land here?"

"Colonel, I am attempting to learn all of G2's sources of information including some of which we cannot speak."

Colonel Obrey studied his face and checked Engelson. Engelson seemed quiet at the moment. "All right, proceed very carefully, Colonel."

"Thank you, sir. Colonel Willoughby, as G2 you had regular sources of intelligence that came from higher authority. Is that a fair statement of fact?"

"Yes sir," came the puzzled reply.

"Is it fair to say you received intelligence from our Allies?"

"Yes, that is also true."

"And, I suppose you have other sources of intelligence, also."

"Yes," warily or uneasily came the reply.

"Colonel Obrey, where is this dance leading? These are very innocuous questions with no apparent meaning." Asked Mr. Engelson.

"Colonel Obrey, those questions are not innocuous. I am operating within guidelines established earlier regarding intelligence. The next few questions should resolve the issue," said Colonel MacIntyre.

"Very well, Colonel, continue."

"Colonel, are you privy to all intelligence matters brought to General MacArthur's attention?"

"Of course," he said.

"Did General MacArthur have access to information that might be denied to you, even though you were his G2?"

Now, Colonel Willoughby frowned and seemed to fret over this question. Coming to some decision he said, "Colonel, to my best knowledge, the only intelligence General MacArthur ever received passed through my hands, personally." He sat back folding his arms across his chest, almost defiantly.

"Did you have advance knowledge through your various intelligence sources that the Japanese military forces were gearing up to attack the Philippines?"

He hesitated.

"Answer the question, Colonel."

"I saw bits and pieces of information over the last few weeks that led me to believe the Japs were up to something but nothing that pointed directly to the Philippines."

"Did General MacArthur see all that information?"

"Oh yes, every bit of it."

"I see. Who all was cleared for your intelligence material?"

"Just The General, sir."

"Not General Sutherland?"

"Well, he saw most of it. He was not cleared for everything, though."

"Are you including the several war warnings you received from the War Department?"

He made a disparaging noise. "No, Colonel, I don't think they knew as much as we did."

Quick as a flash, "Why do you say that, Colonel Willoughby?"

"We had . . . umm . . . confidential sources of information that were usually correct, sir."

"Did you or General MacArthur relay this intelligence to the War Department?" He asked casually.

"Not always."

Colonel MacIntyre chewed on that answer for a moment. He was sure that Willoughby had picked up he was staying away from referring directly to CAST.

"Did some of the intelligence point to war breaking out in other areas in the Pacific?"

"Yes."

"Where?"

Willoughby was silent.

"Did you have reason to believe the Philippines was one of the initiating targets of the Japanese?" Colonel MacIntyre leaned over the podium toward Colonel Willoughby with his hands on his hips, staring at the witness.

Still no answer as Willoughby hunched lower in the chair.

"Colonel Obrey, I wish to declare Colonel Willoughby a hostile witness. Because of that, I request latitude in questioning the Colonel."

"Objection. Colonel MacIntyre is badgering the witness now, Mr. President. He is asking questions about facts not in evidence."

The Colonel looked at both counsels and beckoned. "Approach."

"Colonel MacIntyre, you're skating on thin ice with the intelligence probing."

"Yes sir, that's exactly what I am doing. I am trying to avoid mention of CAST, and Colonel Willoughby has picked up on that. Even so, I believe he has important information about what the accused knew and the time frame involved."

"I see. Mr. Engelson. Do you have any rejoinder to that?"

He shook his head no. "However, I reserve the right to rebut this witness after the Colonel has completed his examination."

"Step back, Gentlemen. We will recess for lunch at this time and reconvene at 1400 hours." He tapped the gavel and rose.

"All rise."

CHAPTER TWENTY-TWO

1400, 2 March 1942
Conference Room #3
Building B-6
Fort Belvoir, Virginia

Colonel Obrey tapped his gavel once. "This hearing is back in session at 1403 hours. Please be seated." He paused while everyone settled in his or her chairs.

"Colonel Willoughby, I remind you that you are still under oath as a hostile witness for the Army."

"Yes sir." He turned to Colonel MacIntyre and waited apprehensively.

"Quick review, Colonel Willoughby. General MacArthur and you had access to intelligence that no one else could see. Is that correct?" Colonel MacIntyre asked.

Hesitantly, "Yes, that is correct."

"I asked you if you had indication that the Philippines might be attacked shortly. Is that correct?"

"No, that is not correct, Colonel. I said we had information Japan was going to move somewhere in the Pacific. I did not say it was the Philippines."

"Did you have knowledge that the Philippines might be struck by Japanese forces, Colonel?" Colonel MacIntyre was snapping out his questions knowing most of the answers. He was searching for something he did not know.

Colonel Willoughby moved about in his chair trying to get comfortable. "The bits and pieces we saw hinted at strikes in the southwest Pacific, but nothing directly aimed at the Philippines."

"In your opinion, was General Brereton correct when he flew over Formosa on November 20, 1941?"

"Why — " Willoughby paused to think through his answer. "What flight was that, Colonel?" Looking puzzled.

"Colonel Willoughby, straight answer, did you know of General Brereton's flight over Formosa on November 20?"

"Colonel, we are waiting for your answer," threatened Colonel Obrey.

Willoughby seemed to shrivel in the witness chair.

"Colonel Willoughby, you are directed to answer that question now." Colonel Willoughby appeared to be near crying but he remained silent.

"Colonel MacIntyre, Colonel Willoughby is in contempt of court and conduct unbecoming, subject to an Article 70 hearing following this inquiry."

My God, he fell on his sword for MacArthur. Unbelievable!

"Colonel Willoughby, you are hereby confined to quarters until further notice." Ordered Colonel Obrey.

Barely above a whisper, he acknowledged Colonel Obrey's order.

"I have no further questions for this witness at this time, sir."

"Very well, Colonel. Mr. Engelson, your witness."

John Engelson stood, thrust his thumbs into his armpits and paced slowly to the lectern. He looked at the shattered witness. "Colonel Obrey, I believe you and Colonel MacIntyre have destroyed any use Colonel Willoughby had. I have no questions for this witness."

Colonel Obrey studied Engelson for a moment and turned to Colonel Willoughby. "You are excused to your quarters, sir."

Willoughby struggled to compose and restore his military bearing as he strode out of the courtroom.

"Colonel, call your next witness."

Colonel MacIntyre sat in his chair and addressed the President. "Sir, as this is Friday afternoon close to break, I request we recess and reconvene Wednesday morning. I believe our final two witnesses will be present at that time."

John Engelson stood. "Mr. President," he said. "We do not have any other names on their witness list."

Colonel MacIntyre looked at Colonel Obrey but turned to Engelson. "If you check your witness list again, I made space for additional witnesses as John Does. These two witnesses are flying in from Australia on a low priority and we do not have their names, ranks, or service organization."

Mr. Engelson made a depreciating noise and started to say something.

Colonel Obrey looked at both counsels. "Gentlemen, please. Colonel, what guarantee do you have these witnesses are on the way now?"

"None, sir. However, this TWX," waving a message blank in the air, "from Sydney was on my desk earlier and reports two people have left there for Fort Belvoir."

Colonel Obrey beckoned. "Approach."

All the counsels came to the bench. Colonel MacIntyre handed the message up to Colonel Obrey who read it. He handed it to Mr. Engelson who also studied it.

"Very well, Colonel, this court will recess until Wednesday morning. At that time, Mr. Engelson may wish additional time to study what is being brought from Sydney.—Is that satisfactory to you, Mr. Engelson?"

"Yes, Colonel Obrey."

"This hearing is in recess until next Wednesday, March Seventh at 0900." The gavel banged.

"All rise."

CHAPTER TWENTY-THREE

0900, 7 March 1942
Conference Room #3
Building B-6
Fort Belvoir, Virginia

Colonel MacIntyre sat slumped in his chair, hands steepled in front of his face. Capt. Millington and 1st Lieut. Worthington sat across the worktable from him; Staff Sergeant Waters leaned against the doorjamb waiting.

Sounding like Charles Laughton in Mutiny on the Bounty, MacIntyre rolled his head toward Waters. "Staff Sergeant Waters."

"Sah!" Said Waters, stamping his boots, saluting and coming to attention like a British trooper.

"Any luck with the Army Air Force HQ Communications people?"

"No sir, not a bit." He said seriously. "It is beginning to look like none of them got out, either." He thought for a moment. "We're hearing that a lot of troops are heading to the hills instead of waiting to surrender to the Japanese. They know of the Japs cruelty in the Philippines already, and in Nanking, China."

"Okay, what about information on the gold?"

"Nothing yet, except we did hear the submarine could not carry all of the Philippine gold and what's left over was dumped in Manila Bay secretly."

"But that is no help for our case. We'll leave that alone."

The Colonel thought and looked around at Lt. Worthington. "Clint, can you toss in anything about that B-17 flight on 20 November?"

"I don't think so, Colonel. Unless you are looking at rebuilding General Brereton's flight plan, times and targets, I think he said it all."

MacIntyre nodded.

"Hey, Sergeant Waters," began Capt. Millington, "you got any more poop on those two guys flying in from Sydney, or what they represent?"

Waters shook his head. "No sir, only a little—they're on their way from Hickam AFB in Honolulu. But I'm working who they are and what they represent."

"They are about the gold shipment, right?"

"Sir, we don't even know that, and still no name, rank, or service—just that they are reporting in to Fort Belvoir."

"Okay, that's it for now unless any of you have something hanging." He ran his pointing finger at all three who shook their heads.

"Okay, 1900 hours at the O Club. That includes you, Sergeant Waters. Go home and get all gussied up in civvies and meet us at the entrance with your wife."

"Sir, I don't want you to get into any trouble. Maybe we should forget this."

"That's an order, Ryan," with a big smile on his face.

"Yes sir, Colonel, see you all at 1900 hours."

He's never ever called me Ryan before.

He backed out of the office, closing the door behind him. Millington looked at his Colonel with puzzlement. "In all this time, I never knew his first name was Ryan. Are you sure this isn't going to get someone's balls in a terrible uproar at the club?"

"Okay, let's tackle that. Ground rules: first names and friendly. Ryan is about to become Second Lieutenant, JAG, in the Army Reserves, attached to this command. And THAT is a secret, okay?"

"Well, I'll be damned," mused Worthington, scratching his beard stubble. "That means you're going to have to break in a new clerk, Colonel."

"And when is this blessed event going to take place, sir?" asked Millington.

"Colonel Obrey is going to jump all over his ass for being out of uniform Wednesday morning as the hearing reconvenes. Should ruin Ryan's whole day. I'm going to take him to the Uniform Store when we break for lunch. Now, let's get out of here. I need to take a bath before we head over to the Club and meet you and yours."

"Yes. Before Colonel Obrey calls the hearing into session, he is going to eat Staff Sergeant Ryan Waters a new asshole. After he is appropriately shattered, Colonel Obrey is going to recognize our General Cramer who will swear him in as a Second Lieutenant, Judge Advocate Corps, USAR. When we recess for lunch, I'm going to get him into the proper uniform of the day. Does this meet with your approval?"

"That's just great," exclaimed Van der Wendt in a loud whisper. Engelson smiled, saying, "This is similar to promoting an attorney to junior partnership, I suppose. Certainly is better than what we are doing, is it not?" Everyone smiled at each other and returned to their seats.

Colonel Obrey had been watching from behind his entry door. Now he entered.
"All rise."
There was a scramble as members of the hearing and visitors stood in respect.

Colonel Obrey smiled and nodded. "Be seated." Hamming it up a bit, he sat and began looking around, frowning. Except for a few members of the hearing, everyone rustled and squirmed at Colonel Obrey's unusual behavior. He half stood, leaning over his table, pointed his gavel, and looked directly at Waters.

"Staff Sergeant, ... I believe your name is Waters."
Waters leaped to his feet at attention. "Yes, Colonel, that is correct."
"Front and center for Office Hours!"
Waters turned pale. He was about to be charged with some wrongdoing—in front of all these people?

What the fuck did I do wrong?

Straightening his tunic, he squared the corners as he marched up and halted directly in front of Colonel Obrey. Saluting, "Staff Sergeant Ryan Waters, reporting as ordered, Colonel."

Returning his salute, the colonel straightened, holding a blank piece of paper and began to read from it. "Sergeant, I have observed you entering and departing this hearing room at odd times for the past weeks. Do you have a drinking problem? Is that why you disappear at odd times?"

In shock, Waters mouth worked as he tried to reply and could not. He shook his head instead. His face turned white and slowly turned pink.

"Answer the question, Sergeant Waters. Perhaps, your bowels are truly in an uproar and that's why you have to leave. Is that it?" He looked down at the sheet of paper again, hard put to stifle a grin or break out in laughter. The Sergeant was turning purple with embarrassment. He looked at Waters again. "Are you the one breaking foul wind every day?" Colonel Obrey slowly shook his head as he frowned at Staff Sergeant Ryan Waters.

Capt. Millington opened his brief case and withdrew a series of contract papers—papers that Waters would sign, acknowledging honorable discharge in order to accept a commission as a Second Lieutenant in the Army Reserve, and various other forms.

1st Lt. Worthington withdrew a new fore and aft cap, also known as a piss cutter or cunt cap, set up with a gold 2nd Lt. bar on one side and JAG emblem on the other. He also had several metal devices designed for officers to replace his enlisted devices to attach to his shirt, tunic, and overcoat.

Colonel MacIntyre withdrew Waters new commission from his brief case, and stood, followed by Millington and Worthington.

This signaled Colonel Obrey to cut to the chase. General Cramer who had sneaked in earlier and sat down in the back row now got up and quietly walked up behind Sergeant Waters.

"Sergeant Waters, You're a disgrace to that uniform. This is certainly a disagreeable situation. I have asked General Cramer to pass judgment." Spoke Colonel Obrey, solemnly. Waters was about in tears in bewilderment.

Now the Colonel picked up another sheet of paper and looked to the visitors' gallery.

"Attention to orders . . ." There was a mad scramble as all military officers stood and came to attention.

General Cramer stepped in front of Waters, unrolled a sheet of thick paper and began to read. As he read the order honorably discharging Staff Sergeant Ryan Waters as an enlisted man, Millington turned to one of the nearby MPs who bore a mystified expression, and signaled him to quietly bring another chair to their table. Lt. Worthington pulled a razor blade out and began removing Water's Staff Sergeant stripes. Then the three officers assembled behind Waters as he was sworn in as a Second Lieutenant in the United States Army Reserves, Judge Advocates General Corps.

"Lieutenant Waters, about face." His three senior officers hastily moved to his side as flash bulbs went off three times, one catching Colonel MacIntyre placing one of his new gold 2nd Lt. bars on his shoulder.

"Gentlemen, allow me to present Second Lieutenant Ryan Waters for the first time." The applause was loud and long. It was needed to offset this grim hearing. Colonel MacArthur's facial expression was sour. General Cramer shook his hand with a big smile on his face, looked at his watch, and left the courtroom. Second Lieutenant Ryan Waters was still in shock.

The gavel tapped twice. "We will come to order now, we're back in session at 0925. Colonel MacIntyre, are you ready to proceed with your next witness?"

"We are, Colonel."

Second Lieutenant Waters was directed to the new chair at the end of the table where he sat down. Millington handed him a pen and a stack of papers. "I've marked where you have to sign, Lieutenant," he whispered. "You should be done in about fifteen minutes. Also, the Colonel is taking you to the Uniform Clothing Store to get you started when we recess for lunch."

Second Lieutenant Ryan Waters, still stunned, nodded shyly.

CHAPTER TWENTY-FIVE

"Very well, call your next witness."

"The Army calls Admiral Hart to the stand."

The Sergeant-at-Arms was back immediately, trailing a man striding ramrod straight. He wore the uniform of a full Admiral of the U.S. Navy.

Colonel MacIntyre approached with the bible. "Place your left hand on the bible and raise your right hand, Admiral." Admiral Hart did this as he looked around the courtroom.

"Do you swear to tell the truth, the whole truth, and nothing but the truth in the matter before this Board of Inquiry?"

"I do."

"Be seated." The Admiral dropped into his seat and looked at Colonel MacIntyre expectantly.

"Please state your full name, rank, and duty station for the record, Admiral."

"Thomas C. Hart, Admiral, USN, currently attached to Chief of Naval Operations, Surface Warfare."

"Admiral, you were stationed in the Philippines previous to this assignment, were you not?"

"Yes, Colonel MacIntyre, I was Commander in Chief, United States Navy Asiatic Fleet, headquartered in Cavite Naval Yard, near Manila."

"Briefly, would you describe your Navy command to all of us Army people, please."

"Objection, is this marching down some primrose path, Mr. President?"

MacIntyre faced Colonel Obrey. "Colonel Obrey, Admiral Hart's command was involved with War Plan Orange 3 and Rainbow 5. We need his input just as much as from other commands."

Obrey looked at Engelson and said, "Overruled."

Admiral Hart looked back at the Colonel again. "The fleet itself was old and small. There was nothing else to send out there after Pearl Harbor. Since a prior decision had been promulgated by the President to augment the Atlantic Fleet, a dozen destroyers were stripped from the Pacific Fleet to add to the destroyers, destroyer escorts, and patrol frigates in convoy duty in the Atlantic." He cleared his throat and took a sip of water. "However, I kept the three cruisers and several destroyers practicing battle tactics for when war would commence.

"Now when the President executed Phase One, we responded, departing the Philippines on December 3, according to our orders and the plans of Rainbow 5. My ships were scattered throughout the Dutch East Indies." He twisted around and looked at General MacArthur and straightened up, and pointed toward MacArthur. "Now he got his dander up because we pulled up stakes. Either he never took the time to read either plan or was just crazy . . ."

"Objection, character assassination!"

"Sustained. Admiral, you must keep your personal feelings to yourself."

"After he called me a coward, Colonel? I think not! That contemptible blowhard can talk forever and never get anything said."

Wham came the gavel.

"Admiral, if you persist, I will hold you in contempt." Colonel Obrey looked into the Visitor's Gallery. "I can clear the gallery, too." The snickering and faint cheering stopped abruptly.

Colonel MacArthur sat ramrod straight, his face contorted with fury. Mr. Engelson patted his arm and whispered in his ear.

"What else, Admiral?"

"I decided to keep my submarines at Cavite where fuel, torpedoes, and stores were readily available. They were to be ordered out into the Jap Fleet's path to report whatever ships were present when Phase One was executed. We did that so General Brereton's Bombardment Group would have the Jap Fleet's location. They were supposed to fly out at high altitude and try saturation bombing on the convoys. But then MacArthur fixed that."

"Colonel . . ."

"Admiral, control yourself and show some respect for his rank."

Admiral Hart peered up at Colonel Obrey. "Colonel, I outranked MacArthur in the Philippines, and I certainly outrank him now. I followed orders then and I will now." He looked at the Colonel. "Are we finished here, Colonel MacIntyre? If so, I have a war to fight."

MacIntyre looked back at Millington and Worthington who were grinning and shaking their heads. Lt. Waters was still signing papers.

"I have no further questions of this witness, Mr. President."

"Your witness, Mr. Engelson."

"I have no questions for this Naval person."

"You are excused, Admiral. Thank your for your time."

Admiral Hart stood, picked up his hat and headed for the door. He stopped opposite the defense table and in a low voice clearly heard throughout the courtroom, "Traitor!" And walked on.

MacArthur leaped up and started after the admiral. Mr. Engelson, Colonel Van der Wendt, and the Sergeant-at-Arms stopped him.

The gavel broke again as Colonel Obrey tried to bring order back into the courtroom. "This court stands in recess until tomorrow at 0900 hours. I shall determine what to do about General MacArthur's violence."

"All rise."

Colonel Obrey got off the stage as fast as he could. Meanwhile, the gallery who had been noisy as MacArthur passed by on previous recesses, stood silently and just watched him leave.

CHAPTER TWENTY-SIX

0900, 8 March 1942
Conference Room #3
Building B-6
Fort Belvoir, Virginia

Colonel Obrey stood for a moment with a new gavel in his hand. "If there are any more outbursts as there were yesterday, I will clear this hearing room."
The galleries stilled, watching. The colonel dropped the gavel once. "This hearing is back in session at 0904. Be seated."
He looked at Colonel MacIntyre.
"Colonel MacIntyre, do you have any more witnesses to present?"
MacIntyre looked at Colonel Obrey for a long minute. "Yes sir, the Army recalls General Sutherland to the stand."
"Objection. General Sutherland has been examined. Prosecution cannot recall this witness."
"In previous testimony by Generals Drake and Gerow, a question came up that only General Sutherland and Colonel MacArthur could answer."
"I'll allow this but you better have something more than wishful thinking, Colonel." He waved at the Sergeant-At-Arms who left to find General Sutherland.
"I believe so, Colonel. That's why I am recalling the General."

"General Sutherland, you are still sworn and a hostile witness for the Army. You will answer all questions put to you by the Army," instructed Colonel Obrey.
"Yes sir, Colonel." Sutherland looked straight forward, hunched in the witness chair.
Colonel MacIntyre stood at his desk, holding a legal pad on which he had scribbled some questions.
"General, I direct your attention to December 18, 1941, Manila time."
"Yes sir."
"You stated earlier you were outside General MacArthur's private office when General Marshall called. Is that correct?"
"Yes sir."

"Then, following that radiophone conversation, General MacArthur called you and Colonel Huff into his office and closed the door. Is that also correct?"

Yes sir," came the puzzled reply.

"Did General MacArthur relate the conversation with General Marshall?" Colonel MacIntyre moved to the podium.

General Sutherland shifted in his seat, showing signs of nervousness. "Ahh, he told us he was fired, that General Wainwright was promoted and relieving him. He said we each had to pack one bag and be prepared to fly out that night."

"We each?"

"Objection. Counselor is quibbling over word and sentence structure."

"Sustained. Move on, Colonel."

"Yes sir. General, you just said we. Who is 'we'?"

"Oh, his family, Huff, Brereton, and myself. General Marshall apparently asked that General Brereton come out also."

"That's all?"

"Yes, Colonel, that's all."

"I remind you you are under oath and required to answer my questions."

"Yes, yes," looking very annoyed with this Colonel.

"Search your mind, General. Is that all General MacArthur said?"

"Objection. Counsel is badgering this witness. He has already answered his question."

"Colonel Obrey, I have to drag the truth out of General Sutherland word by word. Either his mind is slipping or he is deliberately stonewalling this hearing."

"Overruled. General Sutherland, you are again instructed as a hostile witness. You are required to answer every question put to you. Do you understand this?" Colonel Obrey's voice was stern and brooked no cat and mouse games with this witness.

General Sutherland sighed and acknowledged Colonel Obrey with a wave of his hand.

"General Sutherland, you will answer my question, yes or no." Ordered Colonel Obrey.

"The answer is yes," glaring at this insignificant Colonel.

Who the hell does he think he is, addressing me like this?

"General, you are very close to entering the Stockade for insolence toward this hearing. You will conform, do you hear me." Sutherland straightened up; suddenly realizing he had overstepped his bounds. "Yes sir, I apologize, Colonel."

Colonel Obrey pointed his gavel toward Colonel MacIntyre.

"General, was Colonel Huff present for this?"

Sutherland hesitated.

What does he know?

"Right after he announced being relieved, The General sent him to General MacArthur's quarters to prepare his wife and servant for the transfer that night."

"What else transpired between you and General MacArthur—while you were alone, General?"

"Well, we had to hand off the command to General Wainwright and see to other details, as well."

"I see. I find it curious that only General Brereton of General MacArthur's staff came out with you."

"Objection. Where's the question?" Called Mr. Engelson with raised hand.

"Strike that. Did you and General MacArthur discuss which of his staff would come out with you?"

"Why no. Most of the general staff had to stay behind to help Wainwright."

"Were they ordered to stay or did they volunteer to stay?"

"Uh, Colonel, we couldn't locate the others in the short time before we left."

"You tried to call each officer and left urgent messages for them to reply. Is that it? Colonel MacIntyre quietly asked.

"Uh yes, Colonel, I instructed General MacArthur's clerk to call all of his staff officers. It's just that none responded before we departed."

"That is not what General Drake had to say!"

Startled, Sutherland looked up and asked, "What? He's here?"

"He testified earlier, General. According to his testimony, none of the other general staff officers or their senior NCOs WHO WERE ALL NEAR THEIR EE-5 PHONES were contacted. Indeed, they didn't know you were gone until General Wainwright informed them of the change of command. Now then, General Sutherland, do you wish to modify your testimony?"

"There were severe problems, Colonel. Those two B-17s just could not hold more people. Besides, they had nothing to contribute to this hearing."

Colonel Obrey sat back and stared at General Sutherland in disbelief.

"General Sutherland," asked Colonel MacIntyre softly, "did you and General MacArthur decide between you not to bring the rest of the general staff out? In spite of General Marshall's order to bring out MacArthur's staff?"

"Objection. Leading the witness."

"Strike that," stated a seething Colonel MacIntyre. "I have no further questions for this witness."

"Your witness, Mr. Engelson."

John Engelson studied General Sutherland and saw a broken man, nervously rubbing his hands on his trousers again. He shook his head. "No, Colonel, no questions."

"Colonel MacIntyre, is it your intention to prefer charges against General Sutherland?" Asked Colonel Obrey.

"Not at this time, sir."

The Sergeant-at-Arms hurried forward to Colonel MacIntyre, leaned over and whispered: "Sir, this was just handed to me with instructions to urgently deliver this note immediately."

"Thank you, Sergeant," he said absently, as he glanced at the note and did a classic double take.

Colonel MacIntyre studied the note closely and handed it to his staff to read. Fast whispering between all three other officers resulted from reading the note.

Colonel Obrey looked around as people settled down. He cleared his throat and drank some water. "Colonel MacIntyre, call your next witness."

MacIntyre looked up at Colonel Obrey and back at the note. Standing, he addressed Colonel Obrey. "Colonel," holding up the note, "I have just received word of an urgent phone call that has a bearing on this hearing. I request a thirty minute recess."

"How does it bear on this hearing, Colonel?"

"Because the note says 'Regarding the missing gold, please call New York City telephone number Empire 6-5000 at your earliest convenience.' Colonel Obrey. This may be very important information."

"This hearing is in recess until 1400 hours this afternoon. I trust that Lieutenant Waters will be in the correct uniform by then, Colonel."

"Yes sir, at least one uniform," said MacIntyre with a big grin.

Lieutenant Waters looked at the colonel with a shy grin, too.

"All rise."

There was a hasty scramble as everyone came to attention while Colonel Obrey left the courtroom.

"Okay, gentlemen. This note changes things. Clint, would you be good enough to escort Second Lieutenant Ryan Waters to the nearest phone to tell Susan the good news." He laughed at Ryan who obviously had not thought about that. "Also, take him to the uniform shop and get him fitted out for one Class A uniform with new ribbons to wear this afternoon. Use General Cramer's name if you have to. Then, help him order what he needs. Help get his new AGO card, too, if there is time before reconvening this afternoon.

"Yes sir, we're on our way. You, I trust, are going to check out that phone call?"

"Right. Tom, you're on me." They all left the building on their separate missions.

"New Philippines Bank, Mr. Georges speaking."

This may be the ball breaker!

"This is Colonel Leroy MacIntyre of the Army Judge Advocate General's office. I was instructed to call this number."

"Yes, good morning Colonel. Has someone in your office has been trying to track down a missing shipment of gold in Australia."

"That's right, Mr. Georges, my investigator, Lieutenant Waters, has been trying to learn where five hundred thousand dollars of the Commonwealth of the Philippines gold bullion disappeared to after being moved from the submarine. How do you know about this, sir?"

"First of all, I am Anthony Georges, Bank President of the New Philippines Bank. This bank is the official bank of the Philippines in the United States. Our Correspondent Bank is the Chase National Bank. The total value of the missing gold was close to seven hundred forty thousand dollars, Colonel. The bullion, under General MacArthur's Army guard, was taken to Chase National Bank in Brisbane, Australia. Upon receipt, that bank wired seven hundred forty thousand dollars through to our office here. President Manual Queson instructed me to ask General Douglas MacArthur how to disburse funds from that grant."

Colonel MacIntyre's heartbeat was racing with excitement and dread. "Can you tell me or show proof how the fund was disbursed, Mr. Georges?"

"Ordinarily I would not. However, I understand this is an official investigation by the United States Army, and I will. It was in four drafts drawn on Chase National Bank to MacArthur, Sutherland, Eisenhower, and Huff. Strangely, Eisenhower refused his draft and returned it unsigned."

Not so strange, Mr. Georges, not so strange.

"I see. Do you know if the other drafts were accepted and deposited in other banks?"
"Yes, Colonel, they were signed and deposited in separate banks by MacArthur, Sutherland, and Huff."
He was quiet for a moment. "There's more."
"Oh?"

"Yes. I was ordered by the Philippine Treasurer to issue a check for expenses to General MacArthur for $35,000."
"$35,000? Was that in addition to the $740,000 funding? Asked Colonel MacIntyre.

"Yes, and not only that, in a most unusual move, a strange move, I was required to confirm the check was written and delivered to his personal account in another bank. Manila was insistent on a return wire instead of the usual bank procedures of inter-banking."

Colonel MacIntyre was silent for a moment as he thought things out. He was sick inside for which he now had to do. "Mr. Georges, in the strictest confidence, we are conducting secret hearings on General MacArthur's lack of actions at the beginning of the war. I'd like you to fly to Fort Belvoir immediately, if possible, to testify this afternoon. Can you do that?"

"Ordinarily no. But I thought something like this was going to happen. My bank's airplane is ready to go as soon as I get to the airfield. If someone can pick me up at the Washington airport, I will be there in about two hours."
"Oh, you can count on that. Captain Thomas Millington will be watching for you."

CHAPTER TWENTY-SEVEN

1400, 8 March 1942
Conference Room #3
Building B-6
Fort Belvoir, Virginia

"All rise."

Colonel Obrey walked to his table, checked over the assembled officers and saw a civilian in the visitors' gallery. "Will someone explain the presence of the civilian gentleman in the visitors gallery, please?"

"Yes sir, Colonel," said Colonel MacIntyre, rising from his chair. "The gentleman is my next witness."

Colonel Obrey nodded and tapped his gavel. "Be seated, this hearing is now in session."

"Colonel MacIntyre, call your witness."

"The United States Army calls Mr. Anthony Georges to the stand."

Mr. Georges arose and walked to the witness chair. A babble of curiosity followed him.

Colonel MacIntyre brought the bible to him. "Place your left hand on the bible and raise your right hand.

> *Do you swear to tell the truth, the whole truth, and nothing but the truth in the matters before this Board of Inquiry?"*

"I do."

"Thank you. State your name, occupation, and place of business, please."

"I am Anthony Georges, President of the New Philippines Bank in Manhattan, New York."

Leroy MacIntyre turned a strained face to Colonel Obrey. "Colonel, Mr. Georges' note to call him led to a long conversation about the alleged missing gold bullion belonging to the Philippine Treasury. The New Philippine Bank, along with Corresponding Bank, Chase National Bank, represents the Philippine Treasury in the United States. He had information about some drafts that President

Queson and the Philippine Treasurer had ordered and they did not seem proper. Couple that with rumors we were looking for the missing bullion led him to call me.

While he spoke, MacIntyre closely observed Colonel MacArthur at the Defense Table, motionless and wooden-faced whose face was turning paler than usual.

"Will you repeat what you told me earlier on the telephone, please?"

"As I said, I am Anthony Georges, Bank President of the New Philippines Bank: the official bank of the Philippines in the United States. The total value of the missing gold was seven hundred forty thousand dollars in United States currency, Colonel. Philippines Executive Order Number One of 1942, under President Queson's signature made specific instructions. The bullion, under General MacArthur's Army guard, was taken to an Australian bank we do business with in Brisbane. Upon receipt, that bank transferred seven hundred forty thousand dollars through Chase National Bank to our office here. President Manual Queson instructed me to ask General Douglas MacArthur how to disburse funds from that grant."

"Did you follow his instructions, Mr. Georges?"

"Yes sir. As we spoke this morning, one was returned, refused."

"And the others, were they deposited into any bank accounts?"

"Yes sir, they were."

"Do you know the reason or purpose for issuing these drafts?"

"Yes, Colonel. President Queson specifically stated the memo line on each of the four checks should read, 'For Services Rendered through December 31, 1941.'"

"Please repeat that, Mr. Georges." Colonel MacIntyre looked directly at Colonel MacArthur as he asked for the repeat.

"Of course. President Queson specifically stated the memo line on each of the four checks should read, 'For Services Rendered through December 31, 1941.'"

"What is the name of the officer who refused the draft, Mr. Georges?"

He held up the returned check. "Dwight D. Eisenhower." Mr. Georges started to hand it to the Colonel and pulled it back. "I understand you must enter these in evidence but I need the original drafts after you are finished with them, sir."

He turned to his table. "Lieutenant Waters, will you present the new document to the accused, please?"

Lt. Waters, resplendent in his new Class A uniform, walked across the room to Mr. Engelson and presented him with the document, then turned and gave the Court Reporters their copies, the Clerk his copy, and Colonel Obrey his copy. Then, he returned to his seat.

> **To Charge I, the Army adds the following specification:**
> **Specification (4):**

In that then Lieutenant General Douglas Arthur MacArthur committed treason against the United States of America by feloniously accepting a five hundred thousand dollar bribe from President Manuel Queson, United States Commonwealth of the Philippines, not to anger the Japanese by attacking Japanese forces or retaliating from any attacks elsewhere in the Pacific by Japanese forces, causing them to attack the Philippines.

"Colonel Obrey, Douglas A. MacArthur accepted five hundred thousand dollars from President Queson and deposited it in his bank account after he arrived at Fort Belvoir. There can be no question about it. This was a bribe. The memo line proves he was still in the employ of the Philippine government until the end of 1941, six months after he had been appointed Commander in Chief, U.S. Army Forces, Far East.

A savage soto voce whisper cracked across the room. "Benedict Arnold!". Colonel Obrey absently tapped the gavel without saying a word. He simply stared at MacArthur who had whitened but was frozen in his spot. John Engelson and Eric Van der Wendt were carefully reading the additional specification. Engelson looked up at MacIntyre. "May I cross examine now, Colonel?"
"No, Mr. Engelson, I have the proof to enter into the record."

Mr. Georges handed him one check. The Colonel looked at it momentarily and handed it to Colonel Obrey who looked at the front to see the name, amount, and memo line. Turning it over, MacArthur's bold signature was the final shock. He shook his head and turned to the Clerk. "Have all four checks photographed front and back immediately and the originals returned to Mr. Georges as soon as possible."

"Your witness, Mr. Engelson." Colonel MacIntyre returned to his seat.
Mr. Engelson, Colonel Van der Wendt, and The General were huddled in conference.

"Mr. Engelson?"

Engelson turned away and stood. "Colonel Obrey, the nature of this very serious charge requires we study the issues and determine our course of action. We request a two day recess."

Colonel Obrey looked at Colonel MacIntyre. "Colonel MacIntyre, do you have any objection to the Defense's request for a two day recess."

MacIntyre stood with a tight grin on his face. He had MacArthur by the short hairs with no place to go. "The Army has no objection, Colonel."

"Very well, this hearing is in recess until 0900 hours Thursday, morning, March 10th." The gavel sounded once.

"All rise." There was the usual scramble as everyone stood and came to attention until Colonel Obrey departed the stage.

CHAPTER TWENTY-EIGHT

1500, 8 March 1942
General Cramer's Conference Room
Building B-6
Fort Belvoir, Virginia

Colonels Obrey, MacIntyre, Van der Wendt, and Mr. Engleson sat in leather chairs before General Cramer's desk. Sitting on the edge of his chair, leaning on his cane, Mr. Engleson raised a finger toward the general.

"General, using the Reasonable Man theory, it seems Colonel MacArthur will spend a long time in military prison. However, I have strong feelings that General Sutherland is the snake in the grass that will put him there."

Colonel MacIntyre looked over at Mr. Engleson." You are going to have to let General MacArthur take the stand to refute General Sutherland's testimony—if you do that, I will crucify him."

Colonel Van der Wendt asked, "do you suppose Sutherland knows you cannot allow MacArthur to testify, and is covering his skirts?" He turned to Mr. Engleson. "Why not put Sutherland on the stand as a friendly witness, then turn the screws." He thought for a second. "Is there any way we can get him in the Witness chair somewhat messed up? He is a dandy, you know."

Colonel Obrey added, "We all know that MacArthur has been very much upset by some of Sutherland and Brereton comments and charges.

General Cramer tapped a knuckle on his desk. That stopped all conversation. "We've carried this on long enough into very dangerous territory. You each have your jobs to do. Go do it. This meeting is adjourned."

The officers of the hearing all stood and filed out of the general's office. "Gentlemen," said Colonel Obrey. "The hearing resumes at 1400 hours day after tomorrow. Enjoy your lunch," and he walked away.

CHAPTER TWENTY-NINE

1400, 10 March 1942
Conference Room #3
Building B-6
Fort Belvoir, Virginia

"All rise." The usual shuffle and coughing began and stopped. Colonel Obrey entered the hearing room and stopped at his desk. Surveying the crowd quickly, he picked up his gavel and tapped it once.

"This hearing is back in session at 1402 hours. Colonel MacIntyre, continue, please."

Colonel MacIntyre stood, looked at the defense table, then at Colonel Obrey. "Colonel, the Army rests its case against Colonel Douglas Arthur MacArthur," and sat down.

As though there had been no conversation between all the main players, he nodded, "I see." Turning to Mr. Engleson, "does defense wish to present its case now?"

"Yes, Colonel Obrey, Defense calls as its first witness, Brigadier General Sutherland to the stand."

The visitor's section murmured at this recall.

General Sutherland marched in, very relaxed and smiling, and took his seat in the witness chair.

Colonel Obrey looked down at General Sutherland. "I remind you, general, you are still under oath to tell the truth."

"Yes, yes, yes," General Sutherland responded, annoyed at the reminder.

Mr. Engleson looked at him and leaned over to Colonel Van der Wendt. They whispered momentarily, and then Colonel Van der Wendt stood and casually approached the lectern.

"Good afternoon, General. How are you today?"

Puzzled, he responded irritably, "just fine, thank you."

"That's good, we want to review a few points of your previous testimony. As Chief of Staff for General MacArthur, you had to be sharp as a tack to keep up with the general's whims and orders, isn't that true?"

General Sutherland leaned back, relaxing.

This was going to be a walk in the park.

"Oh yes, very much so. I had to know just what he wanted and when to take care of things."

"All right general, then why are you so confused about where you were in the early hours of December 8th? You couldn't recall when you and the general left for GHQ—or even if he left at the same time."
General Sutherland sat bolt upright staring at Colonel Van der Wendt in astonishment.

Is he attacking me? How dare he do that?

While he sputtered, Colonel Van der Wendt asked, "By the way, just what time did you arrive at GHQ, General?"
"0430 hours," he snapped.
"That's not true, General Sutherland. You were still in General MacArthur's quarters at that time."
"Are you calling me a liar?" he shouted, rising from his chair.
"Yes, sir, I am. That's when General Brereton arrived at General MacArthur's quarters. When did you arrive at GHQ?"
"It must have been a few minutes later, then." He pulled a handkerchief from his pocket, started to pat his face, and thought better of it. Instead, he wiped his hands but held onto the handkerchief.
"I see. When you arrived at GHQ, did you sound Call To Arms throughout the command?"
"Ah, no, I did not."
"As I understand it, General, you arrived at General MacArthur's office ahead of The General to prepare for battle. Is that it?"
"Uh yeah, that must have been it. Yes," he said, straightening up.
"And that's when General Brereton appeared at General MacArthur's GHQ door around 0500 hours demanding to see The General again, and you physically forced him away. Is that about right?"
"Absolutely right. He wasn't going in his office while I had anything to say about it."
"Because he was still in his quarters at that time. Isn't that true?"

General Sutherland just stared at him.

"As a good Chief of Staff, you were protecting your Commander. You told General Brereton he had his orders that General MacArthur refused to see him. Isn't that right, too? You wanted The General time to slip into his office without General Brereton interrupting him. Isn't this true, General?"

General Sutherland just stared straight ahead without answering.

Colonel Van der Wendt looked at Mr. Engleson to see if he should continue who waggled his finger indicating no. He returned to the Defense table for instructions, and then sat down.

Mr. Engleson, working on General MacArthur's behalf had a few more questions to ask of General Sutherland.

"General Sutherland, would you say The General was fairly stressed by the turn of events and needed a few minutes to gather his thoughts?"

"Oh no sir, he was right on top . . ."

". . . if he was right on top of the situation, why didn't he show himself to his hardworking staff? As I recall from previous testimony, no one saw General MacArthur until much later that day, not even during that brawl you had with General Brereton. Was that when you had the Stand Down order typed up and thrust it under a confused general's hand to sign?"

General Sutherland sat there stunned, his lips moving without sound.

Mr. Engleson slapped his table explosively. "General Sutherland, you have not answered the last four questions. Are your answers to them in the affirmative or negative?"

The silence was thick in the room. Finally, the gavel tapped quietly. "Mr. Engleson, I am in a quandary." Colonel Obrey chewed on his lower lip for a moment. "Brigadier General Sutherland was the Army's hostile witness and was held in contempt for failure to answer their questions. You also appear to be treating him as a hostile defense witness." He paused, looking at Colonel MacIntyre who looked shocked at the Court's apparent interference. "Where are you going with this, Mr. Engleson?"

Mr. Engleson spoke with care. "Colonel, in privileged conversation, it appears my client had no knowledge of some of the events unfolding . . ."

". . . facts not in evidence, Colonel. General MacArthur has not spoken or written of these allegations."

Mr. Engleson turned to Colonel MacIntyre and nodded. "Withdrawn.

Mr. Engleson lifted his shoulders, took a deep breath and sighed and addressed Colonel Obrey. "It appears that a cocky, self-assured Chief of Staff took too much on his shoulders by issuing his OWN orders while General MacArthur," he paused here searching the ceiling for the right phrase, "was—not available. I submit that Lieutenant General MacArthur is guilty of being the Commander-in-Chief, and therefore completely responsible for everything in his command. He did not expect his handpicked Chief of Staff to be so gauche as to countermand Phase One and Two directives."

He turned to General Sutherland. "Whatever else you are, General, you are a liar and too cowardly to admit your wrongdoing!"

General Sutherland leaped out of his chair, screaming, "How dare you call me a liar and coward, you miserable pimp lawyer." He advanced toward Mr. Engleson who began backing away from him.

"Sergeant-at-arms, restrain General Sutherland," called Colonel Obrey loudly. "Escort him to the witness room." The sergeant saluted and pointed to two of his MP's who immediately came away from their walls and stepped between the defense table and General Sutherland.

"General," spoke the Sergeant-At-Arms in a quiet voice near General Sutherland's ear, "I don't want to lay hands on you, sir. Please come along quietly."

General Sutherland glared at Mr. Engleson, his hands opening and closing while he trembled in heated anger.

"Please General…"

"Come along, General. That's the Court's order, sir."

General Sutherland in a red-faced rage, straightened to attention, pulled his blouse down, adjusted his tie and Sam Brown belt. Without glancing at the MP's or the Sergeant-At-Arms, he strode rapidly to the double doors, slammed them open and departed, accompanied by the MP's.

The gavel slammed down. "This hearing is in recess until tomorrow at 0900 hours. I will see counsel in chambers, immediately."

One of the Recorders called out, "All rise."

Colonel Obrey stood and marched rigidly off the stage to his office.

Colonel Obrey sat in his office chair at his desk. In front of him, pressed against his desk, was a ten-foot long table with chairs along the side and end. As in court, Trial sat on his left and defense to the right. The three Recorders sat at the foot, pencils poised.

He looked around, pointing with his finger: "coffee, tea, iced water, anyone?" Colonel Obrey pressed his intercom key. "Sergeant, we need some liquid refreshments in here -- pitchers of coffee, tea, and iced water."

"Yes, Colonel, right away," came the hollow voice.

"Suppose we begin with the Defense Team.—Wait. Roy? General Sutherland is your witness, albeit hostile. Why haven't you objected to Mr. Engleson's line of questioning? He was certainly badgering and you did not object. What's going on here?"

Colonel MacIntyre had a look of the cat that swallowed the canary. "Hey, he called him and is asking questions that if I tried, he would have been hopping up and down objecting his head off." Mr. Engleson was chuckling on the other side of the table. "Now, I even get to cross examine, if there is anything left of Sutherland after Engleson finishes."

Engleson took a deep breath and let it out slowly as he looked at the others. "It is my opinion that Sutherland has deeply wronged my client. If I can prove that, most of the charges go away."

"Aw come on, Counselor," MacIntyre said disgustedly. "There are the unaccounted ten hours and a $500,000 check he deposited. They are not going away—but he will. Hell, I am willing to drop all the other charges: reduce the whole thing to just these two and you and I can duke it out at MacArthur's General Court-martial."

"Colonel MacIntyre, I have not decided whether or not the defendant is going to any court-martial. I make that decision, not you. Is that clear to you?"

MacIntyre stood. "Colonel Obrey and Mr. Engleson, I am deeply sorry. I made an assumption that got me into trouble. I apologize once again."

Mr. Engleson's smile faded to a serious mien and he tapped his teacup for attention. As all eyes turned to him, he asked tentatively, "Supposing I convinced my client it would be in his best interest to take the stand, Colonel MacIntyre. Would you be willing to contain your cross examination to a narrow field . . . say some of the statements or accusations made by General Sutherland and Colonel Huff?" He pursed his lips a moment and continued. "I believe it would help him if we could make Phase One and Two go away. After all, General Brereton never had any contact with my client, just hearsay from General Sutherland."

"Before you consider deals, Colonel MacIntyre, keep the purpose of Rainbow 5 at the very front of your mind." He stared at Engleson and Van der Wendt. "And, other than enraging General Sutherland, I have not heard your defense program yet. I suggest you have some work to do tonight." He smiled at everyone: "Shall we break now and continue in the morning?"

CHAPTER THIRTY

0900, 11 March 1942
Conference Room #3
Building B-6
Fort Belvoir, Virginia

"All rise."

Chairs scraped, pushed back by people standing up. Wet wool odors proliferated the hearing room. When it was quiet, as now, the roar of heavy rain and flare of lightning and its thunder caused a lot of people to remember battlefields past of what is now called the First World War that ended only twenty-four years ago.

"Gentlemen, be seated." Colonel Obrey continued to stand as he looked around the hearing room. He waited for the muttering to die.

"I do have a smattering of good news to relate. This month, Lieutenant Colonel James A. Doolittle flew off an aircraft carrier in the North Pacific with sixteen North American B-25 Mitchell medium bombers and struck targets across the Japanese islands of Honshu and Kyushu. No great damage except to the Japanese pride." A scattering of light applause increased to a thunderous ovation—we were striking back!

He waited for the applause to die. "Yes. We have business to attend here and now." He looked down at the Witness Chair. "General Sutherland, you are still under oath." Then Colonel Obrey sat down.

General Sutherland stood and left-faced Colonel Obrey. "Colonel, may I address this body?" Obrey looked at him for a long moment. And formally spoke, "permission granted, General."
General Sutherland nodded, looked at Colonel Obrey and did a smart about- face to the remainder of the people. "Members of this hearing and everyone in the gallery, I abjectly apologize for my strong outburst yesterday afternoon and ask your forgiveness." He about-faced to Colonel Obrey, stood at attention for a short moment and sat down in his chair. Colonel Obrey cleared his throat and said gruffly, "Let the record show General Sutherland's apology is accepted. Mr. Engleson, your witness."

A short whispered conversation between Van der Wendt, Engleson, and MacArthur, then Colonel Van der Wendt stood and faced the Witness Chair. It was easy to see that General Sutherland did not like Colonel Van der Wendt asking questions. Colonel MacIntyre and his staff had pencils poised to make notes of this exchange.

"General, let me explain our, that is, Colonel MacArthur's defense position. In the process of probing, you struck back because you believed we were after you, calling you a liar and worse." He looked down at his notes and gathered his thoughts. "We are defending Colonel MacArthur, not you. If you believe you should have an attorney, speak up now, please."

"Yes sir, I need at attorney to look after my interests. I don't want to answer any more questions."

The gavel fell. "General Sutherland, are you invoking the Fifth Amendment?" General Sutherland twisted in his chair to face Colonel Obrey. "Yes sir, I am."

The gavel fell again. "This witness is excused to find legal representation. General, you are still a witness to these proceedings." General Sutherland nodded yes and hurried from the Witness Chair to the door, looked back, and departed.

"Mr. Engleson, call your next witness, please."

Another Defense consultation ensued.

"Mr. Engleson?"

His hand rose acknowledging the call, as they continued whispering.

Mr. Engleson, call your next witness." Colonel Obrey was annoyed and sounded so.

Mr. Engleson faced Colonel Obrey. "We call Colonel Douglas MacArthur to the stand."

Colonel MacIntyre and his staff practically leaped in the air. They would be able to question him on several points if Engleson gave them an opening.

Colonel MacArthur ruffled his shoulders and stalked to the Witness Chair. Colonel MacIntyre was almost licking his chops in anticipation. He got up and casually, oh so casually, walked to the Witness Chair with the bible and extended it toward Colonel MacArthur. "Place your left hand on the bible and raise your right hand . . . "

"Isn't my word good enough without swearing it, Colonel?"

Caught off guard, Colonel MacIntyre struggled for an answer.

Colonel Obrey interceded. "Colonel, this is the standard

format for all hearings. Colonel MacIntyre, please swear the witness now."

Colonel MacArthur gave Colonel Obrey a steely look, which was returned in kind, and placed his hand on the bible and raised his right hand.

> *"Do you solemnly swear to tell the truth, the whole truth, and nothing but the truth, in matters brought before this hearing?"*

asked Colonel MacIntyre.

"Yes, yes, I so swear," he replied.

Colonel Obrey got attention by clearing his throat. Everyone stopped to learn what the colonel had in mind. "Mr. Engleson, Colonel MacIntyre—has Colonel MacArthur had his rights read to him? Does he fully understand the consequences of taking the stand?"

General MacArthur turned to look up at Colonel Obrey with disdain. "Colonel, I am fully aware of my rights and the possible consequences of taking the stand."

"Just his responsibilities he doesn't understand," came soto voce from the military gallery.

Colonel Obrey broke another gavel, and stood up angrily looking at the gallery. "Dammit, I don't know which of you gentlemen was responsible for that remark, and do not want to know. Any further disparaging remarks and I will clear the gallery." He stood motionless staring at the gallery with steely eyes, then slowly sat down. He motioned to Colonel MacIntyre to continue.

"Be seated. Please state your name, rank and duty status.

"Certainly. My name is, as you well know, Douglas Arthur MacArthur, recently demoted to Colonel from Lieutenant General. My duty status is in limbo." His voice was emotionless as he stared straight ahead.

Colonel Obrey quietly tapped his broken gavel head a couple of times. "Let the record show that regarding Colonel Douglas Arthur MacArthur's duty status, he is here to answer charges of deeds or lack of deeds that may have taken place in the Philippines while he was Commander-in-Chief, United States Army Forces in the Far East." Then, he leaned back and waved his gavel at Mr. Engleson.

"Your witness, Counselor."

John Engleson stood by his desk, yellow legal pad with notes neatly arranged, in his hand. He knew this was going to be a delicate surgical test of his skills to come out of this hearing with his client's hide. He took a slow look around the room to judge the sense of the people within.

Across the aisle, Colonel MacIntyre stared intently at Engleson. He didn't feel there was any wiggle room for MacArthur's escape but just to make sure, his senses were sharply attuned.
"Colonel MacArthur, you have heard the witnesses testify to all the charges . . ."
"Yes, I have, and most of them . . ."
"Colonel, please do not interrupt me again."

Colonel MacArthur looked at him in shock. No one spoke to him like that. With great difficulty, he brought himself under control and smiled thinly at Mr. Engleson. "Pardon me, John. As you were saying . . ." And leaned back in his chair.
Colonel MacIntyre and his staff exchanged barely stifled smiles and turned their attention back to the Defense.

John Engleson grasped both lapels and looked down at his feet as though trying to remember where he was.
"Colonel MacArthur, you have heard the witnesses testify to all the charges. I want you to think back to Monday, December 8 past, and tell this Hearing what you recall of the seventh and eighth."
"Do you want me to start at reveille, John?" Colonel MacArthur asked as his gaze wandered about the room.

Mr. Engleson stepped in front of Colonel MacArthur, spread his arms wide, and brought them together. "Please keep focused on me, Colonel. And, no, Colonel, why don't you begin by telling us who was present for supper and continue from there. That will help you remember details more clearly."

"Well, this was en famile, you understand, Au Chew had already taken Arthur to his room, so only Jean, Sidney, and myself were present. Jean had a glass of chardonnay, Sidney and I had scotch—Old Grouse Scotch, I believe. Au Chew made a marvelous fruit salad of papaya, pineapple, mango, and some small nuts. This was following by a light soup. Our main course was lamb chops, with boiled rice . . ."

"That is incredible, Colonel. You have a masterful recall of details." Colonel MacArthur was again shocked at being interrupted by his own counsel. "Let us continue after the Supper hour. What happened next?" Engleson asked, looking a little peeved.

"Hmmm. As I recall, Jean retired to her sewing room while Sidney and I moved to the veranda. I smoked a cigar with another glass of scotch." He leaned forward confidentially. "Sidney can not smoke cigars, you know. His heart condition forbids it." He leaned back and surveyed the room again.

"General, focus on me, please."

"Oh, to be sure, John." He smiled apologetically. "Where were we?" He thought for a minute, dropped his elbow to his knee and raised his hand with a finger pointing skyward. "Yes, Sidney and I chatted about what the Japanese were up to. We discussed the situation in French IndoChina wondering if Singapore would be able to hold when the Japanese attacked.—Yes, that was our conversation." Leaning back, he looked at the ceiling thinking, then looked at Mr. Engleson who was waiting patiently.

"After a bit, I told Sidney I was somewhat tired and would retire for the night." Looking at his feet, he said "I remember telling Sidney to make sure the telephone lines were switched off for the night so we would have a good night's sleep. Since the Japanese had not dropped a surprise attack on us on Sunday as they like to do, nothing was going to happen for a while."

Colonel MacIntyre wrote surprise attack in big letters and underscored it with Millington and Worthington looking over his shoulder.

"Let the record show that Lieutenant Colonel Huff indicated that General MacArthur retired at approximately 2200 hours," said Mr. Engleson. "Is that the last you remember for the evening of December Seven, General?"

"Ummm, yes. Of course, I read my bible, as I usually do, for a while said my prayers and turned off my reading lamp. I usually fall asleep very fast."

"What can you tell us about the early hours of December eighth, General?"

"Early hours, hmmm, yes. I recall that Sutherland shook my shoulder and turned on my reading lamp. Something about a Japanese air raid on Pearl Harbor. I asked him for the TWX about it. He said there were no official TWX's on it yet. I told him to wake me the moment something official came in. Then, I went back to sleep."

"That's it?" Engleson asked.

"Yes—well, no. Later, you see, Sutherland came in again saying that a General Gerow from Washington was on the Radio Phone and wanted to talk to me right now."

He looked up, glaring at Engleson. "And, that's another thing. I have specific orders that my telephone lines are always disconnected between Taps and Reveille. I told Sutherland to handle the call. After all, he was my Chief of Staff. But he insisted that Gerow wanted to speak to me personally. I put on my gray bathrobe and followed Sutherland into my office off the bedroom. I recall that Sidney was there, too.

"General Gerow was all exercised about this air raid in Hawaii, 6000 miles away from Manila. He ordered me—can you imagine that—he ordered me to execute phase two of Rainbow five. Never heard a shot in anger, either. I told him we were ready to meet the enemy and hung up. Is this enough detail for you, John?"

"Yes, General, what happened next?"

"We still had not received anything in writing, so I went back to bed."

"That's all, General?"

"Yes."

"What is your next recollection, General?" Mr. Engleson asked, walking slowly back and forth with one hand on his chin supported by his other hand.

"Something awakened me later on. Some kind of disturbance at the entrance, Sutherland and Sidney took care of it."

"Did you know who it was—or do you now?"

"I understand General Brereton wanted to see me to confirm my orders to his command."

"What orders were those, General?"

"Why, to stand down, Mr. Engleson." He looked up at Engleson with amazement that he couldn't understand. "When I cast out Rainbow five as unworkable in favor of my Beach Plan that included the idea of using those strange B-17's called Flying Fortresses. They were suicidal. Rainbow five was really about our Allies; it had nothing to do with the Philippines. That's why I excluded it. As the on-scene commander, it is my duty and responsibility to act as I see fit and proper."

The gallery became noisy, very restless but did not heckle again.

"Colonel, did you issue Call to Arms when you learned the Japanese had attacked Hawaii?" gently asked Mr. Engleson.

"No. We had not been attacked at this time, you see."

MacArthur's Pacific Appeasement, December 8, 1941
Part II
U.S. Army Article 70 Board of Inquiry

Mr. Engelson frowned at MacArthur and said, "Just answer my questions with a yes or no. Please do not amplify your answers, Colonel."

Colonel MacArthur stared haughtily at his attorney for a moment and nodded his head.

"Let the record show that Colonel MacArthur nodded his head yes," ordered Colonel Obrey.

Engelson looked down at his notebook and considered his next question.

"Colonel, previously you indicated using the Flying Fortress bomber to bomb Japanese installations on Formosa would be a suicide mission. How did you form that opinion, sir? Wasn't that why they were here—to bomb the enemy?"

Colonel MacIntyre waited with pencil poised to write down what MacArthur said.

"Colonel, from special sources you know nothing about," he said rather disparaging, "I learned the Japanese Air Force—IJAF, you may understand—had developed a new pursuit plane manufactured by Mitsubishi Aircraft Company. My special sources also reported that IJAF tests indicated this new aircraft could shoot down any kind of fighter or bomber we or the British Empire had. From that, I concluded those B-17's would not even make it to Formosa, much less bomb Japanese airports and seaports."

"I see," nodded Mr. Engleson, as he leaned over and wrote something on paper. He handed it to Colonel MacArthur, who did a classic double take.

"You cannot possibly know this!" he shouted.

Mr. Engleson picked up the paper and took it first to Colonel Obrey who studied for a moment and handed it back. Mr. Engleson walked across to Colonel MacIntyre. He laid it on the table so all his assistants could see the word CAST.

Colonel Obrey tapped his broken gavel for attention. "Colonel MacArthur, all members of this Board are cognizant of that particular source, even though the initials of the real name is classified secret." He took stock of the members of the Board. "You may use the term special source as often as you wish. Never mention the initials or true name. Is that clear?"

"Perfectly clear, Colonel Obrey."

"Continue, Mr. Engleson," Colonel Obrey ordered.

He nodded and turned to Colonel MacArthur. "Colonel, how many others of your staff were privy to special source reports?"

"Why, no one, Mr. Engleson. Those report were highly classified."

"Not even your Chief of Staff, General Sutherland or Staff Intelligence officer, Colonel Willoughby?

"Of course not. I just told you these reports were highly classified." His response was indignant.

Colonel MacIntyre wrote 'jap attack on manila?' and drew a line under it.

In your recollection, what happened next, Colonel?"

Colonel MacArthur pondered for a moment. "Ummm, as I recall, Sid called for my car and we drove to headquarters."

"By Sid, you mean Lieutenant Colonel Sidney Huff, is that correct?"

"Yes, yes," in an annoyed tone.

"Besides the driver, you, General Sutherland, and Colonel Huff were the only ones in your car?" Engleson asked, gently.

"Yes, no one else was around."

"Approximately what time was that, Colonel?"

"I don't know, John, but Sid's pocket journal will have that detail. He was very good at jotting times and notes."

"Colonel, you ordered him to leave his journal behind when you were ordered here."

MacArthur twisted around and looked directly at Mr. Engleson. "John, you are mistaken. I saw him with it this morning," he responded peevishly.

"Unfortunately, he had to start a new one as soon as you arrived in Australia. What's the next thing you recall?"

"We arrived at headquarters, ummm, well, yes, just before the mess hall opened for breakfast. Not many people were around—before regular office hours, you know. I know the switchboard was up and manned."

"Colonel, when was the message center and radio room opened?"

MacArthur looked at him strangely. "That would be about 0800 hours. We operate our communications network between 0800 and 1700 hours daily, except Saturday, which is 0800 to 1300 hours. We are fully shut down on Sunday—standard peacetime procedures, you know."

"Colonel, you were awakened by General Sutherland to advise you Pearl Harbor was under aerial attack. Why didn't you activate your communications centers and sound Call To Arms, right away?"

"Mr. Engleson," looking down his nose at him, "I don't expect you understand Army tactics or strategy; you are a civilian. Pearl Harbor is more than 6,000 miles away from the Philippines; we had no reason to be excited or go to a defensive posture. The Philippines is not that much of a military target. The Japanese have usually made a surprise attack and mostly on Sunday before dawn. Besides, my special source did not suggest the Philippines would be attacked."

MacIntyre wrote 'special source said attack elsewhere?'

"Did your special source indicate where the initial attack might occur?"

"I'm sorry. I cannot answer that question."

"Why not, Colonel?"

Colonel MacArthur studied Mr. Engleson for a moment. "That subject is high classified; only the Chief of Staff can approve discussing that."

Mr. Engleson nodded. "Very well. Colonel MacArthur, what happened next?" He turned away to study the gallery as MacArthur began to speak.

"Since we were not under attack, I advised Sutherland to wake me the instant we received an official TWX about the attack."

Quick as a flash, Mr. Engelman pounced on that response. "You said the Communications Center was closed until 0800 hours. How were you going to receive a TWX before 0800, Colonel?"

MacArthur looked at him in annoyance. "John, since the Communications Center is closed until 0800 hours, I would not receive a TWX until then." He stared at the ceiling for a moment.

"General Gerow called. I believe he was next. He ordered me to execute Phase Two of Rainbow 5. I advised him my troops were ready to meet the enemy."

"You did not send a B-17 out on a photo reconnaissance mission to Formosa, earlier, and now you refused to permit those bombers to retaliate by bombing the Japanese air fields or ports?"

"That's what I just said. And that's another thing: I did not authorize the November twentieth overflight by General Brereton. I didn't even know of it until this hearing."

"No, Colonel, you said your troops were ready to meet the enemy. Why didn't you send that bombing raid, sir?"

"That would have been an act of aggression attributable to the Philippines. You will recall the Pearl Harbor raid had nothing to do with the Philippines. President Queson was very concerned the Japanese warlords would immediately attack his country and kill many of his countrymen. He did not want to attack the Japanese until they actually dropped bombs on Philippine soil."

"You and the Commanding General, Far East Air Force, General Brereton, certainly had different agendas. He wanted to attack and you did not."

"Mr. Engleson," somewhat heatedly, "we were prepared to defend Philippine soil. We were not going to start a war, based on some chair warmer's opinion back in Washington."

The gavel slowly tapped on Colonel Obrey's desk. Mr. Engleson looked shocked at the interruption, as did Colonel MacIntyre.

Colonel Obrey stood and addressed the Visitors' Gallery and Press Corps.
"These proceedings are on hold pending a complete medical examination of Colonel MacArthur by the authorities at Walter Reed Army Hospital. This will include his mental state as well as his physical being. If they find Colonel MacArthur fit for duty, these proceeding will take up where I stopped Mr. Engleson. You are dismissed."
Everyone was very quiet as they retrieved their hats and coats and shuffled toward the doors. The Press Corps was confused as to their notes.

"Hey, Colonel Obrey. What about our notes and sketches? Do they stay or can we take them with us?
The whole press corps turned as one, waiting for his answer.
"Write your name, organization, address and phone number on the envelope. Place your material inside and seal it. We will be in touch with you."

Colonel Obrey looked down at the counsels.
"Counsel will approach, please."

Everyone stood in front of Colonel Obrey. He was silent, waiting for the press and visitors to clear the room. Meanwhile, he framed his comments to them.
"And, if they do not find him fit for duty, Colonel Obrey, what happens then?" Interrupted Mr. Engleson.

Colonel Obrey looked at Mr. Engleson rather sharply.
"That decision will be in the hands of the examiners at Walter Reed, Mr. Engleson. However, within certain limits expressed by the hospital, you are free to visit with your client, Colonel MacArthur."

Mr. Engleson looked at the others and nodded. He stepped over to Colonel MacArthur. "Come, Colonel, back to our table for a while.

"What is going on, John. Why is this proceeding stopped? I haven't completed my statement yet."

"Colonel Obrey is concerned about your health and wants a full checkup at Walter Reed." Mr. Engleson's comment was soothing.

"That's right, I didn't have my annual physical due to the Japanese attacks."

Colonel Obrey motioned to the Sergeant-At-Arms. "Return Colonel MacArthur to his quarters. Someone from Walter Reed will be in to escort the Colonel to the hospital."

"Yes sir. Are we relieved at that time, Colonel?" He asked.

Colonel Obrey looked down, startled. "No, Sergeant, Brigadier General Sutherland and Lieutenant Colonel Huff remain in House Arrest, pending their respective hearings. Major General Brereton is released to the Air Department's G1 for return to duty status. Brigadier General Drake is released to Army G1 for reassignment."

"Yes sir." He saluted and turned away to take Colonel MacArthur into custody.

Colonel Obrey looked at the Court Reporters. "I trust you got all that."

All three looked up at the Colonel and nodded soberly.

"Good." Pausing, he looked around at everyone. Let's all retire to General Cramer's office and discuss my Finding, and the future of General Sutherland and Colonel Huff."

General Cramer heard Colonel Obrey out, frowning at his finding. After a moment, he asked quietly, "Do you believe he is senile or crazy, Colonel?"

"No sir. I stopped the hearing because something in his responses to John Engleson weren't quite"—he looked at Engleson, as if appealing for corroboration—"what I expected, almost child-like."

John leaned forward. "I put it to you: the whole thing smells to the high heavens. In my opinion, it slowly dawned on General Sutherland that MacArthur was gradually losing his mind. This had to go back to before General Marshall ordered him to take command of the new force, USAFFE."

Colonel MacIntyre nodded. "We know that Philippine President Queson became disenchanted with MacArthur by the beginning of 1941."

Colonel Van der Wendt took a deep breath. "That could explain why the remainder of his general staff was at odds with much of his decisions."

"That's my point," said Engleson. "General Sutherland eased MacArthur out of executive decisions, such as Rainbow and Orange. As far as signatures go, I'll bet it has been a long time since MacArthur's signature has been seen. General Brereton probably saw the stand down order allegedly signed by my client, really signed by Sutherland."

General Cramer nodded and sighed. "So, Colonel Obrey, what do you expect Walter Reed to find?"
Colonel Obrey shook his head with a long drawn out sigh. "It's a crap shoot, General. I believe they will find MacArthur unfit for continued duty in the Army and remand him to a mental institution for the rest of his life." He looked around and stared at Engleson for a moment.

"If Walter Reed finds MacArthur fit for duty Mr. Engleson, I have no choice but to find cause to forward recommending a General Court Martial. That end result will place him in Leavenworth for at least twenty years, if not a full life sentence."

--oOo--

REFERENCES:

Horror Trek, Robert W. Levering, The Horstman Printing Company, Dayton, Ohio, 1948

We Band of Angels, Elizabeth M. Norman, Pocket Books, New York, NY, 1999

An Island in Agony, Tony Palomo, Library of Congress, TXU 109-656, 1984

Midway, Donald S. Sanford, Bantam, 1976

MacArthur, Pocket Books, 1977

Tragedy in the China Sea, Random House, 1942

The Fall of Singapore, Kenneth Attiwill, Doubleday, 1959

Wake island Command, W. Scott Cunningham, Little, Brown, 1961

Day of Deceit, Robert B. Stinnett, Touchstone, 2000

At Dawn We Slept, Gordon W. Prange, McGraw Hill, 1981

Old Soldiers Never Die, Geoffrey Perret, Adams Media, 1996

Thirty Seconds over Tokyo,

December 8, 1941: MacArthur's Pearl Harbor, William H. Bartsch, Texas A&M University Press, 2003

From COMBAT -- The War with Japan, Edited by Don Congdon, Dell, 1961

U.S. Army Articles of War (1912 – 1920, as revised)

Article 70: Board of Inquiry

MacArthur and the American Century, William M. Leary. Lincoln: University of Nebraska Press, 2001. ISBN 0-8032-2930-5.

Douglas MacArthur and Manuel Quezon. A Note on an Imperial Bond, by Carol M. Petillo.

And many Google, Yahoo, and Wikipedia research areas.